Panda Books

Chinese Profiles

Zhang
Centr
publis
by a
memb
comm
Sang
the la
history

Panda Books
First Edition 1986
Copyright 1986 by CHINESE LITERATURE
ISBN 0-8351-1603-4

Published by CHINESE LITERATURE, Beijing (37), China
Distributed by China International Book Trading Corporation
(Guoji Shudian), P. O. Box 399, Beijing, China
Printed in the People's Republic of China

Zhang Xinxin and Sang Ye

Chinese Profiles

Panda Books

Foreword

THESE short profiles are from a collection which aims to present the experiences and attitudes of a hundred Chinese from different walks of life.

During the past year we travelled to many parts of the country and have now finished the bulk of our project. We have a number of places still to visit.

A new age, new impressions, exchanged experiences and methods of feedback call for new literary forms. These faithful oral accounts are based on taped or recorded interviews.

Owing to habit, temperament or other understandable reasons, some of the people we interviewed asked us not to mention their names or where they worked. For similar reasons some of them may not have stuck strictly to the truth. We have respected their wishes and let them tell their own stories.

The hundred subjects chosen are not all "typical characters". Their ideas, lives and hopes may fall short of reflecting the reforms now taking place in our economy. All the same, they still illustrate something of this irresistible trend.

CONTENTS

The Cyclist

One afternoon in April, at the gate of the Beijing Hotel, we saw with surprise the first public mini-bus. Instead of an advertisement, painted on it in big red characters was the notice: Wave to stop us any time. Many Beijingers were even more astonished by the appearance of this new form of transport. They crowded round to look.

Bicycles are the main form of transport in Beijing, which has 3,600,000 of them.

It is 6.40 a.m. on one of the capital's main thoroughfares, West Chang'an Boulevard. Zhao Shulan is a woman worker of twenty-nine. When we ask to interview her we have already been refused by seven other cyclists because they are "off to work" or "have nothing to say".

ALL right, I don't mind talking to you. But I must say I'm surprised. You have to be somebody to be interviewed, I've never heard of anyone being stopped to ask how she feels about cycling. Riding a bike's so common, almost everybody cycles to work in Beijing. Hardly anybody goes by car.

My pay is 47 yuan a month, plus ten yuan or more bonus and food subsidy. We started getting a food subsidy two years ago when the prices went up — five yuan a month it is. Yes, I'm a Hui, so I get another four yuan subsidy as a national minority. Not all Huis get that, only those whose units have no canteen for Muslims. Then there's two yuan to help with travelling expenses, which all regular workers get, and I get two extra because I ride my own bike to work. I bought this bike myself and ride it on public business so I get two yuan more. Quite a sizable sum altogether.

I'm our factory's statistician, so I cycle all over the works. I draw a line between public and private business, don't take advantage of the state. Yes, why do I say I'm a worker? I was transferred from the shop floor to the head office, but I still rank as a third-grade worker. So I'm still a worker.

All my class in junior middle school were assigned jobs in town. I joined our factory at the end of '71, one of the first batch of students not sent to work in a commune. I learned to cycle at school, didn't dare to ride on the main roads at first, only in the alleys, but little by little I stopped feeling nervous about it. I've been cycling to work ever since I joined the factory, for over ten years. My dad cycled for thirty years.

I cycle in wind and rain, not when it snows. Whenever it snows the crowded buses get more packed than ever, because many people stop cycling. The slippery roads cause fatal accidents. As soon as the snow melts I start cycling again. I hate those buses stinking of toothpaste, dirty socks and greasy hair! You're packed in like sardines.

My home's in Yongding Road, the works is at Dabeiyao. That means going from the west suburb to east, it takes two hours there and back every day. Oh there are plenty like me. Some have even farther to go, you get used to it. Get a transfer? Too difficult. Two years ago they gave us forms to fill up, asking where we lived and how far we had to travel every day. That raised my hopes. But it turned out to be for a graduation thesis for some college student, giving the number of people who lived in the east and went to work in the west, and the number who lived in the west and worked in the east, and proposing that they should switch jobs. No use, no use at all. Is a switch so easy? Could a textile worker swop jobs with a steel worker? Scholars are so impractical, they can only waffle. It wouldn't do in any line of production, you can't upset the labour force like that.

You're kidding, what sound grasp of policy do I have? In our shop I used to be Youth League secretary, so I know a few basic principles. Not many of us put other people first, if they did we'd all be Lei Fengs;* but we ought to put the country's interests first.

Buying a bike isn't easy. It's not just the money — getting a bicycle coupon's a headache. I had to wait three years for one to buy this. When I started work I rode dad's bike, so old it kept breaking down. There are lots of bikes you don't need coupons for; if you don't believe that, go and look — the shops are full of them. But no one wants to buy those inferior makes: Unicorns, Butterflies and trash like that. Three of them aren't up to one Flying Pigeon or Phoenix. In less than three months they fall apart. The worst are those from Taiwan, I don't know who gets them in; they look all right but they break down in no time and you can't repair them, can't get the spare parts. They're not smuggled in, but sold in state shops. At first people grabbed them, but now no one buys them. Are there any smuggled bicycles? Where could you pay the tax on them?

You're taxed just the once, then get your licence and bicycle plate. For eighty cents. That's the only tax we pay in China. (In fact, monthly incomes of over eight hundred yuan are taxed, but that obviously doesn't affect a woman worker. — authors' note) We're not taxed but the parking charges mount up. Two cents a time may not seem much to

---

*A young PLA soldier held up as a fine example of serving the people.

you, but if you work it out it's staggering. Parking a bike once a day comes to seven yuan a year, seventy yuan in ten years. And after ten years your old bike won't be worth seventy yuan. Besides you have to park it more than once. One day I went out to buy a pair of slacks, went to ten shops without finding a pair that would do. So I didn't buy anything, but spent 28 cents at different parking lots.

What do I think about while I'm cycling? All sorts of things. The kid, my husband, squabbles with colleagues. Doesn't stop me from keeping my eyes on the road. What was I thinking about before you stopped me? The questions you do ask! Let's see … oh, I was thinking about a poster I'd just seen — that one there. (She points to an advertisement for a film. — authors' note) What a lousy picture, the propagandist in our factory paints better than that! Anyway I just let my thoughts wander.

I've had accidents. Usually because men bump into my bike. They speed along like demons. Sometimes they knock me off and don't so much as look back. No manners at all. They may not have urgent business, that's their way, as if they were rushing every day to buy medicine. My husband's just as bad, dawdles around at home when he gets up, then makes up for it by speeding.

No, very few collisions are deliberate — only hooligans bump into you on purpose. And I don't doll up, I'm not good-looking, so people leave me alone. Except sometimes tiresome middle-school students stand on the pavement and shout, "Hey! Your back wheel is catching up with the front wheel!" Disgusting I call it.

I had ten stitches after my worst accident, and stayed in bed for ten days. It wasn't a crash, I fell into a sewer. The streets at night are badly lit and the men repairing that sewer hadn't put back the man-hole cover. When my front wheel went in I was thrown off and stunned. Had to have a few stitches in my arm and seven on my head, you can see the scar. Ask for damages? Who could I ask? They'd only say: Haven't you got eyes in your head? Of course they were responsible, but I didn't go to complain, didn't think it would be any use. Anyway, with free medical treatment I didn't spend any money. And the bike wasn't damaged, apart from a few broken spokes and a dent in the mudguard — here. One collision did smash up the bike, it was all the fault of the man who crashed into me. He gave me ten yuan on the spot. I didn't call the police, why should I? Cyclists have no use for the police.

Sure, they all salute when they fine you. But that salute costs you at least fifty cents. They fine you for ignoring the red light, not having your licence on you, carrying someone on the back, a whole lot of reasons. If your attitude isn't good, it's a bigger fine. So if the police nab you never talk back, or you'll get a bigger fine. They have the right to fine you. We do resent it. Don't they ever get tired of being so strict and so grim all the time? Those with red armbands (volunteer traffic controllers — authors' note) are even worse. They're all young fellows who slack in their own units. If they worked well, would they be sent out to police the streets? They've never bossed people about before, so they make the most of it. They're tough and won't listen to reason. The first of last month there was a city-wide check-up on traffic, with inspectors at every crossroad, and they'd nothing to do except watch the police fine people. Each time the police stopped someone they yelled, "Fifty cents fine!" What beasts! Of course there aren't too many of them, and the police have their job to do. Wouldn't the traffic be all snarled up without them? So I don't hate them, just wish they'd be less strict. Though they mean well and it's their duty, they should be a bit nicer about it. Why make everyone resent you?

In Beijing your bike's got to have a bell, brakes and a padlock. In fact a bell is no use, no one gets out of your way if you ring it. A padlock's useful, or your bike may be stolen. Brakes are most useful of all, they may save your life! As I told you just now, good makes of bikes are hard to buy. Women often ride men's bikes. It's awkward in summer when you wear a skirt getting on and off. When you swing your leg over, your panties show. But women's bikes are too difficult to come by. Now why ask a question like that? The curse makes no difference, what has it got to do with riding a bike?

You can't make comparisons. None of us know each other, we don't talk to each other, all ride our different ways. So there's no comparison. I think all cyclists are the same, workers, students and ordinary cadres going to work or back. Oh, right, students don't go to work, they go to school. I once thought someone should make a film of us cyclists, and show it scores of years from now to our children and grandchildren. They should see how we raised them, cycling like this, taking our licences, ration books, grain coupons and oil coupons with us.... From early to late, for the sake of the country and our families, we weave in and out of the traffic on our bikes to help to modernize China. The idea of this makes me very proud. Think I'm too naive? That's honestly how it is.

You're wrong! If I were on my way to work how could I natter with you all this time? I'm on my way home. Last night I worked an extra shift to wind up my accounts. Can't you see I'm heading west, going home?

You're welcome. Goodbye!

Translated by Gladys Yang

Her Tribute

The Great Wall Foundation in Beijing has announced that all contributors of five hundred yuan or more to repair the Wall will have their names engraved on a tablet on it, as a lasting commemoration. A considerable sum has already been donated.

She comes out of the foundation's office wearing a white silk blouse, blue cotton trousers, and white-framed spectacles for short-sightedness.

YES, I've just contributed five hundred yuan to repair the Great Wall. It's not worth talking about. Since we in China have this Great Wall I'm glad to contribute to its repair. Besides, I can afford it.

No, I honestly don't want to talk about it. I'm completely unprepared, what could I say?

Well then ... all right, we can have a friendly chat, but don't consider it an interview. No, I've no other scruples, I'm certainly not afraid of any trouble; I just feel I should first ask the higher-ups. And since we're just chatting, don't publish my name, will you. Sorry!

These last few years our economy has got on the right track, and there's more public fund-raising, which is a good thing; it alerts the general public to problems deserving attention. For instance, when organizations keen on preserving cultural relics launch this appeal, it's a good education for the rest of our people. How many of our billion people can make contributions? Not too many I imagine. The starting figure's too high — five hundred or more to have your name engraved, that's too much for most ordinary people. Still this drive should at least have the effect of making everyone treasure the Great Wall and take better care of it. They should realize that they mustn't pull it down. Not now that the authorities and private individuals are raising funds to repair it!

I consider that our generation owes something to the Great Wall, and to pay our debt we ought to contribute our money or our strength, whichever we have. In 1977 my daughter passed college entrance and I went to Gubeikou outside Beijing to fetch her back to town. She'd been working in a commune there for six years. When I reached the village where she lived I was staggered: all the bricks in their houses, pigsties and public toilets had come from the Great Wall! My, that was their idea of "self-reliance" and of construction "in line with local conditions". I understood then why, all along the way, the Great Wall had been reduced to mounds of earth! My daughter said, "The villagers aren't the worst. If you don't believe me go and look at the army. They send trucks and sappers to dismantle the Wall." Can you believe it? To them, the bricks of our Great Wall which symbolizes our nation are nothing but building material. All they think of is how to make use of them. Politically speaking, this demolition of the Wall is an unforgivable crime, yet they consider it perfectly justified, a "revolutionary action"!

Our government had decided that the Great Wall should be preserved as one of our important cultural relics. But in those years between 1966 and 1976, how many important leaders that should have been protected by the state died? Wasn't Liu Shaoqi, chairman of our state, pulled down from his position, struggled against and killed? So what's that about pulling down the Great Wall?

Our people look ahead, that's why there's hope for China. But we're also prone to forget the past and ignore everything except our immediate concerns. We believe in getting things done and have no sense of past debt. That's why I'm all for repairing the Great Wall and inscribing the contributors' names. I'm sure generations to come will say, "Some of our ancestors in the twentieth century destroyed the Great Wall, but others restored it. The names of the vandals have long since been forgotten; now we remember those who repaired the Wall." By then this tablet with names inscribed on it may be a cultural relic too, and they won't break it.

Oh, you mustn't think I'm doing this out of self-interest, spending five hundred yuan to buy myself lasting fame. This money was left by my husband when he died. I discussed this with our daughter last night and we decided to give it to the Great Wall and to have his name inscribed there.

No, I don't know if he'd have done this if he were still alive. Of course, if I could tell you, "This is what he'd have done," that would be splendid; but I'm not sure that he would have. Not because he didn't love his country and the Great Wall but because we had no money. This five hundred yuan was the only nest-egg he had. His prizes, payment for articles and special subsidies came to 523 yuan altogether, of which he never touched a cent. And being strictly logical he might have said, "Other people have wrecked the Wall, why should I spend my money?" He and I were at college together, then became colleagues. We both worked as teachers. And the proudest day in his life was when the *People's Daily* published one of his articles. He had cancer of the liver. When it was terminal and he came out of his coma, sweating with agony, he said, "I'd like to see that again." I knew he meant that article "Notes on Teaching the Prose Poem 'The Sounds of Autumn'", because in his opinion that was his only article worth keeping. That copy of the *People's Daily* was the only proof that he had lived and done some honest work.... So yesterday evening I fetched my daughter home—she's a teacher too, all of us have been middle-school teachers. I told her, "Let's leave your father's name on the Great Wall...." This is the best we can do for his memory, for the Great Wall, and for our country.

Me? I studied in college before Liberation. My ancestral home is in Baodi, but my father moved to Tianjin to work in a foreign firm. No, my grandfather was very poor, a night watchman in a cathedral; but because of that job he was able to educate my father to be a comprador. My parents were both Catholics. So after I finished primary and middle school in Tianjin I entered Furen University in Beiping, a missionary college where I studied Chinese. I was a Catholic too then. Later on I left the Church; I'd lost faith in it. The first time I wavered in my faith was in the third year, when I joined in the demonstration to "oppose hunger, oppose the civil war" — the May 20th Incident. On June the second the KMT reactionaries raided our college to make arrests. An agent of theirs in the college told them who to arrest — God Almighty! Your lamb turned into a wolf! What undermined my faith completely was taking part in land reform just before I graduated. The whole mainland had just been liberated, and our old principal Mr Chen Yuan took us to the southwest, where my classmates Cheng Mingru and Zhang Kun were killed by counter-revolutionaries. That finished my faith in God, he couldn't save people; we'd have to save ourselves by relying on the Communist Party. (She carefully wrote her classmates' names down in our notebook, saying, "Mind you get these names right; they shouldn't be forgotten." —authors' note)

After graduation I was assigned to a middle school to teach Chinese. I taught there for thirty-three years, not retiring till last year. I retired at fifty-seven, teaching two years after the normal retirement age.

Furen University no longer exists, it was amalgamated with other colleges. Its name meant Foster Goodness. Its first principal was an American. Mr Chen Yuan, one of the directors, died in Beijing. Mr Yin Qianli died in Taibei. They were all excellent scholars and good teachers. Our university put moral character first, health second and learning third. We believed that fostering goodness meant refraining from self-indulgence. I don't know if Furen University in Taiwan still abides by this principle. Well, I mustn't go on too long about Furen....

As a middle-school teacher my starting pay was 52 yuan — before that for a time we received wages in kind. Then my pay went up to 62 yuan and finally 78. After that we had no pay rises. Seventy-eight yuan was the most a middle-school teacher earned. My husband and I were the same, first classmates, then colleagues with equal pay for equal work. We had old people to support — his parents, mine had money — and children to bring up too. So we were on a tight budget. After the "cultural revolution", with the children off our hands, our life improved. But we never had money to spare. We saved up to buy a TV set; then saved up to buy a washing-machine. We'd started saving again when my husband fell ill ... not until he was dying did I know that he'd kept this nest-egg of 523 yuan.

Ah, there are some things you may not understand owing

to your different experience and age. This is like teaching, you can't go on day after day teaching the classics, you have to teach practical writing too. So, originally I was a Catholic, a theist; later I believed in communism, but still as a theist, not believing in the cause of communism but deifying our leader. The "cultural revolution" shook me. I went back to being a Catholic; not openly of course, but to find something I could trust in. After the "gang of four" was smashed I started believing again in the Party and the people, this time as an atheist. People like us no longer put our trust in certain individuals; we put the country's interests first and trust the Communist Party. I know the Party has made mistakes; it's not infallible. But only the Communist Party can save China.... I think it's the heart of China....

My contribution to repair the Great Wall is the biggest I've ever made. A few years ago we had an alumnae reunion. My husband and I gave ten yuan, not really knowing what for. I gave one yuan for the disabled, one yuan for the Children's Fund, ten cents for the preservation of pandas. I didn't want to give any money for pandas, but some children pestered me for it so I gave ten cents. I'm not an animal lover; I know pandas are a "national treasure" linked with ecology, but I don't like them. I may have been brought up a Christian, but I take the world as it is, and if some animals can't survive, the sooner they die out the better. No, I dislike all sorts of birds as well.

I haven't any more money. If I had, I'd donate it for the Great Wall too — you know, we're still not sure exactly how long the Wall is. That's right, our funds are still limited, there are many problems we can't tackle yet. I wonder if some of your readers would contribute money to do such a survey of the Great Wall? I don't know how much it would

cost; besides, this isn't for me to suggest or even think of....
Sorry for this digression. Goodbye.

Translated by Gladys Yang

"Why? Why Do I Bum Around?"

Yang Shouqian, nineteen, has a beard about six inches long and shoulder-length hair. His small straw hat has a red tassel on it. People wait outside his hotel just to catch a glimpse of him.

FOR a year and a half, on foot and by bike I've travelled over 35,000 *li*. I've just had my nineteenth birthday.

I wanted to see the country, so I set out.

I'm from Jiamusi. In primary school and up to the first term of my third year in junior middle school I was a good student, always got top marks. But by then I'd had enough of stodgy textbooks, so I stopped going to school in the second half of my third year. I studied at home instead. What if I'd finished school? I'd have gone on to high school, taken college entrance; but thousands of candidates sit for that exam; after graduation I might have been given some job I didn't like, work which didn't interest me, which would get me nowhere. So I thought that rather than be moulded into a screw I'd better mould myself and find a screw-cap to fit me. My classmates and teachers thought there was something wrong with me, that I was off my head. They came to our place to talk me round, steer me back on to the "right track" — get me to crack the standard textbooks. But I stuck to my guns.

This social pressure was mostly family pressure, since

families make up society. By the time we have an ideal society, the family will have to be broken up! My dad — it was mostly him — was a good father, a good feudal father who liked beating us. He beat me when I was a kid, I grew up under the whip of that feudal despot. It was hard to argue with him, he always kept that whip at the ready to give us a beating. He practised Chinese medicine and was polite to his patients, but he hadn't a good word for anyone else.

They insisted on me getting my junior-middle-school certificate. My father said, "D'you expect me to have kept you all these years in school for nothing?" I must have a certificate to show for it. So I went back to take the exam.

When I had the certificate I needed work. Had to wait for a job, right? But what I really needed was to understand society, so as to have some kind of perspective. I worked for three days in a construction brigade, then "retired" to make friends with the local people: workers, peasants, hooligans, drop-outs, all sorts. I wanted to find out, see how these friends of mine lived and what they felt about life. I spent one whole winter on that. Then I made up my mind to leave Jiamusi in spring and travel all round the country.

On March 21, 1983, my father bawled me out again. "For days you've been going on about touring different provinces, but there's no sign of you taking off yet." In fact I'd already made my preparations. "Don't worry, I'm off tomorrow," I told him. "Go on then!" he said. "Good riddance to bad rubbish!" So with this blessing I left.

At 4.30 a.m. the next day I set out on foot on my fact-finding journey. I felt pretty bad as my friends saw me off. "You can't see me off all the way," I told them. "We'll meet again one day." Though it was early spring, the northeast was still covered in snow and ice. Looking back I saw an expanse of white with the smokestacks of Jiamusi sticking up like grey pillars. I headed along side roads towards Harbin....

I had twenty yuan which my granddad had given me for the Spring Festival. He called it money to "weigh down the year", to try to stop us youngsters from growing up. Because if you grow up to manhood, then grow old, you'll die; so better not to grow up at all. That's a folk custom. If you think about it, it may help you to understand some of our people's failings. My parents? Certainly they gave me no money. They cursed me and refused to let me go! They even cursed the secretary of the municipal Youth League Committee. No, I didn't ask him to our place to be cursed. Before leaving I needed a letter of introduction, didn't I? Without one I'd have trouble every step of the way, so I asked the Youth League Committee for a letter. I lied to them, said I was waiting for a job, was twenty-five and wanted to see the country at my own expense. Since this sounded plausible, they wrote me the letter. But when they found out the truth, the fat was in the fire: Yang Shouqian was only seventeen, and his parents were dead set against his leaving home. They wanted the letter back, that's why the secretary came to our place. My dad was fool enough to swear at the man who was on his side, completely confusing enemies, allies and friends. Finally I won the secretary over, since young people can usually see eye to eye. I told him, "You believed me when I said I was twenty-five and agreed to write me a letter; that shows I can pass for a twenty-five-year-old. Now you want it back not because you think I'm not up to going, but because you feel I'm too young. That doesn't make sense. If you think I can pass for a twenty-five-year-old, you should have faith in me. You slipped up, but don't worry about it. My family's opposition is a headache but it's only to be expected. We ought to work on the old people together."

"Comrade Yang Shouqian is on a fact-finding tour; please put him up" — that short introduction smoothed my path for me, though it wouldn't make it plain sailing all the way. After leaving Heilongjiang I tramped through Jilin, Liaoning, Hebei and Tianjin to Beijing, 5,800 *li* in all, pacing out the globe, wearing out three pairs of shoes. The letter of introduction saved me a lot of money, since local governments, Youth League offices and other units gave me board and lodging. Most of them were eager to help me and expressed admiration, scepticism, surprise or even pity. Some of them cold-shouldered me, thinking it was ridiculous, as if I would repent if they didn't give me a bed. Sometimes I stayed with villagers, sleeping with kind old peasants and their equally friendly dogs and fleas; sometimes I slept out in the open in a sleeping-bag I had made, and if it got too cold I would run around to warm up. I didn't mind, it was all my own doing.

I wasn't out to break any marathon record, my aim was to understand society and investigate folk customs; so after reaching Beijing I bought a bike and a simple camera. The money? I earned it! While finding out about local customs and listening to the villagers' tales and gossip about their neighbours, I practised medicine. With the prescriptions passed down in our family I cured quite a few patients, all with fairly common diseases. The countryside's still short of doctors and medicine, as the "barefoot doctors", who had a little education, had gone off to be entrepreneurs. So I took their place as an itinerant quack.

By the time I left Beijing I'd picked up a couple more ways of earning cash by teaching martial arts or coaching youngsters in philosophy and history for their high-school entrance exams. All this brought in a bit of money. But I never had any to spare. Right now I haven't got a cent to my name. The other day I figured out that in eighteen months I spent altogether 1,800 yuan. People don't believe this, because it costs that much to live in town, and I'd bought a bike too, a camera and several hundred yuan worth of books. But I honestly spent only 1,800. And I earned it all myself apart from twenty-five ill-gotten yuan, the twenty given me at the Spring Festival and five more you'll hear about presently — they were really ill-gotten gains. I didn't mind being broke, I could always earn more.

In Guangdong I couldn't be a quack, there were no patients, and no chance to teach martial arts; so I went to a restaurant and told the boss that I was starving, please would he give me some work. Helping him wash up and chop firewood I got my keep and three yuan on top of it, enough to keep me going for two more days. Someone said my behaviour was first-rate publicity, and I should ask some factory to pay me for advertising their goods. Or I could take a collection; but I didn't know who to approach or how to do that. Various local papers wrote me up, but still no factories recruited me, only an unemployed youngster tracked me down, dead set on coming with me. He was the end! He really disgusted me, he did. Once I went without food for three days and asked him for a bite, just a mouthful of his malt extract; but he wouldn't give it to me for fear he might starve to death! I'd done my best for him, taken him to Shanghai with me, so I just sent him packing. I can't stand guys like that. The people I met along the way were better.

I cycled through Hebei, Shandong, Jiangsu, Anhui, Shanghai, Zhejiang, Guangdong and Guangxi, and stayed three months on Hainan Island. That part of my journey was about 30,000 *li*. The south wasn't like the north — they were big on class struggle! I kept being detained by police or by militia. My letter of introduction didn't wash with them, they simply didn't believe I could come all the way from the northeast on my own, so they put me in the poky as a vagrant while they checked up on me. After I got used to this it didn't bother me. I would tell them what I was doing and ask them to contact Jiamusi, then cool my heels for a bit. Sometimes it took a couple of hours, or seven or eight, depending on their telecommunications. If they got a long-distance call through without any trouble, I would be let out very soon; otherwise I had to hang about a bit longer. When the Jiamusi Public Security Bureau assured them that I wasn't an escaped criminal, they'd cheerfully let me go, even say nice things. That was how they were. At the border checkpoint in Shenzhen I got detained as usual. When they let me go I said, "Letting me go isn't good enough, I must see your special economic zone." "Can't be done," they said. "For that you need a permit from the Provincial Security Department." "Well, then ask for one," I said. "You've called up the northeast, what's so hard about calling up Guangzhou?" As a result the Provincial Security Department gave me permission to see round the Shenzhen and Zhuhai special economic zones.

Sometimes I get taken for a "healer with magic powers", sometimes for a schizophrenic. In one temple the nuns kowtowed to me as a "reincarnation of Buddha". But very few people believed that I was investigating local customs. (He picked up a mug and took a sip, then tapped the mug. — authors' note) Take this mug for instance. Someone calls it a golden rice bowl, someone else a piss-pot; it's obviously a mug but no one admits it. And me? I call myself a "high-class beggar" or a "semi-itinerant quack". Aren't begging and cheating social phenomena too?

My three days in Shanghai were the most frustrating. I'd collected a whole mass of material and written a long account of my observations, as well as an article on marriage. I showed it to an old scholar who studied folklore. "This article of yours," he said, "well, it.... It smacks of spiritual pollution." Why? Because I mentioned communal marriage and promiscuity. "These things, well, the masses have forgotten them. So why bring them up?"

That wasn't the first time I met with this kind of reaction. I feel we've got to analyse our Chinese folk customs and the inner logic of the development of folk literature. Stands to reason, doesn't it? But when I speak of a cultural transitional zone between relatively backward and relatively advanced cultures, the usual reaction is, "What's a 'cultural transitional zone'? Did you make up that expression?" Language is a tool to express ideas so that men can communicate, so why shouldn't I coin a phrase? But no! "You haven't got the right!" Because I'm too young. They claim that old terms can express new ideas quite clearly. I must look up the first paper on atom bombs to see if it left out "atom" and just said a "super bomb". I'm not joking. You may think it funny but I don't.

Touring the northeast and the north I was left alone, basically, by the police and militia. But I ran into bandits. That was when the whole country was searching for two gangsters, and quite a few bad characters in the cities had taken to the hills. I ran into some of them. Once two young fellows held me up. I told them "I haven't got any money. I'm on a fact-finding tour." They told me to strip, and we started arguing. After arguing with me for a while one of them dodged behind me. I stepped aside just as he lammed out with his stick. Wham! Luckily for me he missed me, but he bashed the face of the guy in front of me. I kicked him and jeered, "Fine stick-up men you are! You should take a few lessons from an old hand like me." With that I took off. Believe me, that was a narrow escape. If that blow had landed on me I wouldn't be here today.

Another time I bumped into a "good bandit". When he grabbed me I told him, "I haven't a cent, haven't eaten for a whole day. I'm on a social study tour." He didn't believe me of course. Demanded to see my papers. Who ever heard of such a thing, a bandit wanting to see your letter of introduction! When I showed it to him he said, "Good for you, brother! I haven't made any hauls the last few days, all I've got is five yuan, but take that." I didn't want his stolen money. "I'm helping you out," he fumed. "If you insult me I'll kill you!" I looked at his club and was afraid he'd really beat me to death, so I took the money and ran. Behind me I heard him saying to himself, "Not take money? Who on earth refuses money?" That five yuan was a headache to me. If I left it by the road somebody else would pick it up and spend it. How could I hand it in? I had to keep it and try to put this ill-gotten gain to good use. That was the five yuan I spoke about earlier. I often think about that guy and hope he's straightened himself out.

By now I've written over three million words, I keep a diary every day. I've also taken nearly four thousand photographs. Different Youth League committees and cultural bureaux have helped me develop them. Seems to me that from the thirties to the eighties the study of folklore was at a low ebb in China. Practically nothing new came up. Folklorists abroad have taken a big step forward, and we've taken over some of their new ideas, jumping up as it were from grade three to grade five. But it's no use just blindly copying foreign methods. The study of folklore isn't the same as building a computer. You've got to draw on different social sciences, on natural sciences too like maths and statistics, to study our Chinese customs. No. I am against the study of folklore based on statistics. Foreign theories aren't always correct. We must keep our priorities straight. So I say that the study of folklore in China today is just in an embryonic stage, not fully systematized.

I've been asked about the political significance of what I'm doing. What the motive behind that question was I don't care, but the man who asked certainly didn't know anything about folklore. I'm studying these social phenomena, trying to understand the emergence and development of different cultural groups, with the aim of reforming some of our national defects. If you don't understand them, how can you reform them? For instance, why are peasants everywhere so afraid of family planning? Why do women go into hiding to have their second baby? Better first get some idea about the influence of material life on people's thinking, on their views on existence, clan relationships, their sense of family responsibility and so forth....

I plan next to study the aboriginal wild men. In the history of civilization, or in the history of mankind you might say, could there have been a group that turned away from modern civilization? Is there a community that has stopped evolving, a community still in a pre-historic stage? These things are mysteries. I want to discover some wild men — the missing link in human evolution — and find out how they developed. Out of the world's four big mysteries, two, the Loch Ness Monster and the Bermuda Triangle, are abroad, out of my reach; I haven't the equipment or theoretical know-how to study UFOs: I can only study the wild men. That's why I've kept my hair long and grown a beard, and got my mother to make me a fur coat. In December I'm going to Guangxi, next spring to

Hubei, to Shennongjia. I know plenty of people have searched Shennongjia already without catching a single wild man. If I find any, I may not catch them, I'd rather live with them. That's the only way to get to know them and study them. I have to be among them, not with them in a cage and me outside it. Genuine zoologists don't study tigers in zoos. So when people ask me, "Young Yang, when are you going to catch a wild man?" I just laugh. At most I may bring one back with me.

I shan't leave the mountains until I've succeeded. A few days ago when I was in Beijing I climbed the Great Wall, as a sort of farewell gesture. Standing on the Great Wall I found myself really moved, quite carried away. The Great Wall is our national symbol, but it's no longer able to protect us. It's a wonderful part of our cultural heritage, but now it's falling to bits, ruined by people and by the elements, like a dragon hacked apart and left on the ground....

Let us build our new Great Wall with our flesh and blood.
The Chinese nation faces its greatest danger.
From each one the urgent call for action comes forth....

That's from our national anthem.

I'm not up to that, don't know enough. What do I need? Photographic equipment and a small tape-recorder, that would do me. I shall borrow the money and pay it back later. No, I don't collect contributions, don't know how to. But if some of your readers want to help me, they're welcome to.

Translated by Gladys Yang

A Young Section Chief

Liu is a salesman in a Xinhua bookstore. He was cagey, as if suspicious of us two strangers. He didn't volunteer any information and refused to answer some of our questions.

I'M twenty-seven. After finishing secondary school I was assigned to this bookshop. I'm in charge of the literary section now and thirteen shop assistants. Of course I serve behind the counter too.

Yes, we serve behind the counter, can't let the customers help themselves from the stacks, or we'd lose books. As it is we still lose some. Last year we tried opening up the stacks for a month and our section lost over seven hundred books. The state had to make good the loss. Open stacks are convenient for readers, but they're convenient for thieves too. That won't do. We opened them up on instructions from the higher-ups; when they told us to close them because we were losing money we did. I don't know about other countries and can't remember what it was like before the "cultural revolution", but it wouldn't do nowadays to open the stacks. In future maybe, when there's a higher standard of public morality, but right now you can't ask our shop to solve the problem. Even selling over the counter we still lose books. If we catch a thief we fine him.

True, we haven't got any legal right to fine people, but we have our way of doing it: we charge for the book, then confiscate it and tell the thief he can have it when he brings a written self-criticism with his unit's chop on it. Since he doesn't dare let his unit know, he doesn't come back for the book. So we fine him its cost. I see nothing wrong with this, it's the thief who's in the wrong. Even if this method is wrong, you should blame our manager, not me.

Thieves usually hide books in their satchels or clothes. If we suspect someone we make him undo them to show us. We seldom make a mistake; when we do we apologize. Whether we have the right to do that or not, I've yet to see any honest customer refuse to open his satchel or unbutton his jacket. If he hasn't stolen something he's eager to clear himself, right?

I make thirty-eight yuan a month. On that I keep myself without any help from the family and without helping to support my parents. I'm saving up ten yuan a month for my marriage. Now I've saved up more than seven hundred yuan.

I've gone out with several girls, but each time it came to nothing. The girls always called it off. No, I didn't feel it a loss of face. Do you mean that I lose face when I can't get a girl? I don't feel ashamed if she ditches me. It's her fault not mine. I don't lose face, I can relax.

Of course I meet these girls through introductions, and first we go out together to try it out. If we click we can go steady; if not we part. I want a girl of good character with a clean political record and good-natured. Her looks don't matter. No, they really don't, so long as we hit it off.

We haven't got any university graduates here. Our leadership is basically two sorts of people. There are old army cadres who know next to nothing about the job and have to learn once they're here. Then there are people like our manager. In 1951 he was a sales assistant in a Xinhua bookstore in the northeast. Then he was gradually promoted to be a section chief, vice-manager and manager. Of course he knows the ropes, but he's not top-notch. He's a decent sort and reliable. Our ablest people are usually the heads of different departments — they're the most competent professionally. In the old days of joint state-private ownership, most of them worked in the secondhand bookshops. They can't be managers, not yet anyway. Our manager's worked faithfully for thirty years, he sets a good example for us all. No, I don't want to become manager, I'll do whatever job I'm needed for. Some of our manager's old colleagues are still shop assistants. Shen Rong once sold books too, and now she's an author writing books of her own. But she's exceptional. I don't envy her, I know my own limitations.

Yes, some of my colleagues say my only good point is that I'm not hot-headed. No good comes of being hot-headed. I think it's a failing. Do something rash and you'll suffer for it all your life and involve your children too. Haven't there been a lot of cases like that? It's better to be cautious and not ambitious.

Of course I can tell you how I came to this conclusion. In middle school I joined the Youth League and was active with the Red Guards. I was really somebody! But a few years in the shop opened my eyes, I grew more experienced. In the campaigns to criticize Lin Biao and Confucius, to oppose the Right deviationists' attempt to reverse correct judgements, to smash the "gang of four", to clean up spiritual pollution ... each time we took a lot of books off our shelves. We stopped selling them and sent them to be pulped. The writers had to make self-criticisms. Of course, since the smashing of the four pests there's been no literary inquisition; still, writers who make mistakes have to criticize themselves, and that can't be comfortable. So I've always swum with the tide. Besides, I couldn't write a book if I tried. That's one obvious example. Here's another. In our district shop (this helps to administer smaller branches in that district — authors' note) one comrade told me she studied in senior middle school and did brilliantly, but because her father was a Rightist no college would take her, she had to work in a shop. Now her father's been cleared, rehabilitated, but she's nearly forty, completely disillusioned. So people should toe the line, not play with fire to make trouble for themselves and their children.

I can't tell you that, it's a trade secret. Generally speaking, the biggest circulation, nationwide, is about two million. That includes political works, selected writings of heads of state, collected works and regulations. In special cases, Chairman Mao's works for instance, ten million copies are sold. The only books in our literary section which sell like that are thrillers. The lowest circulation for the whole country is about two thousand copies, for rather nondescript poetry or boring history booklets.

If books on government policy lose money, the publishing house stands the loss, it doesn't affect us. But we know some books are bound to lose heavily. Art albums for example, with only a few thousand copies on octavo copperplate, printed in colour — they're certain to lose money. That doesn't affect us either. Some books sell like hot cakes but don't get reprinted; there are a lot like that. The readers and bookshop would like to have them reprinted, but they don't appear in the distribution index. Recently there haven't been many like this, but there are still some. We don't have any say in this.

Well ... that's very hard to say. For instance the Chinese translation of *Decameron* isn't being reprinted. No, I can't give you any examples of Chinese books.

Now you're putting the same question another way. I have to be responsible for what I say. Well then, *Ren A Ren** sold out very fast, but can it be reprinted? It's an unhealthy book.

No, that's not my opinion. It must be objectionable. Why else should it be withdrawn? Hasn't it been criticized in the press? We have to do as the higher-ups say; they have a grasp of principles and understand the overall situation. We can't just stock best-sellers, we have to take politics into account, not go all out for money. We know the value of money, but have no way of measuring the political damage done.

Yes, sometimes we make package sales. In theory we shouldn't, but actually we do. For instance, *Huo Yuanjia*** with history booklets. Too many adventure stories are bad for young people, so with each goes a copy of *The Unification of China by the First Emperor* to counteract their influence. *The Facts of Life* and *Required Reading for Newly-Weds* sell quickly too, each with a copy of *How to Repair Electrical Appliances.* You'll find that other shops go further. They foist off two works of literature with each copy of the picture book *The Champion Boxer.*

That ... it's another trade secret I don't feel I can tell you. Generally speaking we make twenty cents on each yuan-sale, but we're taxed and have to pay for deficits, building repairs and wages. We tried the responsibility system for a month, then gave it up for various reasons. For one thing, prizes were given to those who overfulfilled their sales quota. But the prizes were such a small fraction of the gross

---

* Dai Houying's novel. Recently it has been translated into English and renamed *The Stones of the Wall.*

** A popular novel about a Tianjin athlete at the turn of the century.

profit, it wasn't worth their while. Instead they took good books, best-selling books home to sell in their spare time — and pocketed all the profit. We couldn't have that, could we? There were other reasons too which I'd better not go into.

Of course not! I'm in favour of reform, the Party Central Committee has called for reform! The question is how to do it. We can't break up the iron rice bowl to sell scrap iron. If we're all determined but have no definite plan, each tugging in different directions, that won't do. As I see it, we should listen to the higher-ups, those experienced old comrades know what to do. What's meant by going all out to mobilize the masses, by democracy, by centralization? These questions need a lot of studying. Especially in a bookstore which isn't a purely commercial set-up. No, there's a big difference between selling books and selling vegetables. Books are propaganda.

I hardly ever read novels, I like seeing films. Chinese films preferably, the foreign ones are too confusing, too muddled for me to follow. In this I'm not like my colleagues: they go for Japanese and American films which I don't care for. In the evenings at home I watch TV or think over my work. After all I'm a section chief.

I'm quite content with any job I'm given — I'm out to serve the people! I've never thought of becoming a manager or asking for a transfer.

No, I can't answer that. No comment.

I can't tell you that either. What an extraordinary question.

We look at this question differently. I don't think we're overstaffed. Some of us sell books and make out bills, others take the money; that's our system. The sales assistants aren't in charge of receipts; the payees aren't in charge of books — what's wrong with that? If you don't believe me, ask the others; they think this saves trouble. To handle both books and receipts wouldn't do. It really wouldn't. Apart from the fact that a few backward people might embezzle cash, just suppose you were suspected of embezzlement, how could you clear yourself? This is our system! (Judging by what we've seen, apart from a few private bookstalls, in all Xinhua bookstores and the second-hand bookshops, there is this division of labour. — authors' note) I'm not convinced by those examples of yours; that's the capitalist style of business when a shop belongs to the boss.

I haven't got any special worries. I can't think of any.

I don't want to tell you. Still less would I want your readers to know. I've already said too much, more than I'd normally say in ten days. A section chief has to set a good example.

What do you mean by cagey? Oh — well you can think what you like. Anyway I've been telling you nothing but the truth.

Of course I'm like the rest of my generation, but I'm quite satisfied, I'm not looking for trouble.

No, or would you like to talk to our manager? All right then, goodbye!

Translated by Gladys Yang

A Riot of Colours

He Be, masseuse in a clinic

APART from the things that people with sight talk about, my mates and I discuss questions that would only occur to us. For instance, which is better, to be born blind or to lose your sight later on? Some say it's less upsetting to be born blind, with no notion of green or yellow; others say it's better to lose your sight after you've seen daylight, seen what your parents look like. Those who've gone blind retort, "No, we're worse off, because we've lost what we had." Then those blind from birth argue, "We've never even had it...." This is a vexing question that we argue about without coming to any conclusion. Once one of my colleagues said, "What we can grasp is our whole world, because like everybody else, each person can only grasp part of the world." Still the rest weren't convinced, they went on arguing that what he'd said was only one side of it, only partly true....

Have I got a standard Beijing accent? No, it's because I model myself on radio announcers, this is part of my world too. On the one hand I want to be able to pass on news correctly, on the other it's by way of compensation since our hearing is better than that of people with sight, so why shouldn't we speak more nicely? Ah, I can hear you leafing through my books, that's braille. Braille is the written

language for blind people the whole world over. It's been in
use for 155 years, this year is its 155th anniversary. We use
braille in China too, but it's not the generally used braille
because it's based on our alphabetic script and phonetic
notation. We can tell the approximate sound of each term in
braille books in English, and presumably blind people
abroad can tell what our words sound like, but they don't
know their meaning. For instance ... well, the Chinese for
"us" *women*, means "women", females, in English.
They're both written the same in braille. Yes, it should be
easier for blind readers all over the world to communicate,
as the script is the same; but far from it — we have no
dictionaries. Braille words are simply symbols for sounds in
different languages. We really need a Chinese-English
braille dictionary, it's too bad there isn't one. I've got a
phrase book printed abroad — not on sale — of common
expressions in Chinese and English braille, intended for
blind tourists. When I've time I "read" it. First of all I
looked up what my name means in English.... My name's
He Be. In English Hebe means "the goddess of spring".
That bucked me up, but rather disturbed me too. Still I'm
grateful to my father for happening to give me such a name.
Then I "read" "By extension, a barmaid". No, I wasn't
upset. There's not the remotest connection between me and
the goddess of spring or a barmaid.

I wasn't born blind, I lost my sight completely when I
was eight, in 1955. In 1945, when the war ended, my father
came back from France eager to help rebuild our country;
but instead of building it up the Nationalist government
was preparing to fight a civil war, so it was hard for him to
find a job. I was born in September 1946, when he was
working in the Jiangsu provincial government, completely
disillusioned. Later I discovered that he named me He Be
because the proudest day in his life was when he got a

doctorate,* and he didn't imagine he'd ever do better than that.

I started primary school in 1953 and was a very ordinary child. Red-letter days for me were when I got full marks or wore a pretty frock. In the first term of second form I began getting headaches from time to time, not when I was playing, but when reading or looking at the blackboard. The harder I looked at anything, the more it hurt, and there was always a black cloud in front of my eyes. So gradually my work suffered, and I stopped getting good marks. Especially in maths, the teacher wrote so faintly I couldn't see clearly. She came home to report this, and father scolded me for not working harder. I told him my head ached but he didn't believe me, thought I was shamming. He took me to hospital and, strange to say, I had no trouble at all in reading the visual chart. Later on my headaches got worse, and when I had vomited twice the family realized that I wasn't shamming or slacking.

"A tumour in the retina." Such tumours are always malignant; the only thing to do was remove the whole eyeball — that's still the practice today. The doctor said ninety-five per cent of such cases occur in children under three, so I was one of the other five per cent. First they diagnosed a tumour in one eye only, and I had to be hospitalized to have it removed. All I thought was: How ugly I'll look with only one eye! When they said I could have an artificial eye, so that no one could tell the difference, I stopped worrying. I'd still be able to see and would stop having headaches.... Father was very upset. He'd heard that this trouble was hereditary. He said: No one in my family ever had it, it must come from your mother's side. Whether that was so or not nobody knew, as she had left us in 1949 to

_____
* Be or Bo means "doctor".

go off with some high official in the provincial government — I learned later that he was a section chief and she'd been his secretary. They went to Hongkong. Later still, a few years ago, I heard that he'd died soon after, and she was teaching in a Chinese primary school in Indonesia. We never write to each other. Getting letters written in braille is very expensive, very difficult, and I don't want her to know that she has a blind daughter on the mainland....

After the operation, father bought me lots of good things to eat and ordered the best food in the hospital for me. My teachers and classmates came to see me too, and I felt very happy thinking, how nice it would be to stay on here enjoying myself like this!

Several months later my headaches started again. I didn't breathe a word, for I knew it would be all over for me — I'd become blind. As soon as I got an artificial eye, the headaches got even worse; but if I took it out they eased a bit; so I hoped for the best, thinking the artificial eye was to blame. Then the pain got so bad I had to tell my father: I seem to have rather a headache.... A check-up in hospital showed that there was a tumour in my right eye too. Seventy-five per cent of tumours on the retina occur on one side only, but I belonged to the other twenty-five per cent. I felt I was finished.... The doctors wanted to operate at once, but father wouldn't hear of it. He insisted on waiting two months. The doctors said that would be risky. He said, "I'll take the risk, I won't hold you responsible if anything goes wrong. I want to take her on a tour, as this is her last chance to see our country before she loses her sight. This will make all the difference to her later on...." He wept, and so did the doctor. I was eight then, but I'll never forget what he said.

We weren't well off. Though my parents' divorce had been announced in the paper, she was abroad, and father was only a middle-school teacher. He already owed money to his school for my hospital expenses, and now he borrowed eight hundred yuan from friends. Eight hundred yuan! At that time it was an astronomical figure! Setting out from Zhengzhou the two of us, father and daughter, went to Beijing, Xi'an, Chongqing, then down the Yangtse to Nanjing and Shanghai.... We both knew this would be my last sight-seeing trip, every day I was farther from home, and then every day nearer home, until not many days were left.... Last of all we went to Kaifeng, our old home. Step by step I climbed up the seventy-eight stone steps of Dragon Pavilion, then looked down on Lake Pan and Lake Yang. Lake Yang, the lake of the Yang family generals, had clear emerald water; Lake Pan, the lake of the treacherous minister Pan Renmei, was muddy. We visited Fan Pagoda too. Its dark wooden stairway had golden veins in the wood. On each grey brick was a Buddha. Our home was under Iron Pagoda, which isn't iron but dark brown brick.... After leaving Kaifeng, on the train, father said: Little Be, look back, there's Iron Pagoda and below it our home. Have a good look....

I looked hard, but my memory of it is hazy now. I can describe it in detail because afterwards I conjured up mental pictures of it over and over again.

The evening before my operation we went to see a Henan opera with Chang Xiangyu acting. Before the operation all that I could see was light grey. I counted one, two, three.... I knew that when I came to there wouldn't even be that light grey, there would be nothing at all.

Since then, day or night, waking or sleeping, everything has been black. At first I didn't even have the faintest sense of direction. I mixed up everything, even the things just beside me. Each time I bumped into the corner of the bed or the table, I was sorry I hadn't looked more closely at them before my operations, so as to memorize their exact position....

By degrees though I was able to "see" again, relying on my hearing or sense of smell and touch. Sometimes without relying on any of these I sensed changes in the world around me.... Father slowly paid off his debts, ten or fifteen yuan a month, not paying when I was ill, but he didn't run up fresh debts. My health was poor after my two operations and other treatments. When he had paid off all but fifteen yuan he suddenly fell ill with hepatitis. That was when I was about to graduate from the school for the blind. My teacher said, "Don't be upset, but your father's ill and wants you to go and see him." I realized, sensed it somehow that it was serious.... Very soon he was in a coma. He was forty-four when he died. In his obituary his school described him as an exemplary teacher.... Actually he died of cancer, but they kept that a secret from me. No, he hadn't been persecuted or struggled against, so there was no question of having his name cleared.

I was left all on my own. That was at the start of the "cultural revolution", so I stayed on in the school for the blind. All the welfare factories and clinics for the blind were in such disorder they couldn't give us work. I was relatively lucky. My classmates, especially those who could distinguish between light and darkness, were sent for treatment to the June 26 Medical Corps. I believe June 26th was the date of the publication of a talk Chairman Mao gave on medicine, but I'm not too sure. Their treatment was mainly acupuncture and moxibustion, and mostly ineffective. To prove that more and more cases were being cured, they kept looking for new patients, and to start with all my friends were very pleased, thinking that after one needling they'd see light. Later they lost faith in it but were still dragged there for treatment which hurt or numbed them or made them feel sore or bloated, but didn't restore their sight. The few who were cured were those with some blockage of the optic nerves. That acupuncture made some of my classmates "see stars". The medical corps said that was the start of a cure, so that bucked them up, but then it came to nothing. It wasn't a cure, just the result of over-stimulating the optic nerves, because they had something wrong with their eyeballs though their optic nerves were all right. So all those with some perception of light were put through the mill for nothing. As I had no eyeballs they left me alone. That didn't worry me. I don't believe any way will be found in my lifetime to restore my sight. I had my work cut out looking after the house my father left, because if it was taken over in all the disorder I wouldn't even have a home.

Staying at home I couldn't manage on my twelve yuan relief each month. My father's school had given me over three hundred yuan after his death; but as I had to get someone to help me light the stove, buy coal and do repairs around the house, that was very soon used up. I hadn't even the means for bare subsistence. Some neighbours might have helped, but our home was in what was called an "upper-class" district, where practically every family was in trouble, so none of them could take much care of me. No, by the means for bare subsistence I meant those twelve yuan. After all organizations stopped functioning, I didn't know where I could turn for relief. Just then, though, one of my first-form classmates saw me. He took pity on me, and told me that several of my old school friends were keeping out of the Red Guards' activities, not joining any fighting brigades but staying at home to make radios. They all lived in working-class districts in cramped quarters, and would like to use some rooms in my house to assemble transistors.

For that they could provide me with free meals. They hadn't much money themselves; to get transistor parts they'd raided the broadcasting room of one Red Guard contingent. I didn't know that at the time, not until they were discovered and those Red Guards arrested them. The next day the military control commission of the Public Security Bureau took me in too for questioning, because after the Red Guards had beaten up my old classmates and taken the things from my house, they'd turned them over to the public security. I was arrested for hiding stolen goods. And besides, I'd done something wrong with one of them. He'd confessed it.

I was put in the same cell as a woman who was paralysed. Nowadays they might not imprison a sick person, but in those days they did. And I heard her case was serious. I don't know what crime she'd committed, we weren't allowed to discuss our cases together. I didn't dare snuggle up to her to sleep, and I was scared, afraid that crippled woman might be a murderess. She said, "Don't be afraid. Come and feel my legs, my feet are hot." That was an awful shock to me, I still haven't forgotten it. When the police had questioned me and locked me up for a few days, they let me go. One of them told me, "You've been let off lightly. Have you anything to say before you leave?" I blurted out, "I'm longing to leave, to tell people that a paralytic's legs aren't cold, they're hot...."

The school had been notified by the Public Security Bureau, and there was someone at the gate to meet me. Not long after, at the end of 1968, I was assigned work. Since then I've been a masseuse in this clinic. I meet all sorts of people here, people of every kind, and can sense how big yet how small the whole world is. I listen to the radio too, and "read" all sorts of books in braille. I try putting myself in the place of the characters in books and on the radio.

My pay is thirty-six yuan, not bad. (One of her colleagues puts in, "I'll say! In the old days how could the blind earn thirty-six yuan! They sang in the streets or else told fortunes or begged. Some people really believed in blind fortune-tellers. I could tell fortunes too but I couldn't tell where my next meal would come from. You could fool people with sight, but couldn't fool your belly." — authors' note) But I don't save money, what use would it be?

What I'm most sensitive to is changes in moral standards. Old people can compare the old society with the new, but I can't. Nowadays I'm offered a seat in the bus and helped across the road. These last few years we've been well treated by more and more people. From our patients' talk we learn about social changes too, who's under fire and why, who's been commended and given a prize of five yuan. So it seems the system of prizes has come back. Sometimes they swear at the peasants for making so much money.... The things they talk about change from year to year as our country moves ahead. That's how we can sense our country's new look now we're taking the right road, are on the right track. One day, suddenly, we hear cars sweeping the streets. I ask what they are and I'm told they're mechanized road-sweepers. I think: So the old road-sweepers have gone. By the roadside there's a new line of bins, there every day. I feel them and ask what they are. I'm told: Dustbins. Trucks come to empty them. So I realize the old garbage heaps have gone.... People are eating better than before, wearing better clothes, I can sense that too. I've bought stylish clothes myself, I can "see" what's good-looking, and how many people in the street are well-dressed.

I can "see" everything. When the authorities gave me 132 yuan—my relief for eleven months· — then I saw, didn't just hear it over the radio, that the "cultural revolution" had really ended. My mates have asked me to describe Deng Xiaoping, is he especially short? I can't remember clearly, I was so small when I saw the photographs of the heads of the Party Central Committee at Tiananmen. They, no, we blind people are funny that way, we want to hear what people with sight say, but we've got to hear our own mates' descriptions too.... I said: I believe Deng Xiaoping is rather short, but he's a great man! Without him we'd be sunk! And I meant that, every word. One of my mates said, "If I could see just for one minute, I'd first see what my dad and mum look like, then look at a photograph of Deng Xiaoping. Wouldn't mind if I had no time to look at my wife and kids." I don't know what you think. I see nothing wrong with that order, that way of talking.

But some people jeer at us for being blind. Some kids yell, "Dump the blind in the river to feed the turtles." Because they've got sight and we haven't, they feel superior. On a bus once a man said loudly, "Huh, this blind girl's quite a beauty. Too bad her eyes are glass!" People shouldn't think the blind are deaf. Can you judge others just by their faces and figures? Handsome is as handsome does. Plenty of people with eyesight are ugly. They can't see as clearly as we do the difference between ugliness and beauty. Once one of my mates bought an opera ticket and went off to the theatre in high spirits, but the ticket collector stopped him — someone with sight had palmed off a slip of paper on him. Just that once, but we won't forget it! ("In his next life that fellow will be born a monster!" one of her colleagues puts in. — authors' note) This doctor was born blind, so he can't control his face muscles and often his face twitches; he looks quite a sight, but he has a heart of gold.

How do we manage? Our sticks help us to see the road. We don't walk on the pavement but at the edge of the lane for slow traffic, tapping the kerb. So what we hate is when a lorry parks by the roadside, and before you know it you've bumped smack into it. That's never happened to me, but one of my colleagues is careless, keeps bumping into them and cutting his head.... Recently they've invented some ultrasonic glasses for the blind. If you wear them with earplugs, you hear a warning buzz if there's something in your way. I don't like using them, too noisy.

I haven't married. I'm living in my father's house with a friend from another clinic. She's single too. We turn on the light in the evening and don't forget to switch it off before we go to bed. We're human too, and can't live in the dark.

We can tell notes of different denominations by the paper and the size, but we can't distinguish between the coupons for half a pound of flour and ten pounds of flour — they "look" alike to us. We can't tell the difference either between coupons for rice, flour and oil. But we ask people who can see to sort them out for us and put the ones for the biggest amounts at the back. We remember what order they're in and don't mix them up. Our hands are our eyes, so I don't approve of giving the blind heavy rough work which gives them calluses, because that makes it hard for them to "see" and may retard them. Our hands are very sensitive, so we can cook and do housework just as well as people with sight. We can knit, and "see" what we're doing by the feel of it, and learn all sorts of stitches. So our hands are our eyes, and when some factories get the blind to mind a furnace or shift goods about, that damages their hands. One of my friends works in a book-binding firm, which has roughened her hands so that she can't read. But she says, "How many people are there with eyes who read books every day?" It's really too bad.

Apart from "reading" I like going to "see" films. I can follow all the action, even "seeing" where an actor is using sign language and his expression.... I'm not all that keen on operas. Though they talk of "listening" to operas, I can't understand all that's sung, and there's such a din, I don't know whereabouts on the stage the actors are or what they're doing. It's not too easy getting to see a good film. I know some people in cinemas, but when they get good tickets they sometimes forget me. I go and wait for tickets to be returned, there are generally some. Once they showed a good Japanese film. After one day's showing word went round that it was to be withdrawn. I badly wanted to "see" it, but couldn't buy a ticket. That was my birthday, and I was longing to "see" a good film. So I asked our accountant to write on a piece of cardboard: Today is my birthday, please let me have a ticket.... Very soon I "saw" people gather round, and someone put a ticket in my hand. I felt the warmth of his hand....

......

Don't cry, don't cry....

Translated by Gladys Yang

The Head of a Ten-Thousand Yuan Household

Tianjin. One of the best tables in the Dengyinglou Restaurant.

A young married couple. The woman is wearing a semi-transparent pink nylon blouse and a pair of standard black trousers. A "Seagull" twin-lens reflex camera lies on the table. They have ordered six dishes and two litres of beer, then hurried out to buy a fried chicken in the street. They tear it apart with their hands, spitting the bones on the floor.

A few minutes later we get into conversation with her. Her husband is extremely taciturn and only puts in the very occasional remark.

YOU'RE very observant. We're both peasants. From Jinghai County, where Huo Yuanjia* came from. Have you heard of Huo Yuanjia? He was a real hero. That TV serial's really hot stuff. Huo Yuanjia's grandson still lives in Jinghai. He's a schoolteacher: doesn't know the first thing about martial arts.

Where are you from? Hey, that's a good place. Never mind Jinghai — it beats Tianjin too. We came here early

---

*An exponent of the martial arts early in the twentieth century who was the hero of a popular TV serial shown more than once in China.

this morning, and we'll have to be going back tonight.
We're very busy, but before the wheat harvest we can have a
bit of time off on the quiet to come to Tianjin for a day out.
How much do you make a month? Hey, that's not much: it's
nothing.

Just look at how we eat: we really do it in style. Fish, king
prawns, over thirty smackers' worth in the meal. We're
burning our money. Doesn't matter. We've got plenty.
We're not short of the readies. We've got great wads of
tenners. Honestly, there's nothing to worry about. Making
money's the way to glory now. (She is not happy with her
husband, who discreetly shoots her an angry glare and
denies what she has said. — authors' note)

You're wrong. We haven't just got ten thousand flaming
yuan — we're got ten thousand *jin** of grain too. I rake the
money in by raising martens, and he grows grain on the
land we've contracted for. Last year we earned 11,000 yuan
and harvested 13,000 *jin*. So we've really made it. Ha! The
townies are failures. We poor and lower-middle peasants are
ahead: we've left the working class behind. They had it fine
for thirty years, the stinkers, but now they're only getting
bonuses of ten or twenty yuan. They're crawling along by
oxcart. ("Never mind what she says," her husband puts in.
"Once she starts talking there's no controlling her. The
workers are the leading class." — authors' note) Leaders,
that's right, but would you become a worker if anyone
asked you? And why not? It'd be because you couldn't
make any money, wouldn't it? We two can pull in a
thousand a month — more than those workers see in a
whole year. Ha!

We've only got rich in the last few years. We were really

---

*A *jin* is 500 grammes.

poor some years back. My family and his both come from
the same commune, but from different villages. When I was
nineteen he was chosen for the army, so I got engaged to
him. That was because we were poor. When you're poor you
don't have much principles. When I saw he was going for a
soldier I was really keen. Although soldiers are demobilized
after three years and sent home to work in the fields, there
was just a tiny chance that he'd be promoted. Then I'd have
been able to move into army housing and eat government
grain. Of course, the odds were ten thousand to one against,
but it was better than marrying a peasant: they didn't even
have that one chance in ten thousand. ("Just look at her,"
her husband interrupts. "That's the way she thinks, and
she's shameless enough to tell everyone." — authors' note)

What do you mean, shameless? Have I ever disgraced
you? Times were hard then. Apart from having to "learn
from Dazhai" from one year's end to the next, we had to
learn from Xiaojinzhuang.*

"Learn from distant Dazhai and from Xiaojinzhuang
nearby;

Thoroughgoing revolution: red hearts to the sun."
Can you remember that couplet? It was issued to every
household to be pasted up. The work team issued them just
before New Year.**We didn't get any money — just those
damned bits of paper. After he went there was an earthquake. The house fell down, the well dried and his dad was

---

*The village of Dazhai was held up as a national model for many years,
though its supposed achievements were later said to have been falsified.
Xiaojinzhuang was a local "Dazhai-type" village in Tianjin.

**Auspicious couplets on red paper are pasted beside doorways at
Chinese New Year.

crushed to death. People say my father-in-law wasn't a bad sort, but everyone in his village hated him. He was the brigade leader, good at bawling people out but not up to much when it came to work. Hunh! If his old man hadn't been the brigade leader he'd never have got into the army. (Her husband refutes this: "That's rubbish. Don't believe a word of it. We soldiers were chosen by the county armed forces office. We didn't go round by the back door and pull strings."—authors' note) What? What's that you're saying? If he couldn't get in by the back door your dad would have made himself a back window. The people in the armed forces office didn't go short of booze from your family, did they? Did your family slaughter those "revolutionary chickens" to feed to your dogs? Let me explain. A family was only allowed to keep two chickens. Any more and it was "spontaneous capitalism". That's why the two chickens people kept in the village were called "revolutionary chickens".

Anyhow, we two have always got on famously. He came out of the forces in 1980 and we got married. I didn't get many presents from his family: two outfits of clothes, a watch, and a bike, only a "Red Flag" — they couldn't get a good make. ("Well, those things cost the little amount of money we had accumulated for years," her husband puts in. — authors' note) Some friends and relations were invited to a meal, but there wasn't much meat — they were putting beancurd and turnips into the food for all they were worth. Never mind that it was four years since the fall of the "gang of four" — our standard of living had only just started getting a little bit better. Two years before that it was still all that nonsense about learning from Dazhai. Things only got better after Old Deng came to power. If you want to know who's popular, the people the peasants most trust and respect are Old Deng and Zhao Ziyang.

My man's able and he's got guts. When he was in the forces he really got to understand what the Party Central Committee wants. He came home just when the land was being allocated to families. There were two ways it would be done. One was for it to be contracted out by head — so much land per head. The other way was for it to be contracted out by how much of it you were able to work. In their village — well, I ought to say our village now I've married into it — a lot of people have gone off as traders, so the land was contracted out by ability to work it. You didn't have to take any land if you didn't want to. ("She's talking through her hat," her husband says. "She's never got it into her head that when the land was contracted out by ability to work it you had to take some. If you didn't, who was going to provide you with grain to eat? What not taking the land meant was doing a deal on the quiet with someone else to work it for you. You had to pay them to work it. It was only last year that you could buy grain and not take land." — authors' note) He contracted for fifteen *mu** and started work. In '81 we got over seven hundred *jin* to the *mu*,** just eight hundred*** in '82 and about the same last year. So we were a ten-thousand *jin* household three years running. The first year we got a prize of a hundred yuan, the second year it was a bike coupon,**** and last year it was just a certificate. ("No. All she notices is the money. We were given chemical fertilizer too, and priority in buying pesticides. Besides, there were a lot more ten-thousand *jin* and ten-

---

*A hectare, or 2½ acres.

**5,250 kg/ha.

***6,000 kg/ha.

****Authorizing the holder to buy one of the better brands of bicycle.

thousand yuan households last year. If they'd all been given prizes that would have been a hell of a lot." So says her husband. — authors' note)

But he wasn't making any money! You've got to pay for the use of a tractor or a car, to pump water to irrigate your fields, and for chemical fertilizers and insecticides. You've even got to pay for the use of a donkey now that they've all been contracted out. On top of that, we've put a lot of fertilizer into that land and levelled it too. If the top officials ever put out an order to take the land back we'll have been had. All that investment will be down the drain. ("It won't happen," her husband says. The Circular Number One put out by the Party Central Committee this year says the contract system won't change for the next fifteen years. She's getting herself stewed up about nothing." — authors' note)

I go in for sideline production, because that's the way to make money. What do I do? Raise martens. I buy the cubs from the state. They cost eighty yuan each. If you buy a pair and look after them for a year or so you can sell them for three hundred yuan. They breed too, and when the cubs grow up they have cubs. So in a few years you can have a whole lot of them. Me, I spend all my time with my "three hundred yuans". I love it. I got someone to buy me my first pair of cubs down south in 1981. I borrowed the money from the bank and bought two pairs. It's bloody hard getting a loan from the bank. You've got to have official letters and official stamps. They investigated my credence. ("Not your credence, your credit," her husband says. — authors' note) Anyhow, it sounds much the same. They were worried I wouldn't pay the money back.

You wouldn't understand the technical stuff, so I won't go into it. Anyhow, you need a lot of technique to raise martens. The most important thing is that you absolutely mustn't let one of the cubs die when you start raising them. They're your capital, and you depend on them to give you more little ones. But it's very easy for them to die on you when you start keeping them. It's only when you've got some experience that you don't lose so many. But there's nobody to teach you that experience. I can't just write off the dead ones like in a state enterprise and just treat it as an experiment. Besides, when one of a pair of martens dies the survivor won't mate with another one. They've got real feelings — not like people. When people have had enough of sleeping with one partner they go off and find another. (Her husband opens his eyes wide in astonishment or anger. — authors' note) I've been lucky. None of my martens has died. ("Shit! At least a dozen have died on her." Her husband has finally found a way to get his own back. — authors' note) They don't count. Once I'd got a whole lot of them, losing one or two didn't matter. The thing is not to let any die when you start raising them. When I'd got a whole lot of them I started selling cubs. I couldn't raise that many. Martens eat meat, any meat, and when they get in a bad mood they bite. Look — see how they've bitten my fingers.

Last year I did really well — I made over ten thousand yuan. The state makes them into sable coats to sell to foreigners. It gets several times as much as I do. I've got a conscience and I won't do the state down. Smugglers from the south have offered me a colour TV for my pelts, but I wasn't having anything to do with that. Besides, we've got a colour television already. I won't do private customers down either. There are some people about who'll put a widow marten and a male who's lost his old woman together as a pair to sell to folk from other parts. That's a terrible thing to do. When a marten of mine loses its mate I feed it up till I can sell the skin. Of course, I lose out by raising one of those because it won't breed, but I'm not prepared to do anyone else down. If the first two pairs I was sold had been like that my money would all have gone down the drain, and my credence at the bank would have been finished.

Sometimes when marten cubs die, people cry. It really tears you up — worse than losing your own father. It's money that dies. People are really great, I must say. They don't lift a finger to help you. All they're interested in are the readies. The township head's just as bad as the old commune head. One day he makes us pay this or that tax, and the next he's holding an on-the-spot meeting at our house with everyone feeding at our expense. I'm no fool. What I say is, "If you're going to tax us, do it openly, and make it a good big round number. I'll contribute two thousand for the primary school." Get it done once and for all, then they won't be going on at us all the time. What? It's not allowed under central policy? They think they're the Party Central Committee. They don't understand what the Party Central Committee wants.

If we gave money to the primary school the teachers would bring the kids along to thank us and promise to teach our son well if we have one. We haven't had a kid. I've been to the hospital for check-ups a lot of times and there's nothing wrong. It's just that I've never got pregnant. ("We're fine without a kid," her husband says. "Saves us a lot of worry. Besides, births are planned now." — authors' note) Crap! Only a real clod wouldn't want a son. Pay no attention to the relaxed way he's talking — he's even more desperate than I am. I'm desperate too. I want to send my son to university. Money's one thing we aren't short of.

Some people don't know how to get rich sensibly. They do it stupidly. I don't know how it happened, but there's a fashion for clay pots in the village. It's all nonsense. ("They're not clay pots, they're Yixing stoneware teapots, which are very famous." Her husband keeps having to correct her.—authors' note) All the men of thirty or more want one to drink their tea out of, but you can't buy them now. So some people use china pots to drink out of. They aren't really teapots — they're those things they put vinegar in in the big restaurants. His fourth uncle is terrific. He went all over the place to find a coppersmith to make him a copper teapot. Somewhere or other he dug up a couple of those Bighead Yuan silver dollars* and he got a silversmith to use them to cover the whole thing with silver. He calls it his silver teapot. But he made a real fool of himself. He couldn't use it — it burned his hands. The boys in the village said, "You won't burn your hands if your wear gloves when you hold it, grandpa." (We all laugh except her husband: "Those silver dollars were part of his share when they struggled against the landlords. Fourth Uncle was saving them to pay for his coffin." — authors' note) Yes, they're so rich now, they don't have to save up for their coffins any more. Besides, you get cremated now. You're not allowed to have a coffin made.

Goes without saying, everything you've got we've got too: colour TV, a tape-recorder, a bike, a fridge, and a house. Have you got your own house? ("But you haven't got their education," her husband says. — authors' note) Education? Education's useless. If you've had the first three years of middle school that's all you need to get rich. Education's not worth anything.

---

*Issued during the presidency of Yuan Shikai, 1912—1916.

Yes, we have, and plenty! Didn't I tell you just now that some people get rich stupidly? Some people think they can get rich by getting pictures of Old Man Zhao printed. Where we come from there are a lot of people who know how to make woodblock prints. But they don't make respectable New Year pictures: they reckon it's too much trouble and doesn't pay. They just print pictures of Old Man Zhao and the Kitchen God. As the state won't print that sort of thing there's a gap in the market for them to fill. Where do they sell them? They set up stalls at markets, and charge very high prices. What? You don't know who Old Man Zhao is? He's the God of Wealth! The one with a moustache and a beard. Of course he's called Zhao, Marshal Zhao. He comes into Chairman Mao's works. ("Look at you! How can you make up quotations from Chairman Mao?" Her husband gives her another long glare. — authors' note) Of course there are customers for them, but people don't call it buying — they say "inviting them". They hang him up in their homes and make offerings to him when they have a free moment. At any rate the bastard doesn't eat. We don't have one. What's the point? They're useless. That's not the only thing those people print. They print banknotes as well. From the "Bank of Heaven" — a piece of old paper is "a hundred thousand yuan". You give them to the dead. It's just superstition. We bought some for one *fen* each. A hundred hundred-thousand-yuan notes that we burned at my grandad's tomb, so he wouldn't be short of ready money. Hunh! A load of nonsense!

Go on, have some of this food. Then have a drink. Go on, eat! We can afford it. No? Do as you please: we won't force you.

The clothes I'm wearing are all from Hongkong. I got someone to buy them for me in Shenzhen. Cost me seventy.

It's a big place — everyone's rich there. ("Anyone'd think she'd been there herself: she's talking nonsense," her husband says. And we tell her, "Those trousers aren't at all classy, not even medium-quality. And the style doesn't suit you. For the same amount of money you'd have done a lot better to buy clothes made on the mainland. For seventy you could have got worsted." — authors' note) Cut it out. You're just trying to make a fool of me because I'm from the country. Of course Hongkong stuff is good. Why do small traders go all the way to Shenzhen to buy Hongkong stuff? I know perfectly well. When I can spare the time I'm going to Shenzhen to take a look round, and I'll go to Shanghai while I'm about it. I've been to Beijing five or six times. The Temple of Heaven, the Summer Palace, the Dongfeng Market — that's all there is to it. The roast duck's not bad, but it's not worth all that queuing.

What are you laughing at? We really are rich. The policy of the Party Central Committee is good: everyone getting rich. What's the Communist Party for, if not to rescue the poor from their sufferings? ("That'll do. If you go on talking any longer you'll start singing opera and playing Yang Zirong and Shao Jianpo,* " says her husband with a smile. —   authors' note)

Soon we'll be going to Water Park,** not that there's much to it, just boats and water. After three years as a ten-thousand yuan household never mind Shenzhen, even a trip to the US wouldn't be such a big deal for us.... To hell with passports. We're poor and lower-middle peasants, we've got tens of thousands of yuan, and we can go anywhere we like.

Translated by W. J. F. Jenner

---

*Characters in the "model" revolutionary Beijing operas of the "cultural revolution" era.

**In Tianjin.

Certificate

Li Xiaohang, born in 1949 — the year of the establishment of the People's Republic of China

I need a university qualification if I'm going to get security in the job I have been doing for four years. The management is going to start to grade our posts and without qualifications we'll be nowhere. At the moment, there are several ways to get the qualification: there's the television university or you can do a correspondence course, or, if your unit agrees, you can follow special training courses laid on by the university without leaving work. I have been doing a course, then sitting an exam, then doing another course, then sitting another examination. Altogether I need to do nine courses then I'll get a certificate — equivalent to a university degree. So far I've done four. Actually I'm too old for exams now, yes really. But if I learn the subject up and then sit the examination, I don't have time to forget things. I'm studying Chinese. Why? Is that my special interest? No, I just need the certificate.

In 1966, I was in the first year of senior middle school. I hadn't yet thought what university I would try to get into nor what I would study there. I played volleyball. At that time, although our national team was nowhere, they were ambitious to do better. Our government invited a Japanese expert to come to coach us. His method of coaching was really quite cruel by our standards. I was in a special school for coaching amateur sportsmen and sportswomen. I never took it easy, I wouldn't let myself. In fact, looking back on it now, I can see I pushed myself really hard — almost to death.

I also learned to do oil paintings. As far as I was concerned, volleyball was a sort of duty, but painting was my pleasure. I couldn't decide whether I should really try to be a professional. At home they hoped that I would go to fine art school, but I also like music and other things. In fact, I feel a bit embarrassed to say so now, but dancing was what I liked best. But what everyone seemed to agree was that whatever I did in the end, I should get a university degree first.

In early summer that year, I first learned to swear. The first time I heard one of my girlfriends swear, I was astonished, it was so unlike her. But the first time I swore, I felt a little faint, then I thought my friend must have felt that way too, although she didn't show it. She looked quite ordinary. The day before I had been criticized by the "advanced elements" in my school for dressing in a bourgeois way. I had been wearing a frock. Next day, I wore trousers and joined a Red Guard organization. But there had been already established an organization in the school which was called "The Red Guards". To distinguish ourselves from them, we had to add something to our name. I remember we met in the school playing field and spent a whole evening arguing whether we should call ourselves "The Red Guards of Mao Zedong Thought" or "Mao Zedongism Red Guards". This came down to whether it should be "ism" or whether it should be "thought". The basic question of whether to use "thought" or "ism" linked with the whole revolutionary future. Everybody went up and took up the microphone to put their point of view. I didn't say all that much, I just listened to what the others said, but all the same, the next day I'd lost my voice.

Of course, I also took part in the movement to search people's homes and confiscate things. Sometimes, I had no idea who the people were. You would just hear the summons and then everybody would stop a truck, scramble up onto it, and go off to "clean people out". Sometimes we didn't know what we were up to, what we were confiscating, nor did we know the names of our companions or what schools they went to. We also caught the members of street gangs, like "the nine dragons and one phoenix" for example. They sounded frightening, but when we caught them, we beat them until they begged us for mercy. Of course I don't like talking about those things now, it's something I'm rather ashamed of. The funny thing is when I do talk about it, I remember all sorts of other things. Can you understand that? I remember cutting off girls' plaits; delivering leaflets; confiscating other people's leaflets; endless activities and meetings. Of course I went on the great expeditions to exchange experience as well. That was the first chance I'd ever had to go a long way from home—it didn't seem far then. Trains would be full of figures clad in khaki wearing red armbands. If all the seats were full, then people would sit under the seats; if it was full there, they'd sit in luggage racks. Sometimes the luggage racks couldn't hold them all and would fall down. You'd get a dozen or more people cramped in the little space between two carriages of the train and they'd all be squatting. You just can't imagine it. There was nothing to drink, no way of going to the lavatory and everyone would be playing the mouth organ and singing.

After these mad, single-minded days, many people began

just to live for pleasure. They cooked at home and went out to buy vegetables. Before this, I'd never cooked in my life. Then there was the business of making boyfriends. In 1968, fashionable dress for young people in the street in Beijing was a blue outfit from top to toe, with black slip-on shoes and a surgical mask hung round the neck. The mask itself had to be hidden from view leaving the tape showing. The girls wore their hair in short bunches. If you went out dressed like that, then boys dressed in the same way would greet you, and come over to chat you up. The street gangs called this "hunting the birds". At that time, the older Red Guards who had been amongst the first to rebel had begun to get on quite well with the street gangs. They had begun to feel such people were pretty easy to understand. Not long ago, I met up with a classmate from middle school and we talked about all sorts of things. She asked me whether I'd slept with a lot of boys at that time. I said I hadn't slept with a single one. She was very surprised and told me a lot of stories had gone around about me. When she thought about it a bit, she could see she jumped to conclusions because we had all been brought up so strictly. In fact, I didn't know anything at all about sex at that time. That was something I learned   later.

Although our life as students had really finished earlier, it formally came to an end in the summer of 1968. A lot of us went down to the countryside. I was sent to Inner Mongolia — to an area inhabited by herdsmen. This time too I went off playing the mouth organ and singing, but I did feel it was a long way from home. We educated youth had a Mongolian yurt to ourselves. To start with, life seemed very fresh and full. I learned to ride a horse and control it sitting upright in the saddle while it was trotting — much more difficult than just hanging on as it galloped along. At first, I felt rather sick and giddy. I was chafed between the legs. I learned to drink tea with milk in it, to speak a bit of Mongolian and to milk. I began to understand the beauty of the great outdoors. When I was riding in the great grasslands, it was very beautiful. If now I have a sense of wonder, or I sometimes feel nostalgia for something, if I have an understanding for remoteness and quietness, it was there that I learned it all.

Afterwards something happened. I got on very well with the herdsmen and their families. I often used to go to visit them, and to help with their work. They looked after me. They used to ask me to come over. But then, one evening the son of the family I knew very well raped me. The whole family was there and they helped him. Several of the girls who went to Inner Mongolia as educated youth met this fate. Some of them settled down there. Later, some educated youth asked me to do self-criticism. Yes, that's right, self-criticism! They said I had been doing my best to seduce the young herdsman, because my father hadn't yet been freed. Make a plaint? Who could I make a plaint to? They were national minorities, this was the custom. This is something I've never told the people at home.

Later, I met somebody who was recruiting workers. I went to work in a small chemical factory. I worked there for five years and it was there I met my husband. He's from a worker's family in the countryside. He was very good to me, he helped me wash my clothes, gave me eggs, all that sort of thing. That's how we got together. When we were going to get married, I told him what had happened to me. He was very upset; he almost couldn't take it. I hadn't expected this — we nearly didn't get married. But I still feel his kindness to me was one of the best things that ever happened to me. I'd never known anything like it. I learned to make clothes and pickles, to cut my husband's hair and to curl mine, to chat and gossip with other girl workers. I found out how to pull strings with people who worked in the shops when we needed things that were not easy to buy. I managed to get hold of some timber, and I found a carpenter for whom I cooked special things so that he would make furniture I designed myself. In other words, I learned everything that a housewife should know. Furthermore, I made a good job of it. In that little town, we got together a cosy home and then I gave birth to a boy.

In 1978, the universities started to organize entrance examinations again. Lots of young people were taking up their studies again. They worked at maths, at physics, and at chemistry. Whenever you met somebody, they would say: are you going to take that examination? What speciality are you going for? I didn't join in. I just didn't have any wish to go to university. I had a home and my child. And yet, at the same time, I did have an ambition or a sort of desire to do something, which I felt I couldn't control. I had already adjusted to my life and I felt satisfied, but it couldn't hold me forever. I was still able and ambitious, and I couldn't go on living in that little town indefinitely. I wanted to get back to Beijing. I wanted to return to the political and cultural centre I knew so well.

It seemed very ambitious. Getting my residence permit transferred to Beijing was really going to be very difficult. I didn't think it was going to work just to stick a little advertisement on one of the telegraph poles in Beijing. And what's more, it wasn't just for me; there was my husband's residence permit too. The residence permit of the child normally went with the mother's. But on the other hand, I'd already understood one thing: it's no use worrying too much, but it's no use being afraid to act; you must grasp the opportunity.

To transfer your residence permit, you had to move on several fronts at once. There is the official in charge of the bureau that looks after entry to and exit from the city, and there's the unit in Beijing that you want to work for. Obviously the first thing is the bureau in charge of entry to the city, and for this you have to find somebody who wants to exchange with you. There are a few people who want to leave Beijing. I found some. They were working in the track maintenance department of the railway bureau. Their household registration was with the railway bureau which meant it counted as Beijing, but actually they were moving about all over the place. There were two of them and they had originally come from the town I worked in. They'd reached an age when they felt they would like to come home. They lived in workers' accommodation in the suburbs. I went to see them on my bicycle. It was a windy spring day in Beijing, I had to pedal against the wind the whole way. When I got there I had a chat with them. I found a lot of them wanted to go home. I felt quite sorry for them, but I couldn't tell them all about the advertisements of people who wanted to swap places with them. If I had, there would have been no one left to maintain the track. Anyway there might have a fight over who would swap with them. These two people made a couple of conditions: firstly, one of them wanted me to help him to find a job, a good job, in that little town. The other one wanted a flat there. They were in Beijing after all, so their bargaining position was strong. I managed all this but then the personnel department wouldn't let them go. So I had to think up some way to overcome this new problem. You think presents would have done the trick? No, too easy. It's no good just spending money; you have to make sure you spend it the right way.

The thing to do is to see what they need for their families —
you have to use your eyes or make enquiries. The son-in-law
of this official was in the army, and would soon be demobilized. He'd gone into the army from the countryside,
but his wife was in the city. So he wanted to return to the
city. This wasn't at all easy to arrange and I had to use the
influence of old friends of my parents to do it. It was no use
going to my father or my mother because they wouldn't
have known how to set about it at all — they would be afraid
to open their mouths. So that was how it was. I knew the
right way. Again and again I had to work out how to do it
and then get it done. Finally, I got my residence permit and
that of my husband and my son transferred to Beijing. In all
this I had to use the knowledge that I had learned through
ten years' hard life in the big world. In fixing everything, I
discovered just how able I could be.

Now I am working on archival materials about old buildings. This is a job I found myself. The educated youth of my
generation had one thing in common. When they got into a
work unit, they didn't mind a bit of hardship, they were
good at seeing what needed doing, and they could cultivate
good relationships with people. They were easy-going and
pretty flexible. At the beginning, the boss in this outfit
didn't want women working under him, so I was sent off to
do odd jobs. I used to do things which I didn't really have to
do. So in the end that boss kept me on. I'm very interested
in my work, although I never expected to make a career out
of anything like this. But I feel this work needs imagination
and a feeling for history. It's pretty steady too. Just over a
year ago, they began to talk about introducing grades.
During the ten years of chaos, lots of young people lost their
opportunity to study, but now you'll find lots of them in
jobs which they got through their own initiative, like me. In

this way, they've managed to attain the status of specialists. Our country is developing, it needs standards, and it needs educated people. The scientific research institutes want people with university qualifications. So are we all done for? Well, some people say, "Oh, what a waste. Everything is ruined." But I don't think it's quite like that. These days you need a junior middle school certificate even to work in a factory. And to tell the truth, I'm not sure I could get that, if I had to do it again.

I decided that doing one course at a time, then taking an exam and getting a certificate for it would be the best method for me. After all, in several of these courses I've already studied the material a bit in junior and senior middle school and in my ten years in the outside world, so it shouldn't be too much to learn. Take history for example. Even in primary school we learned a bit about peasant rebellions. Then, in middle school, we started all over again on the same material. In the "cultural revolution" and in the movement to criticize Lin Biao and Confucius we looked at the same stuff all over again, and at the Warring States Period. The whole population was asked to study all this, to make criticisms and to write poetry. Of course it goes without saying that the concepts were wrong, completely wrong. But now we are still studying the same things, though the standpoint is different. So you could say it's familiar, yes; it's true it's familiar, but you could also say it's strange and that would be right too. Furthermore, studying on your own there's nobody to get on to you each day to do a set amount of work. It is difficult to be disciplined about your time. Sometimes I get really fed up with studying. I go through things again and again and I still can't remember them. I've been going on like this for more than ten years; I've studied these things so many times and I still can't remember them.

How can this be? Last time I took an English test, I didn't pass it. Several thousand people did the exam but only about two hundred got the certificate. I'll take it next year. I'll only finish with it when I pass it. Sometimes, I lose confidence and feel very frustrated. I've been through all this so many times before. Going one, two, three, four again makes the whole thing seem like an endless circle. Now ten years on, here I am on the same point of this circle again. And who knows what sort of practical value this certificate is going to have anyway? When they introduce grading and a new wage scale, I don't think it will really count as a proper university degree. Let's not think so far ahead anyway. I despair about each course. Sometimes I like the content I do with history for example. When I go right back and look at it again, I feel that it's something totally new, although in fact I studied a lot of it before. But when I look at the whole course of Chinese history — I don't know why — it makes me think a lot, makes me look at my own past. I particularly like contemporary history, but when it comes to the exam, you just have to reproduce a few pages and then that's that. It doesn't matter how much you feel about it, or how keen you are on it.

My younger brother got himself into university and graduated properly. He studied Chinese too. He often tells me that I'm working myself to death quite pointlessly. According to him, there's no need to work hard. You shouldn't put your feelings into working for your course. The texts are full of old ideas anyway; you just have to learn things off by heart and then pass the exams like that. I can't take his frivolous, cynical attitude towards it. I don't want to grumble to him about my problems either. What's the use of doing that? We are not of the same generation; he is eight years younger.

We do all have our grumbles though. We grumble about the classes and the exams, about our children being sick, about having to go to buy coal or to fetch milk. We are busy all day long and yet we don't seem to get anything done. When I went to get the certificate for the first course, the room was full of my classmates. They were all the same generation as I am, so they are all parents. Yet every one of them was sitting at a table crying. Yes, they were all in tears.

Translated by Delia Davin and Cheng Lingfang

The Old Man

Mr Zhang is seventy-eight. He has worked all his life in a bank, the only differences being the changes in the bank's name and his promotions and demotions.

He lives in two north-facing rooms inside a dark little doorway at the end of a cul-de-sac of an alley like an appendix behind the Beijing Hotel. The wall is covered with little packets that look like packets of Chinese medicine. On them is written with a writing brush, "Day lily", "Tree-ear fungus", "Beanstarch vermicelli", "Cooking soda" and a date. Apart from beancurd, which cannot be put on the wall, all the non-staple foodstuffs sold in set quantities to local residents each month when they produce a non-staple foodstuffs ration book are on that wall.

I don't go in for *taijiquan* exercises, I don't diet, I eat fat pork, and I don't bother at all with methods of living longer. I go out every morning at about nine, walk along East Chang'an Avenue to Dongdan to buy food, and buy whatever's available. Throughout the year I get what's in season. I don't insist on eating hothouse Chinese vegetables and tomatoes in the middle of winter. Hothouse vegetables are expensive, and they aren't necessarily very nutritious. Then I walk back. I cross the southern end of Wangfujing,*

* Beijing's best known shopping street.

turn back in here when I see the traffic lights, and come straight home. I never go into the shops. Wangfujing isn't a place for us Beijing people to do our shopping. And when you get to my age there isn't much that you want to buy. So on the way there and back I cross the road twice and see traffic lights four times. In the afternoon? I walk to Tiananmen and stand under the gate tower watching the traffic. Then I come back. That also involves crossing the road twice, but there are six lots of traffic lights as there's a pair at the western end of the Beijing Hotel. They're not usually in use, and there are concrete bollards in the road. Those are the two routes I follow every day.

My wife died eleven years ago. I'm from Hebei. I came from there when I was eighteen to be an apprentice. I started in the Salt Bank, which was a Chinese bank. When Xuantong (i.e. the last Qing emperor, Aisin Gioro Pu Yi — authors' note) pawned his treasures for silver the Salt Bank was involved. Later on I worked in the Huifeng Bank and the Banque de l'Orient et d'Indochine. That was when I learnt English. The Huifeng was called the Hongkong and Shanghai Banking Corporation, Peking in English. Originally it wasn't called Peking but Peiping. (Now the spelling Peking has been changed to Beijing. — authors' note) I didn't work in the Banque de l'Orient et d'Indochine for long, so I didn't master French. I didn't make a proper study of it. There were two kinds of banks I never worked in. One was one of the official banks — the Central Bank, the Bank of China, the Communications Bank and the Agricultural Bank. The other was the Shyokin Bank. That was a Japanese devils' bank.

A bank's a good place to work. "Get in the railways, the post office or a bank and your worries are over." People always want to move things, send letters and spend money.

That's why those three jobs were iron rice-bowls in the old society. Being an official wasn't an iron rice-bowl. Wasn't President Sun Yat-sen kicked out by Bighead Yuan?* And didn't old Chiang have to step down in favour of Li Zongren?** Mind you, old Chiang was just putting on a show: once he got to Taiwan he chucked Li Zongren out as acting president.

To get back to what we were talking about, I spent my whole life in banks, from when I was an apprentice to when I was deputy manager of the credit department. But I never worked in a bank that had the right to issue currency notes. After Liberation I worked for the Bank of China. *Bank of China* sounds better than *The People's Bank of China*, doesn't it?*** But the Bank of China didn't have the right to issue banknotes either. It was only after I retired that it livened up and started printing banknotes — Foreign Exchange Certificates.**** They're worth the same as Renminbi, but they can buy things that Renminbi can't. Take that bean vermicelli on the wall, for example. You can only get it with Renminbi if it's written down in your ration book. But with Foreign Exchange Certificates you can get as much as you like. Hunh!

Of course I've got some Foreign Exchange Certificates. I've got all the denominations. I got someone to buy them for me. I keep them to look at.

When I was an apprentice I earned a few silver dollars each month. When I'd paid for my board and lodging and was free in the evening I used to go out. I went to the theatre

---

* In 1912 Yuan Shikai replaced Sun as president of the Republic of China.

** In January 1949 Chiang Kai-shek resigned as president.

*** Italicized words in English in the original.

**** A parallel currency to the ordinary Renminbi currency for use by foreigners and purchased with foreign currency.

and sometimes down the "alleys". That was outside
Qianmen Gate, Yangmeizhu Angled Street, Hanjiatan, and
those places. The "alleys" were the brothels. In those days
nobody thought anything of going there for a bit of fun. My
parents arranged my marriage back at home. We'd never
met. After I went home and married her I brought her back
to Beijing. In those days there was plenty of housing and
not many people. If you wanted to buy or rent a house you
could take your pick. Despite all the big blocks they've put
up now there's still a housing shortage — too many people.
All the people in the streets are young. This place of mine
was bought fifty years ago. In those days it really wasn't
difficult to buy yourself a small courtyard. It's near
Dongjiaominxiang, and it's very quiet too, being at the end
of a little alley. In those days all the big banks were in
Dongjiaominxiang or in Qianmenwai Street; you could be
there in no time by rickshaw. This house isn't any good
now. The new part of the Beijing Hotel blocks out the
sunlight. The original Beijing Hotel was just the grey
building in the middle. The red west wing and the yellow
east wing were built after Liberation. I don't think the
yellow wing is right for the Beijing Hotel: it's too foreign.
I've heard it's all very splendid inside, but terribly
expensive. Anyhow, it's no place for Beijing people to stay.
It makes a lot of money out of foreigners.

As for prices, that depends on how you look at them. In
the old days everything was very cheap except calico, grain,
and foreign oil — what's called paraffin these days. A one-
way tram ticket cost three coppers and the circular round
the city five. You got five hundred coppers for a silver
dollar. Now it costs five *fen* to get on a bus, and how many
five *fens* are there in a yuan? But in '47 and '48 money
wasn't worth anything. A sack of banknotes wouldn't buy

you a sack of grain. With those so-called gold yuan and silver yuan you didn't bother counting low-denomination notes: you just sorted them out into their different values and weighed them. Later on accounts were kept in millions and tens of millions of yuan — rows and rows of noughts. So no wonder a peach cost tens of thousands of yuan. In those days a hundred-yuan note was worth less than a sheet of toilet paper. Well, no: people didn't take banknotes to the toilet with them. That's just a figure of speech. By then low-denomination notes had gone out of circulation: all the notes were for ten thousand or more. That's where the Communists are better than the Kuomintang. You have to admit it. There's no inflation. Soaring prices and recklessly printing money doesn't work. Old Chiang didn't care whether he had gold reserves and backing in foreign currency or not, he just printed banknotes like a madman and did for the common people.

But when we changed from the old currency to the new, prices went on rising. The high-cost sweets put on sale in 1961 were a price rise. Later prices came down a bit. A few years back there were pay increases, and last couple of years they've been issuing exchequer bonds. Things really are more expensive than they were. But the standard of living has gone up in the last few years, and everyone's got things like televisions, refrigerators and electric fans. That's good. It gets money circulating faster, and the state is deliberately encouraging people to buy things. After a lifetime in banking I sometimes like to think about things like that: it's become a habit with me. We won't go into anything else, but there's no other country in the world with inflation as low as China's. What does the reputation of Renminbi depend on? Stability. You can put your money in the bank and forget about it. No need to worry about it losing a lot of value, and there's no hope that it'll shoot up either. Foreign currency's hopeless. It's always changing in value. Look how the Hongkong dollar collapsed a few months ago.

As I told you, I was involved in credit before Liberation. Credit means loans. I didn't make the loans: I used to work out the value of assets. That meant checking up on a factory's ability to repay before the bank made a loan, so that the factory wouldn't default. That wasn't quite what I was doing, actually. We had specialists to do that. They used to estimate what potential the factory had for development. The main thing was that you had to keep your wits about you. I depended on a very sharp eye. I was in charge of estimating the value of assets when a factory went bust. If we made a loan to a factory and it went bankrupt I'd be very busy. I'd have to work out what their buildings, machinery, raw materials and so on were worth. When the case came up the capitalists would try to get out of their obligations and talk all sorts of nonsense. Then I'd bring out my assessment, and say how much it was all worth, and what percentage was owed to the bank. No, I didn't appear in court: the bank had lawyers. If they'd had to depend on me they'd never have won a case. I never fought a case. "Even if you're in the right it's a disgrace to go through the books in open court." We Chinese! In the last years before Liberation the bank simply stopped making loans. Things were in such a mess that no factory stood a chance. There was no point in throwing money away on them. The banks lent out gold, but all they got back were banknotes: only an idiot would do a thing like that. Old Chiang Kai-shek couldn't get at us as we were a foreign bank. After Liberation we went in with the Bank of China, and I suppose you could say that I joined the revolution. I counted as a senior official, so I kept a good salary. The

Bank of China specializes in foreign exchange dealing and doesn't make loans. Later on it also went in for foreign currency credits, but there was never any bankruptcy work. All I had to do was supervise the removal of money from the vaults: it was very easy work. Goes without saying — if the state's prepared to lend you money you can be sure you won't go bust. The factories and the bank both belong to the state.

I didn't have any talent; there were people a lot cleverer than me. Talented people will always come forward. The Central Bank had Xu Yizhuang. He became a branch manager when he was very young. He was honest, he didn't go whoring, he didn't take bribes and he was a hard worker. But he came to nothing in the end. Old Chiang treated the state bank as his private money-chest. Whenever he felt like it he'd write a note, "Give so-and-so so many tens of thousands", and they'd all go to Xu Yizhuang for their money. Xu Yizhuang ended up in a terrible mess. The last time I saw him was in 1947. He was involved in speculation, he'd lost his job, he couldn't keep away from the whorehouses, and to top it all he was on opium. Chiang Kai-shek destroyed him. If you ask me, someone like Xu Yizhuang would have made managing director of the bank. They said he died young, but I can't remember whether it was in Taiwan or Hongkong.

I used to collect coins from every dynasty, and I had quite a collection. I had *wuzhu*, *bu* and *dao* coins — those are what people call "trouser" and "big sword" coins — and even ones from the Wang Mang usurpation and the Taiping Heavenly Kingdom.* I was a collector from when I

---

* *Wuzhu* cash were first issued in the Western Han Dynasty; *bu* and *dao* coins, also called "spade" and "knife" coins, date from the Warring States period; Wang Mang's usurpation lasted from AD 9 to 23; and the Taiping Heavenly Kingdom from 1851 till 1864.

was a boy, and I loved it. During the "cultural revolution" I handed my whole collection in. Nobody was in charge of me then as I'd already retired. Nobody asked me about it, but I was scared. You just had to look at what was happening in the streets. Even the shop signs in Wangfujing were smashed up because they were supposed to be part of the "four olds".* The smashing up reached this alley. Duke Xia's Palace — that was feudal, you see. The Red Guards had their Red Guard logic. They did not come to this courtyard, but my neighbour to the east was raided. He used to have a shop selling silks and cottons, and from the way he lived he can only have been prosperous in a small way at most. He liked paintings and calligraphy, and his place was stuffed full of it. If you ask me, nearly all of his stuff was fakes, and there were virtually no genuine pieces. But he had one painting by Qiu Shizhou** that was the real thing. People had come from the city Cultural Relics Bureau to see it. They wanted to buy it, but he wasn't selling. The old woman from the street committee brought a whole mob of Red Guards in to raid his place, and they burnt all his pictures, including the Qiu Shizhou. It was torture for him. He kept saying, "Don't burn it, don't burn it, I'll give it to the state." But the Red Guards paid not a blind bit of notice. They just beat him up. "What would the state want with that 'Four Old' of yours?" the old woman from the street committee asked. That's why I took the initiative in getting rid of my stuff by handing it over to the state. A few years ago when old wrongs were being righted they compensated me for my collection by giving me some money. That was supposed to settle the score. But I didn't

* Old culture, old ideology, old customs and old habits — a formulation much used during the "cultural revolution".

* * Qiu Ying, one of the most famous painters of the Ming Dynasty.

want the money: I want my old coins. I know what old coins fetch on the black market these days, but I never once did any foreign currency fiddles when I worked in a foreign-owned bank in the old society. Would I sell my coins on the black market in New China? Wouldn't it have been enough if I'd left them to the state on my death? But let me have them now. I do miss my old coins....

I've got three children but no grandsons of our line. My eldest girl's a cadre — she and her husband are both quite high-ranking. Before Beijing was liberated she was a student, and she joined the underground Communist Party. It was a secret. None of us knew anything about it. Now she's the secretary of the Party committee. She can talk and she's capable — not much like one of our family. During the "cultural revolution" she got criticized and struggled against. She always comes to see me at holidays and the New Year with her children and some presents: she knows how to behave properly. My second child is a son, and he's very dutiful. He studied water conservancy, but he's too far away: he was sent to Yunnan. He happened to graduate just when the "cultural revolution" came along, and he had to spend years and years on a state farm. The army had to be matchmaker for him — he married a painter's daughter. Both of them are well into their thirties, and their child's a girl. He's always concerned about me, and often gets people to bring me big containers of rapeseed oil from there. He says pork fat isn't good for old people. I don't like that sort of oil myself — it's got a peculiar taste. It's not as good as peanut oil, but they'll only sell you half a *jin* of that a month. My youngest, a daughter, graduated from senior middle school and had to spend ten years in the countryside before she was allowed to leave because of our family difficulties. She married late. She and her husband are both primary-school teachers, and they haven't got a place of their own. They had to borrow a room from a colleague to get married, and now she's had to come back here to live with the baby. She has the inner room. There's a lot of noise, and the baby cries. It's a boy. But none of them gave me a grandson of my own name. I've only got granddaughters and grandsons that belong to other families.

Apart from my little strolls every day I go out for a meal with some friends every Friday. We're all retired. We get together and say, "Let's go to Quanjude and have duck this week." Come Friday we all head off to Qianmenwai. When the bill comes we split it equally. At the end of the meal someone'll say, "Let's go to Senlong and have puffed rice next week." And that's what we'll do. There are so many restaurants and so many different styles of cooking in Beijing. This week we're going to the Laijinyu Pavilion in Zhongshan Park to have steamed buns with dried cabbage stuffing. The Laijinyu still looks the same, but the fillings fall a long way short of what they used to be. The dried cabbage isn't fresh enough, and they're too greasy. Eating out's expensive these days; you have to know the right people. I can't take having to queue up and wait for an empty table. Last time we got someone to fix us up with a private room at the Hongbinlou so we could take our time over the meal. It was very comfortable. We usually get someone to put in a word for us beforehand. If you get someone to fix things and make contacts beforehand you can usually get your meal a bit cheaper. Some dishes that aren't usually on the menu you can only get by using contacts. The hot bamboo shoots at Makai's are never on the menu, nor is "Buddha jumping over the wall" at the Zhensuzhai vegetarian restaurant. But if someone puts in a good word for you they'll serve them up for you. They're perfectly ordinary, traditional dishes, but the restaurants can't be bothered to serve them as they're too much trouble. A couple of years ago restaurants didn't even look like businesses: bureaucrat business methods. In the last couple of years things have got a bit better, but they only want to cook the dishes they make a big profit on. They'll be damned if they're going to put low-profit dishes that are a lot of trouble to make on the menu.

We all got to know each other on our strolls. We used to do all sorts of jobs before — a doctor, a gardener, a professor, a worker. But we don't ask each other where we live. We get on all right. Even when we make friends with each other we don't visit each other at home. We just meet every Friday for our meal. If someone fails to turn up the next time and we think he might be sick we'll arrange for a message to be sent to him. Whoever sees him will tell him where we're eating next week. If he still doesn't come the time after that we reckon he's probably passed on. But nobody says so in as many words.

Next week we're going to Donglaishun to eat instant-boiled mutton. If we don't go now it won't be on the menu any longer: it's getting too hot. We're not like you: if we don't have it this year we can't be sure we'll be getting it next year. We can't tell whether we'll last till winter.

Translated by W.J.F. Jenner

The Hunter

He Guangwei is a 76-year-old member of the People's Political Consultative Conference of Henan Province.

I can't really say I'm much good at anything apart from hunting. I'm all at sea when it comes to meetings like this; but the government's thought enough of me to make me a member of the conference, so it's only proper that I should come along and do my share in ruling the country. The only problem is that food they feed us. No, I can't quite put my finger on it. Seems a bit off, you know; none too fresh. Maybe it's because it's high-class tucker.

I live at Wu Family Bridge, it's due north of the Meng County Seat. There's a story connected with the place that says it's the place where Wu Song was banished and had that drunken spree in Jiang Menshen. (A delegate at a neighbouring table breaks in: "The people where he comes from say Comrade He is a reincarnation of Wu Song. No, really. But he has a more impressive record than Wu Song: over the last sixty years he's killed or captured seven tigers and over 330 leopards with his bare hands, not to say anything of the 2,000 or so wolves and wild boars he's hunted. Wu Song would've been no match for him, believe you me.") Thanks very much all the same, but you're laying it on a bit thick. I'm a hunter pure and simple, it's my job.

Who do you reckon's the king of the mountains? The tiger? You're way off, it's man; man's the real king. Say when you're after a leopard, all you need is the right method, the strength and enough pluck and you'll be able to do the job. Leopards don't go for people, they try and run away the moment they catch sight of a human being. But you've got to stick with him, rile him. You keep at him until he turns on you in anger, then you stand your ground and wait for him to come at you and you aim a solid blow at his snout. That'll knock the wind out of his sails. There's 200 catties behind him; add the same again for your strength, and that means he takes 400 catties on the snout. He'll be so dazed he'll forget all about biting you. It's when he's panting and wiping away the tears that you have to go straight up, grab him by the head with one hand and by the tail with the other, using your legs to scissor his head, and press down on his pelvis. Then you wait for the cage you've made to be brought along. And there you have it: catching a leopard is no harder or simpler than that.

They're funny things, leopards; they care more about eating than staying free. They're not like other wild animals that refuse to feed in captivity. You hold him down and make him eat a bit of meat and once he has he'll be as good as gold. You have to tie him proper around the legs and he's ready for the cage. You take him down the mountain in a small cage and put him in a large one later. You have to drug him to prevent shock. Leopards are easier to keep alive and transport since we started using sedatives.

What's the key you say? Well, the thing you have to watch out for is flies. Every creature has its natural enemy, and leopards don't take to flies at all. Now if a fly fouls his eye then he'll be sure to get sick. And once they get sick they're as good as done for. What are you laughing about? It's true. Forget that stuff you've read, that's just the way it is.

Originally I'm from Hejiapaifang, southeast of the county seat of Suxian in Anhui. I finally settled in Mengxian County. My dad was drowned by a landlord's lackeys when I was only ten. After that I was forced to go to work for a landlord too. He was all smiles on the surface — they're the worst kind. He was scared I'd steal from him and so one night he spread some coppers in the courtyard and waited to see whether I picked them up. I did because I thought I could use them to pay for a doctor to see my gran. But then I reckoned I'd sooner starve than steal from someone so I put the damned lot down on his doorstep. We've been submissive villagers, my family, for generations.

During the autumn wheat harvest of the year I turned fifteen I got news from the village that both my brothers were dead. The elder one had been sold to be a soldier by the village head and had died on the way to Suzhou. My other brother hung himself after he was caught stealing some wheat stalks and beaten. You couldn't even eat wheat stalks; people used them for kindling. The landlords couldn't use them for anything. My second brother was only nine when he died. I had a dream in which my father and brothers said to me, "Don't work for the landlord any more, break away and make a life for yourself." I hugged them and cried, "The world is a large place, there must be somewhere for me. I'll go and learn a trade and when I'm rich I'll be a good man and show them all."

I went to a fortune-teller who said to me, "It's a wide world and there's no end of places where you can settle down and make a life for yourself. Go out and make your own way." He wrote the words "He Guangwei will prosper anywhere" on my waistband. He was very kind and refused to accept any money. "You can make a donation to me when you've become a rich man, that'll satisfy me."

I met Master Wang in Luohe. He was a short man with very smooth skin, something feminine about him. But you couldn't let that fool you, he was a talent. He had a reputation all over the place as a "two-in-one": small like Wu Dalang, but as deadly as Wu Erlang. His speciality was tigers; he caught them unarmed.

He wouldn't take me on as a disciple, though I approached him twice. He refused to teach me, but I pestered him so much that in the end he offered me money to go away. "I know all you want is enough money to feed your family. Well, here, take this." I knelt down in front of him and pleaded, "I'm the only family I have left. All I want is to learn something to keep myself going. I have nothing to live for." When he heard that he decided to take me on. "It's not that I didn't want to accept you," he explained, "but you have to understand that whoever lives by catching tigers will one day be killed by a tiger. I've got a bad back and it's getting worse all the time. I don't even have a son who can keep my name alive when I'm gone. But the reason I never got married was that I didn't want my son to follow in my footsteps. Now I'll take you on as a disciple on the condition that you're only to stay with me for three months."

For the first two months I studied eagle kung fu, then pushing techniques and the use of fists and legs. Finally my master took me out into the hills. He showed me how to catch a tiger in the Dabie Mountains. I remember it was snowing that day and what seemed like a whirlwind came rushing up out of a hollow. My master shouted, "He's coming," and pushed me aside with the words, "Watch me carefully." He crouched down in the eagle position, straightened his shoulders, using his left hand to block the sun out of his eyes and his right fist was clenched and raised to protect his chest. He let out a mighty yell and knocked the tiger down with one blow. Then he called me over to help tie the beast up and take it out of the mountains. We sold it for over 100 yuan and we split the money between us. My master said to me, "Here, take this money; this is the end of our acquaintance. I've taught you everything I know. You can only expect your children to be yours for life; disciples always leave you sooner or later. I'm nearly done for, and you've got a long way ahead of you. Let's call it quits now If you ever think of me go into the hills and call out; I'll hear you whether I'm in this world or the next." I searched for him for years after that, but never got any news. I don't know if he was killed by a tiger, or maybe he died in a fall in the mountains. Possibly he was shot by stray soldiers. I guess I'll never know.

After that I caught five tigers in Hunan. The first was in Changde. But once I became famous things became very sticky—bandit gangs were always after the tiger bones and leopard skins I had; the KMT people had an eye on the money I made; and the girls kept chasing me, too. For a while there it was so easy to get into trouble that I gave up hunting altogether. Since I was out of work I learnt to make "refugee cigarettes". I started out in Dong'an and Quanzhou, then I moved on to the Talisman Cigarette Factory in Guilin. The cigarettes we made were a local version of Manila cigars. That's right, cheap cigars; they stunk.

I got married in Quanzhou, though I was introduced to my wife in Dong'an. I don't want to go into any of that if you don't mind. But there is one thing about that first meeting I should tell you. I ate a whole bucket of rice at her parents' place and two huge bowls of pork gelatine. I've always been a big eater and I'm not the type to pretend I'm full when I'm not. I could tell they were shocked at how much I ate and so I figured it was a lost cause. That afternoon I gave the matchmaker some money for the parents — I hadn't gone there just to get a free meal. Then I left for Quanzhou. It was the last thing I thought'd happen, but she followed me there and we got married. Know what she said to me? "The spirit in my dreams told me it's my fate to cook for a big eater." Dreams and all; sure, whatever you say.

We spent time in Guangxi during the War of Resistance Against Japan. The KMT came along with all that stuff about taking a side track to achieving national salvation. They screwed up the locals something terrible. We were running from the Japanese all the way to Guilin. Our first boy died not long after he learnt to walk. We had another one but he died too. God, we were poor, and things were really hard for us. There was no way we could keep the little ones alive, and it wasn't safe to stay in Guilin so we moved on to Panxian County where we had a little girl. At the age of three she fell into the wok when she was crawling around the stove looking for food—scalded to death.... I got blind drunk and jumped into the pond and started drinking the mud. Then I turned a gun on myself, just wanted to end it all. But I used too much strength and the barrel slipped over my shoulder. Didn't shoot myself but I did get the house.... My father, two brothers, then my own two sons and my daughter. Six lives. Then there was my master and my friend, a guy who worked with me in the tobacco factory in Guilin. He was a Communist and the KMT killed him. Eight people in all. The world was a rotten place, and I didn't want to live any more.

I went hunting all over the country — Yunnan, Sichuan, Hunan, and finally ended up in Mengxian County. That was after Liberation.

I've caught over three hundred leopards in the past sixty years. I remember this really wild fella in Shanxi — he used to chase trucks on the road. He ran after the mail truck once and forced it right off the road on a corner. Then he'd scamper away to make trouble somewhere else. But I took care of him, sent him packing. Off to a big place where he'd see lots of action: the zoo.

They've got my leopards in zoos in Shanghai, Qingdao, Jiaozuo and Anyang. Sure. Why, just before this conference started a fellow from Xinjiang came to see me. Said he wanted me to capture a snow leopard for their zoo. I told him to hang on till the conference is over. This is important to me; anyway, Xinjiang's a long way away.

Sometimes I do make a slip. Once I came a real shocker. It was over in Hongdong County in Shanxi. There was this leopard there, you see, a real brute. They got me in to trap him. I knew it wasn't going to be an easy job as the locals had spoiled him rotten, feeding him like a prince for years. Every time he came out of the hills he'd take a leisurely look around, and having tired of that he'd walk straight into someone's place and make off with a pig or a dog. The locals would just stand by and watch. I put up at an old boy's place in a village. Boy, his daughter-in-law sure had a mean mouth on her. The very first night she came out with something incredible while we were having dinner. "Sure you're still up to catching leopards at your age? Better watch out or the leopard will end up catching you." There's lots of superstitions attached to catching animals in the hills, and one of them is that you shouldn't jinx a person by saying things like that. Puts a fella right off. I was feeling edgy all night. First thing the following morning she had another go at me, "You really should take care, you know. The leopard made short work of Shuanquan from over the back yard just a while ago." That really knocked the wind out of me. Then on the way into the mountains I kept coming across snakes, rabbits and such. That decided it; I wasn't in the mood, so I turned back.

I started back up. I reckoned the locals would all laugh at me for being a coward; then if I went on would I come across more bad omens? I ended up going on. I caught the leopard and my son came up with the cage. We'd just got his head inside it when things went wrong. As I was holding him someone came up behind me and tapped me on the shoulder, "Hey, so this is the old man-eater, isn't it?" That gave me such a start — I'd told them to make sure no one followed me. So what was this guy doing there? The shock made me loosen my grip for just a second and that wily old leopard slipped away from me and went straight for the guy who'd tapped me on the shoulder. I grabbed hold of his tail just in time and swung him over a cliff that was a dozen or so feet off. It took every ounce of strength I had to do it.

Now I just had to cage him. He'd had a narrow escape and it'd be hard to get close to him again. If he went free he really would be a wild man-eater. So I jumped down to see where he'd landed; he was stunned but the moment I went to grab him he came to and got up on his hind legs and hugged me. We ended up rolling around on the ground for a while but I eventually got the better of him. I'd captured him alive, but it was a first for me: I spent nine days flat on my back in a hospital. They gave me injections, medicines, the lot. I'd been wounded in over ten different places. Oh, him? The guy who patted me on the shoulder was the head of their production brigade. Bit of a slacker. But I wasn't meant to die in Hongdong County.

I make enemies easily. The government put out a new regulation about not killing river deer, red deer, wild bulls and tigers, so I refuse to. Even in the case of leopards I make sure I catch them alive. I know it's all got to do with ecology and making sure there'll be wild animals around for our grandchildren. I've studied all about it like everyone else, so we don't shoot protected animals even if they're staring straight into our guns. But there's some local bigwigs—blokes on the county or commune level who rule the roost—and they want to show off a bit by getting their own tiger skin and they try and force me to shoot protected animals. I refuse and that makes me enemies. They foul-mouth me behind my back.

And there's catching monkeys. Nothing to it really; once you've got the knack you can catch them by the dozen. But it's prohibited. People who want monkeys come after me offering money and just won't leave me alone. It's a real pain in the neck. And there was this time in Linfen when I caught a leopard for the people at Luoyang. A group of locals took it off me on the spot and wouldn't give it back until they'd held an exhibition in the county township for three days. They said they could get two cents a head and at least 10,000 people would come to see it. They even promised me all the takings. But the weather was boiling hot, don't you think it would have been damned cruel on the animal? So I refused. I told them the heat would kill her. They wouldn't give in, so I told them just what I thought of them. "Look, I'll pay you if you'll only let us go, alright?" Acting like that doesn't make you any friends.

The zoos can upset you at times, too. You hand over a leopard that's pregnant and warn them that whatever they do not to watch it when it's giving birth. Then they go and ignore your advice because they're curious. And it's a loss to the state when the mother gets all riled and kills its cub. And everyone knows you shouldn't separate a pair, but they go sending the male off to Anyang and the female is sold off to Qingdao. I tell them, "You can't do that. They care for each other, go on, get her back from Qingdao." The zoo keeper only says, "Come on, old man, why all the fuss. If they don't have cubs it'll mean all the more business for you." Now that really got my back up; I was furious. "If that's how I wanted it then I wouldn't waste my time coming here to Anyang." In the end they took my advice. Good thing, too.

A man's integrity is more important than money. You've got to have a heart. It's just not right to be too carried away by money.

I've got three sons. The eldest is called Zhenqian 'cause he was born in Guizhou. The second is Zhenxiang: he was born in Hunan; and the youngest was born in 1949 so we called him Zhenqi. They got it wrong on his birth certificate though. The wife of the eldest boy is a kind lass and she's in complete charge of the kitchen. The other is a hard worker, good as a man, and she comes hunting every time we go out — a regular Mu Guiying or Sister Gu*. The wife of my youngest son is clever and pretty. My three boys are good workers and big eaters — they can polish off eight or nine catties of rice a day, even when they don't go hunting.

Now that I'm well-off I reckon it's my turn to do my bit for others and work for the common good. You've got to do what you feel is right. The Communist Party has been good to me, they've treated me with respect; so I figure I owe them.

Problems? Sure I've got problems. You're from Beijing; do you have any friends who have contacts with the Minister of Forestry? My permit to go into the mountains has expired, can you pass the word on for me? To get some

---

* Two heroines in ancient China.

things done you have to go straight to the top man. The local authorities are useless. Oh, and there's another thing. Nowadays it's real important to develop transportation; you can't do a thing without vehicles. If you have any connections ask around for me whether I can buy a motorbike in Beijing. I want a three-wheeler, one of those jobs with two wheels on the back. Yes, got two. Money? No problem.

We've been written up by lots of people. Just about have to get 'em to line up. And how they fight over whether a story or a photograph is real. But all in all I'm nothing more than a hunter, so don't go getting carried away. Otherwise people will think I've been bullshitting.

Sure could. Use it to record a sheep and then turn it on in the woods. Ba-a-a, ba-a-a. The leopards an' all would be out in a flash....

Translated by Geremie Barmé

Marriage

Aisin-Gioro Pu Jie is the senior surviving member of the Qing imperial house. The younger brother of Pu Yi, the last Qing emperor, he is also the highest-ranking Manchu as a member of the Standing Committee of the National People's Congress and deputy head of China's Nationalities Commission.

As there has been so much written about him we confine ourselves here to a subject that has a little news value: his reunion with his wife.

He sits in his Japanese-style sitting room. He is seventy-six.

His wife Saga Hiro speaks from the inner room from time to time. She is ill.

Young Bu, the housekeeper, sits down for a while to hear her employer talking about the past.

IN the winter of 1935 I graduated from the Japanese military academy and came back to Changchun. Someone in the Guandong Army* suggested to me that I ought to get married. He said, "A man needs a woman to serve him, and Japanese women serve their men better than any others," and all that sort of thing. Later on Lieutenant-general

---

* The large Japanese military force occupying Northeast China when it was the Japanese puppet state of "Manchukuo" under the nominal rule of Pu Jie's brother Pu Yi.

Yoshioka Yasunori* suggested formally to my brother Pu Yi, "Pu Jie ought to set an example of close friendship between Japan and Manchukuo by marrying a Japanese." Pu Yi was very strongly against it: he didn't want a Japanese agent around him as his sister-in-law.

My brother and my second sister (Princess Wen He — authors' note) were very anxious. They decided to move first and sent someone to Beijing straight away to find a wife for me. A few days later he came back with a pile of photographs of the daughters of leading families and I chose one of them. The man was then sent to bring my fiancée and her mother to Changchun.** Who was she? Don't ask! This arrangement did not work out. I don't know what's happened to them now.

The Japanese couldn't be kept in the dark. My brother was only a puppet emperor, after all. Yoshioka Yasunori came and said to me, "You are the emperor's younger brother. Close friendship between Manchukuo and Japan is the Guandong Army's wish. We only want what is good for you. You must think very carefully before taking any action." What he meant by "thinking very carefully" was that I'd be a dead man if I didn't do as they told me. Yoshioka went on to say, "General Honjo Shigeru would like to act as your matchmaker, and he is finding you a bride in Tokyo." This order was not to be disobeyed: Honjo Shigeru was the Japanese emperor's senior military aide.

In the autumn of 1936 I went back to Japan to study infantry command. Honjo and General Minami, the army Minister at the time, gave me a pile of photographs of Japanese girls and told me to choose one. The one I chose

---

* The "Attaché to the Manchukuo Imperial Household" who was simultaneously a senior staff officer in Japan's army of occupation in the Northeast.

** The capital of "Manchukuo".

was my present wife Hiroko.* It was love at first sight for us.

("I was twenty-four when we were married. I'm not the emperor's sister — that's a rumour, and it's wrong. I'm only from a noble family that is related by blood to the emperor. My grandmother was the younger sister of the Meiji Emperor.** At first I didn't agree to be married to a Chinese, but my parents told me it was in Japan's national interest, so I had to obey." This is what Saga Hiro said in another conversation.)

We were married in 1937. Nearly all the top people in Japan came. It was lovely after we were married. ("When the July Seventh Incident happened Pu Jie didn't say a word all day," Saga Hiro interrupted. — authors' note) I can't remember that. At the time I was hoping for a Japanese victory so that our Great Qing Dynasty could be restored, but I was also worried that if they really won the Japanese might replace the Aisin-Gioro clan. I was torn by contradictions.

Ten months after we were married we had our elder daughter Huisheng. Two years later Hiroko went back to Japan where she gave birth to our second daughter Husheng.

On 8 August 1945 the Soviet Union declared war on Japan. Yoshioka told me, "We are going to move the capital to Tonghua. If the decisive battle for Tonghua ends in defeat after the move you and I must both be ready to kill ourselves." From that I realized that it was all up with us, so I decided to die there and then. When I got into the car, I lifted up my revolver to shoot myself, but Hiroko threw her arms round me and said, "Put your gun down. Whatever

* A more familiar form of the name Hiro.
** 1852—1912.

will I do if you die?"

As it turned out, Yoshioka didn't kill himself either. We were all captured by the Soviet army.

When we parted Hiroko didn't shed a single tear. She was wearing a blue cheongsam and Husheng was standing beside her. I wrote to her twice when I was in the Soviet detention centre for war criminals. ("I only got one letter, only one," Saga Hiro put in. — authors' note)

In 1952, when I was in the Fushun War Criminals' Prison, I received a note with Hiroko's address in Japan on it, and from then on we were in contact again. It was only later that I found out that Premier Zhou Enlai had received a letter in Chinese from my elder daughter in Japan asking if she could write to me. He told the comrades in charge to arrange it. I'll always be grateful to Premier Zhou. The tragedy was that because of mistakes by Hiroko and myself our elder daughter Huisheng killed herself for love. At the time I didn't understand what it was really all about. All I knew was that Hiroko was against Huisheng marrying a Japanese and insisted on finding a Chinese husband for her. The result was that soon after getting a letter from me telling her to follow her mother's wishes in everything she and her Japanese fiancé killed themselves....

After ten years in the war criminals' prison I was given a special pardon and allowed back to Beijing. Premier Zhou Enlai invited our family to Zhongnanhai to have "democratic discussions" on whether or not Hiroko should be invited back. My brother Pu Yi was against it. As far as he was concerned, the marriage had been a dirty trick by the Japanese, and as the Communist Party had remoulded us and made us into new people our family should sever all connections with the Japanese. My feeling was that a clean break was out of the question: Hiroko had already suffered terribly and had been waiting for me for over fifteen years. Japanese militarism had nothing to do with the feelings we two had for each other.

Premier Zhou put pressure on Pu Yi for me. "People can change," he said. "If we welcome Saga Hiro back one possibility is that they will live together happily, and that will be fine. The other possibility is that they'll be disappointed and she'll go back to Japan." The premier was a good man. All the dozen or more members of the family who went to Zhongnanhai that day agreed with his suggestion, and even my brother nodded his head.

When Xu Guangping, Lu Xun's widow, visited Japan she took a message from me asking Hiroko back; and when Liao Chengzhi made his visit to Japan he took a letter. The following spring she came back.

I went to Guangzhou with my younger sister's husband to meet her at the gateway to China. Hiroko stood there, her head bowed, holding Huisheng's ashes in an urn. Husheng was standing beside her. Not a word was spoken. There was absolute silence. There was too much to say after sixteen years' separation. The "wandering princess" had come home.

Of all the descendants of the Qing house my social status is the highest. When my elder brother Pu Yi was alive he was only a member of the Committee of the Chinese People's Political Consultative Conference. Materially we live very well. I value the confidence new China has shown in me and the honours it has given me, but I'm very dissatisfied too. As one of the billion Chinese people I feel worried as well as gratified.

Translated by W. J. F. Jenner

An Urbanized Peasant

In a signed article which appeared in Outlook, *China's only weekly news magazine, the author made the following statement regarding the future of China's agriculture: All of the grain, vegetables, cotton and sugar required by the state will be produced by a small percentage of China's farmers through contracts and cooperatives, freeing the remaining seventy percent of rural residents from working the land. In other words, some six hundred million Chinese peasants will eventually no longer engage in traditional farming. This is a major force to reckon with.*

Though many of the urbanized peasants now engaged in peddling and other small business in Beijing are further removed from the soil than their counterparts in other cities, few of them regard themselves as urban residents.

Zhang Baojian is twenty-nine years old. At the time of this interview, he was wearing a woolen suit and had a white measuring tape hanging around his neck. The following was recorded at the Donghuamen Gate pedlars' market near Wangfujing Street in downtown Beijing.

YOU guessed it, I'm not from Beijing. And don't believe that "Shanghai Tailor" sign I've got hanging up there. I'm not from Shanghai either. My hometown's Qingpu. That's a county right outside the Shanghai municipal area. It's late now and business is pretty slow, otherwise I wouldn't be talking to you this way. Usually I'm much too busy. If I didn't have this sign up, no one would give me any business. But I'm not trying to fool anybody; Qingpu's actually run by the Shanghai government.

I come from a family of farmers. We don't get grain coupons like you people in the city, so we have to grow our own food. I finished junior middle school, but it was only a rural school for us country folk. When I graduated, there weren't any college entrance examinations to take. But even if they'd had them then, hayseeds from the country like me wouldn't have had a chance of passing. Both my parents are still alive. They're illiterate farmers. Qingpu's a pretty poor part of the world, you know. A few years ago there wasn't a single light bulb in the place. But because it's so close to Shanghai, nobody believes me when I tell them that. Things have gotten a lot better the last few years. A lot of people have TV sets now. My family? Sure, we have one, we've got a real fancy colour TV. Both my younger sister and I learned a trade; that's a surefire way to make money. Now we've got plenty of money, but no education. I'm living here in Beijing now, but I hardly ever write letters back home. Writing letters is too much trouble.

The year I graduated was the same year that old baldy Lin Biao got himself cracked up in a runaway airplane. After graduation all of my classmates went back home to work on their family farms. Middle school kids in the countryside had no other choice. At that time they were using the workpoint system like up at Dazhai. Young people like us worked our tails off from morning till night for a paltry seven workpoints; ten was the most anybody got in one day. They didn't figure out how much each point was worth till the end of the year, so none of us knew how much

money we were making. The most they ever paid was 29 *fen*
per day, but that was for ten points. If you want, you can
figure out how much I earned. What a grind! The worst it
ever got was the year they raised all that commotion about
eradicating the "four pests".* That year we had to pay the
production team one-point something workpoints each day
out of our own pockets. It was bad enough slaving out in the
fields for close to nothing. But then we had to sign IOU's for
grain (actually borrowing grain from the production team
or brigade before the harvest — authors' note). There was a
saying going around at that time, "If the Tangshan
earthquake had hit Qingpu, it would have been a hell of a
good deal." There's nothing funny about that. When
there's an earthquake, at least you're sure of getting some
emergency grain rations.

With an empty wallet, what's the use of going into the
city? You can't buy anything there. All you can do is walk
around window-shopping. In those days everybody was
jealous as hell of people from Shanghai. We all felt like
failures, and people started saying fate had it in for us. But
things are better now. What's so great about Shanghai
anyway? The people there hardly have any money. They
don't have colour TV or decent places to live in either. But
they keep on making fun of us, like we're their stupid
country cousins or something. But you know what? My
wallet's bulging and their salaries are so low it'd make you
cry. In fact, in one day I can make as much as they get paid
for two weeks' work.

I started studying tailoring the year they began the
production responsibility system. At first they called it the
"field responsibility system", but the two are actually the
same thing. Our family, a total of seven people, had a little

* Rats, sparrows, flies, mosquitoes.

over two *mu* of land to work. It wasn't enough. There were
too many people and not enough land. Since they divided
all the land in the brigade up evenly among the households
without counting how many mouths you had to feed, the
more able-bodied workers in your family the less you got to
eat. I wasn't stupid. I knew the new policy was to let
everyone make money and get rich, but with so little land
you could only earn shit. So I went out and learned how to
be a tailor. My older brother stayed home and worked the
fields.

The production contract system meant dividing the land
up among individual families. At the beginning these plots
were called "responsibility fields", but actually assigning
production quotas and dividing up the land is the same
thing. The idea is, the fewer people on the land the more
money you can make.

Some people were pretty poor at farming and couldn't
make any money at it, so they rented their fields out to
others on the sly, freeing themselves to do other work. This
was legalized two years ago, and now people can take on
more land if they've got the manpower to work it. In
addition to turning in your state grain rice quota you've got
to pay a sort of land use tax to the brigade based on the
amount of land you farm. Don't forget, they still own the
land. Anyway, when everyone else was sweating away out
there like a bunch of idiots, I went out and started learning
a real skill.

Learning to be a tailor is no simple matter. The first thing
you've got to do is pay someone to teach you the ropes,
since nobody's going to give away their family trade secrets
for nothing. I made up my mind not to improve the lot of
any tailors in Qingpu in this way. I wanted to learn in
Shanghai. The last few years, everyone and their uncle in

Shanghai's been opening up tailoring schools. The neighbourhood committees have them, the districts have them,
the educated youth organizations have them and there're
even privately run ones now. But I decided to keep away
from those private ones. The good thing about the places
run by the city government is that if you're one of those
unemployed educated youths you can study for free, or at
least pay half tuition. Naturally I wanted to study for free.

There's no way I was going to pass for an unemployed
educated youth, but I found a way around that. I asked my
uncle to write a letter of introduction for me saying that I
was his son. Those schools don't really care who you are, all
they want from you is a letter of introduction. You don't
have to give them any photographs either. So I borrowed
my cousin's name for a while. Those schools give out
diplomas if you graduate, but who needs it? When I
graduated I didn't even pick mine up. It had my cousin's
name on it anyway, and with my picture on it it would have
looked pretty silly hanging up here, don't you think?
Anyway, the only thing that matters is whether or not
you're a decent tailor, and that has nothing to do with a
diploma. Later on I took intermediate and advanced classes,
each time switching to a different school. Getting a letter of
introduction from my uncle's factory was never a problem.
I was there to learn something, not to take anybody for a
ride. In those days I didn't have a spare penny to my name.

But when I finished the advanced class, I felt, I needed a
diploma. Why? Because I wanted to find work in north
China, and that diploma was the only proof I had that I was
a real Shanghai tailor. So I asked the teacher about it. He
was a real bright guy. He told me, "First time I set eyes on
you I knew you weren't from Shanghai. It's written all over
your face." He told me to fill in the blanks on the diploma

myself, which put all the responsibility on my shoulders. Worse come to worst, he could say he didn't know what was going on. When I was about to leave, I offered him a little gift in an envelope, but he wouldn't take it. He said, "If I accept this it means I've sold you a fake diploma." You don't find too many honest guys like that in Shanghai. Most people there wouldn't give a guy from the countryside the time of day. Look here, that's the diploma I'm talking about.

I studied in Shanghai for a year altogether. Then I went back to Qingpu and spent a few months teaching my younger sister what I had learned. We practised on newspaper instead of cloth. Who would be crazy enough to use cloth to practise making clothing? I got all the old newspaper I needed for nothing from the Party office of the brigade. You know how it is.

They did me a favour, so I owed them one. Every time I go home now there's always someone in that office waiting for me to make something for them. Is my time worth less than a pile of old newspapers? I tell you, owing people favours is a hell of a lot worse than being in debt.

The next step was for me to apply for a small-business license from the local bureau of commerce. Normally this takes a lot of sweet talk and a bit of cash under the table. Sure, you have to give them something, otherwise you'd never get your license, or they give you one marked "Valid Only in Qingpu". If I worked in Qingpu I'd starve to death! I wanted to work up north. The moment you cross the Yangtse River, the price people are willing to pay Shanghai tailors starts going up. The first time I offered that guy in the commerce bureau a gift was in 1980, but he made up a million excuses and finally refused to give me the license. That didn't stop me, though, and I made up my mind to give it a go without a license. So I spent the next seven months working in Tianjin and Harbin and ended up earning more than five thousand yuan. Without a license you can't work in the street or even rent a room in a hotel. That makes things pretty tough. Fortunately I had a distant relative in Tianjin who let me stay in his home. I paid him one hundred fifty yuan for three months — a lot more than it would have cost to stay in a little hotel. In Harbin I stayed with an old friend from Qingpu who had worked for a while at the Daqing oilfield and then got transferred to Harbin. People from your hometown often turn out to be a hell of a lot nicer than your own relatives. Business was good in those days, much better than it is now. There are so many Shanghai tailors running around now, it's like everyone in Shanghai's in the business. A few years ago I got one yuan twenty for cutting out a pair of pants. Now I'm lucky if I can get sixty *fen*. But earning that five thousand yuan was a breeze. I didn't even have a license then, and I didn't have to pay any taxes either.

When I brought all that money back with me to Qingpu at New Year's, the people in my family nearly jumped out of their skins. They thought I'd committed armed robbery or something. My father didn't say much, but my mother kept asking me, "Xinna, you didn't steal that money, did you?" My sister didn't do as well as I did, though. Where she was down in Changzhou she could just make enough to feed herself. You see what I mean when I say you've got to go north to make money.

A few days after the New Year, the head of the production brigade came to see me and said, "You've been running around free as a bird for a whole year now." Then he told me I had to pay the brigade for my grain rations and a management fee of one yuan a day. He ended up squeezing three hundred and sixty yuan out of me. I didn't have a choice, you know. If I thought he might start making trouble for my family, I'd never be able to go away and work in peace. That sort of thing's no problem any more. Now I've got a contract with the production brigade. All I have to do is pay them a management fee. Then the brigade head asked me how I got my grain coupons. I told him I bought them, how else? Twenty *fen* a kilo. But that's better now too. You can trade rice for grain coupons at the state grain stores. Grain coupons are almost totally useless anyway. They're bound to do away with them sooner or later just like they did away with cotton rationing. Finally he asked me to take his son along with me and teach him the ropes. Not me, boy! What was in it for me? I had to ease my way out of that one pretty carefully. Had I done it any other way, I would have gotten into a heap of trouble.

After talking it over with my parents, I decided it would be better to spend a thousand yuan for a license rather than keep on doing business on the sly. But then it turned out I got my license without having to spend a penny. At that time the central government came out with a new policy. Fortunately for me, it was not out of the hands of the guy I'd been dealing with in the local bureau of commerce, and everything went fine. I have to pay taxes now, a five percent commercial tax and a two percent management fee. They call that progressive taxation; the more you earn the higher the rate you pay. I was in the seven-percent bracket. The very lowest anybody has to pay is five percent. The people in the bureau are a bunch of clever monkeys. They can pretty well figure out how much business you're doing. Of course, the amount I report each month is totally up to me. But I never evaded any taxes. If they fine you that's one thing. But if they take away your license that's the end.

That new policy is a good one. The more money I make, the bigger my contribution to society. That actually makes a lot of sense. In addition to the business tax and management fee for the local bureau of commerce, and the management fee and reserve fund contribution for the production brigade, I've got to pay a daily management fee to the people who run the pedlars' market where I set up my stand. It's higher in the city than in the countryside, naturally, but you can't make any money in the countryside.

The last two years, I've worked in nearly twenty different places, both big cities and little towns. Even though I can make any style of clothing you can think of, I've been earning less recently. The reason is that there're too many people in business now. If things stay the way they are, though, I can pull in about three hundred a month, no problem. That's more than a college professor earns. The most I ever earned in a month was 1,200 yuan.

There've been some hard times too. Last November when I was in Chongqing there was hardly any work to do. Remember that anti-pollution campaign? (The campaign to combat spiritual pollution, though it was not a political campaign — authors' note) At that time the people in charge of the market wouldn't let us make any so-called weird fashions. Actually there was nothing weird about the clothes we were making. All the patterns came out of books and magazines they sell in bookstores. Maybe they were a little different from that tired-out stuff they've been selling in the state-run stores for years. But if they weren't a little different, people wouldn't come to me. Let them try to find stuff like that in the state-run stores! When I heard that they weren't making such a big fuss about weird fashions in Beijing, I decided to come here. What I heard turned out to be true. Whenever one of those campaigns hits a small town, the officials blow things way out of proportion. Those people never watch television, so they don't know what's really going on. I was staying in a hotel where they had a TV and watched it every night. Sure enough, when they showed Hu Yaobang meeting a bunch of foreigners he was wearing a good old Western suit. I've been in Beijing for about six months now. When I go back to Qingpu this time, I'm going to have to write a self-criticism, since I didn't pay my taxes last year. They're going to charge me a late fee too. I don't care, business is good in Beijing. I've got it all figured out already.

I never send any of my money home through the post office, since if you do it that way everyone in the production brigade and the post office knows exactly how much you've got. They say things like, "He's sending so many yuan home this time." Also, there's a charge for sending cash through the post office, ten yuan per thousand. What a waste! I deposit what I earn in the bank every three or four days. I've got a regular savings account. I've also got it worked out so that I'm the only one who can take money out of the account, even if I lose my passbook. Another good thing is that you can earn interest on your money this way. The people in the bank keep calling me a millionaire. What's the matter with being rich? I made my money with my own hands thanks to the government's policy. The thing is, though, if you've got the skills but there's no policy to protect you, they'll attack you sooner or later for being one of those "four baddies,"* or a member of the "new bourgeoisie". On the other hand, with a good policy and no skills, there's no way you're going to make it through either. What good is a person with no skills? Even if the

---

* Landlords, rich peasants, counter-revolutionaries, bad elements.

government forced you to get rich, you'd never make it.

Sure there're a lot of people out there getting rich in slippery ways. I've never been in an airplane, or on a sleeper train for that matter. I always buy the cheapest hard-seat tickets. It's not worth throwing away a few days' income on a single night's sleep. Even if I were rolling in money I'd never travel that way. There're too many better ways to spend your money. I'm still single and I don't have girlfriends. That doesn't bother me, though. If you've got money, a skill and enough energy to keep yourself going, it's no trouble finding a decent wife.

I'm all in favour of the government's new policies. If Deng Xiaoping wanted a suit made, I'd do it for him for free. But he'd have to promise me that they won't fool around with those policies. I'm just kidding, of course. What does a bigshot like Deng Xiaoping need me for? Hey, don't record that, alright? Rewind the tape. I know how to work a tape recorder like that, I've got one at home. It's better and a hell of a lot bigger than the one you're using. It's made in Japan.

I bought government bonds for a thousand yuan. You see, the government is starting to borrow cash from the people now. I'm willing to do that since there's a pretty good chance they're going to pay me back. In Shanghai, whole work units buy bonds and split the cost evenly among the workers. That's a pretty piss-poor way to do it.

This is the first time I've ever heard the term "urbanized peasant". There're a lot of urbanized peasants out there who are a lot richer than I am. They make good money cultivating mushrooms and raising chickens. They can earn a lot more than I do without ever having to leave home. Some of those families can earn ten thousand yuan a year. But there are also quite a number of people worse off than I am. Since they're totally unskilled there's nothing anybody can do to help them. There're also people who get rich one day and lose it all the next. They buy clothing in Guangzhou or Shanghai, or even in Shenzhen, and sell it up in the northeast. Some do real well at it. But others lose their shirts at it. It's a pretty chancy business. Better to make your money with your own hands, I say. When someone else gets rich, I don't never turn green with envy about it. People have told me that I should get into selling clothes as well. No way! I don't think anyone who goes into business can beat the state at it. Can you beat their set-up? Can you beat their prices? I really believe what Chairman Mao said: "Ample food and clothing through self-reliance." You call peddling clothing in the northeast self-reliance? Don't laugh. This is what I believe and nobody's going to make me change my mind. Commodity circulation? That's just buying and selling. You can't really call that work.

You know, if you write about me in the newspapers everyone in Qingpu's going to make fun of me. They'll say, "He's no ten-thousand-a-year household, what's his name doing in the paper?" Actually, my family earned more than ten thousand yuan last year. But since on the books I don't live with them any more, they didn't count my income in. Families that earn ten thousand yuan get a prize of a coupon to buy a Phoenix bike.* Doesn't bother me. You can buy one of those on the black market pretty easily now for about forty yuan over the regular price. Who's going to ride it? Everyone I know who rides a bike has a Phoenix already.

No, I don't have any plans worked out for the future. I can hardly write in the first place, so what good is a plan

---

* Phoenix bicycles are the most sought-after brand in China and hence are in short supply. The coupon gives the holder the privilege of buying one.

going to do me? I wasted nine years in school already. But I can get by using the northern dialect now. I've learned to use *nin*, the polite form of "you", as everybody else does in Beijing.

I plan to keep moving around like this for another couple of years and then open a little shop of my own somewhere and settle down. Maybe I'll earn a bit less that way, but who cares? I'll have a wife and child to take care of by then. Everything'll be alright so long as I can keep my capital. It's going to take me another couple of years to put enough in the bank. I need twenty thousand at least. With any less than that, the interest isn't enough to support a family.

Translated by Don J. Cohn

The Forty-Minute Night

From the names of the stops, we can learn the names of the former and extant city gates of Beijing: Deshengmen, Xizhimen, Chongwenmen.... The Number 44 bus runs along the former site of the city walls, which once surrounded the former imperial capital. Bus Number 3715 is a large articulated model with three doors. It has 69 seats and can hold a total of 120 passengers. The two conductresses are wearing identical grey cotton overcoats. One is seated at her ticket desk; the other is standing.

An entire journey on the Number 44 bus route takes 65 minutes. We board the bus in the middle of the route, leaving us forty minutes to chat with them.

Their names are Wang Lian and Bao Mujie. They're both twenty years old.

I'VE been working for the bus company for more than a year now. My mother was a ticket seller too. She started working in 1958, during the Big Leap Forward. When she retired at the age of 50, I took over her job for her.

In general now, the bus company doesn't recruit new workers from the outside. That's one way of providing jobs for the children of the people who work for the bus company. My father was a bus driver. He was born in Beijing and never left.

My mother didn't like the idea of me working for the bus

company, so when I graduated from senior middle school I signed up for the university entrance examinations. At that time there was a rumour going around that they were going to revise the policy about kids taking their parents' jobs, so I changed my mind and signed up for a job. In those days I wanted to study engineering. What did I want to be? I would have been happy with any kind of work. I probably wouldn't have got in. But still....

I started working for the bus company when I graduated from junior middle school. I've been here four years now. I started out on the Number One route, one of the busiest in the whole city. It stops at Xidan, Tiananmen Square, and Wangfujing. It's so crowded all the time you can hardly breathe. On that line we used to change shifts in the middle of the route, and those buses were always so packed that it was almost impossible to get on, not to mention get over to the ticket counter. When I got off work at eleven o'clock, my older brother and sister had to take turns coming to meet me, since the *hutong* we live in is in a pretty out-of-the-way place.

Route 44 is a new line. From the beginning they assigned six crews of drivers and ticket sellers to work it. This has to be one of the easiest routes in the whole city. The peak and off hours are as different as night and day. From ten to eleven in the morning and from two to four in the afternoon there are hardly any passengers, and late at night like this there are even fewer. How many bus companies are there in Beijing?

Six motor bus companies and three electric bus companies.

Each bus crew has eight ticket sellers divided into shifts. The early shift goes from five thirty in the morning to twelve noon and the late shift goes from twelve to eight at night. Each shift makes a total of five trips around the city. Once you start working the night shift you don't change; there's no switching shifts, so we hardly ever get a chance to watch television. When I get home sometimes I can catch the late news. I don't get to see too many movies either. The bus company gives out movie tickets about once every three months.

She's not kidding, only once in three months!

Sometimes I buy my own ticket. In any case, once you get up in the morning, clean up the house; go shopping, cook and eat, it's time to go to work.... Show your ticket, please. I'm talking to you, miss! Stop! (A girl in a red ski jacket who has already gone a good distance from the bus slowly reaches into her pocket and takes out her monthly ticket. As she flashes it in the direction of the bus, she gives the ticket seller a dirty look. — authors' note)

Disgusting! Some people think each time we catch someone copping a ride. But that's not the way things work.

You don't know what copping a ride means? That's Beijing slang for riding the bus for free. Copping a meal means eating at someone else's expense.

You can always tell who's copping a ride by just looking. When they get on the bus, they always head for the crowded places, and when they get off they try to get away quickly, or don't get off until you're just about to close the door and the bus is about to start. People from out of town are honest and buy their tickets, but there are some soldiers who don't, so you've got to say something to them. Maybe they do it because they don't have any money. Then there are all those young housekeeper types from Anhui who get on the bus and try to play dumb, and those guys who sell stuff in the free market. They're so cheap they'll do anything to save a few pennies. We can pick them out just by looking; never

miss, you know. Thing is, we don't stop people too often....
Look over there. One year ago, there wasn't even a single
house here, not to mention those little trees. This place was
like a desert. Look at those streetlights....

At the end of one month and the beginning of the next,
we inspect tickets a lot, since that's when monthly passes
have to be renewed. If we catch somebody without a ticket,
we fine them the price of a round trip ticket. If someone's
got a fake monthly pass we've got to charge them a round
trip fare for every day of the month, about six yuan altogether. If the route supervisors find that someone's gotten
off the bus without a ticket, they can take part of our
bonuses away.

(People are arguing in the front of the bus. The two ticket
sellers turn to listen and tell us that it's a fight between two
passengers who bumped into each other. — authors' note)

We generally avoid getting into arguments with passengers. This is a "Civic Virtues" bus. There's a sign which
says that hanging on the front of the bus, so we try not to
get into too many arguments. Whether an argument breaks
out or not usually depends on the way we handle the situation. For instance, if someone gets caught in the closing
door, I might apologize, and that will be the end of it. But if
I happen to be in a bad mood, I might not say anything, and
if the passenger starts making a fuss, I'll let'em have it!
Sometimes the shouting match won't end until the passenger gets off the bus, but that always leaves me feeling lousy.

Sometimes I'll get fed up about something and start an
argument. You know, we spend a lot of time with the same
bunch of people both on and off at work, and it's all pretty
monotonous. Sometimes it seems like everyone who gets on
the bus comes out of the same mould.

Make friends on the bus? That's impossible!

Some guys start talking to you and never shut up.

(Bao Mujie's name could pass for a character in a martial arts film. She's also extremely attractive. — authors' note) You gradually get to know the people who ride the bus all the time. Once there was a guy who proposed to me. Should I tell them about it?

Go ahead.

There was this guy who used to ride the bus every day. He'd come up and start talking to me, even when I ignored him. This guy was really good looking. He told me he worked in a song and dance troupe. He even showed me his identity card. He really was an actor or something. But it never worked out. You never can trust the kind of people you meet on a bus.

Most of the people who work for the bus company go out with the people they work with. For example, a ticket seller might date a driver, or two ticket sellers might get together; it makes life a lot easier. You see that guy selling tickets up by the front door? He's a ticket seller, but he's not part of our crew. It's his time off now, but he's standing in for his girlfriend so she can go home a little earlier tonight. What about us? We take care of ourselves.

What do I like to do after work? Well, I read magazines and novels. I go out and buy them myself. What do I like to read? I read everything I can get my hands on. My favorite magazine is *The Younger Generation*. There's a lot of interesting things in it. What article did I like the best? I can't recall right now. The two of us are taking classes at a tailoring school. The tuition is six yuan a month. I earn about seventy yuan a month. That includes my basic salary, bonus, and bathing and bicycle subsidies. I give it all to my mother, and ask her for money when I need it. But it's not enough for me. Who am I closest to? My mother and father, of course! At work? Well, there's this ticket seller in our bus crew.

I handle my own money. I manage to save about twenty yuan each month. Is that for my dowry? Are you kidding?

The best thing is to get a promotion and become a driver or a dispatcher. A lot of drivers start out as ticket sellers. Sometimes you can move up after a year, but sometimes you can go on selling tickets for years without getting promoted. How would I describe my ideal mate? I think I'm too young....

I want to marry someone who I can look up to, someone who doesn't work for the bus company. I don't care if his job's worse than mine, but I really think he's got to be someone better than me. We can't help getting dirty. If you look at your shoulders after just one run, you'll see a layer of dust. There's no way we can take a bath at work. The hours at the bathhouse are the same as ours. By the time we get off work, they're all locked up. That's why they give us a five yuan fifty bathing subsidy.

Five fifty isn't even enough for one trip to the Silian Bath House and Beauty Parlor, but it's alright if you go to a cheaper place.

Getting a permanent's out of the question. You can't even use hair cream on this job. Otherwise you'd end up with your hair all dried out and full of dust. It's bad all-year round. It's hot as hell in the summer. This bus's like an oven; and it gets worse when people start squeezing in next to each other. There's a ton of dust in the springtime, and you freeze to death in the winter. Aren't your feet cold? I bought this overcoat with my own money. The bus company gives out uniforms you can wear in spring and fall. There always seem to be a lot more people riding the buses in late spring and early summer. A lot of guys like to take their girlfriends for rides around the city then. They've got monthly passes.

Look how beautiful Beijing can be. It's a completely different scene every season....

I've never made any friends on the bus. People get on, people get off.... (The eerie light of a streetlight flickers over her shoulder. — authors' note)

So long now! So long!

Translated by Don J. Cohn

The Wooded Hill

He is twenty-seven this year, not tall, neatly dressed, back in Beijing from western Hunan to take an examination for acceptance as an M.A. student.

Two years ago he volunteered to work in very poor hill country, and was for a while and to a certain extent a man in the news.

He refused a formal interview, and only agreed to a serious informal conversation with us. In our two hours of talking he drank five glasses of water.

SOMEONE wrote me up into a short story, but it wasn't like me or anyone else in the real world. To be honest, I really did want to go back to the countryside, to a country-side with no woods and no rivers and no mountains and no brick houses. I wasn't as bent as that writer tried to make me out to be. You must tell the truth if you're going to write about me — don't tart it up. Of course I'll be pleased if this really is oral documentary literature — but that means you'll be pushing the responsibility on to me, doesn't it? No, that's not what I mean. What I mean is that as it's oral documentary I'd be responsible for the contents if it went into the ·People's Daily.

Let's start with my name, Yang Shangshu. When I was in middle school another kid who lived in the county town teased me about it because it sounds like "sheep in a tree" in Chinese. When he said "There isn't a single tree in your village," I was so angry I blacked both his eyes, the little swine. I was punished for it, and got a black mark on my record. Everything on your record from junior middle school onwards goes into your personal dossier, and I've had that black mark against my name ever since. There used to be trees in our county — the year I was born the province was still calling for tree planting. But the next year it was "Everything for steel", and all the trees old and young were fed into Field Marshal Steel's home-made blast furnaces. My grandfather chose my name, Shangshu, which means "honour trees", like in the saying "honour trees and care for people". He was a doctor of traditional medicine. But I still think of "sheep in a tree" whenever I hear my full name, and it makes me feel uncomfortable. I prefer being called Little Yang or Shu Er, my nickname when I was a kid.

I'm one of the first group of students who got into university on our real merits. I was the only one to pass the entrance exams in the whole commune. All the students in my year were very big-headed — we thought we were the greatest. It didn't take me long to get stupid. I didn't get wise — I got stupid.

I got into the department of pharmacology of the medical college, specializing in Chinese traditional herbal pharmacology. In my village I'd been a high flier, and in the county town I was the life and soul of the propaganda team. I played the Chinese flute and fiddle and sang too. When we had the first party at college for students from our faculty I thought I'd show them what I was capable of, so I put myself down for a flute solo. Imagine what I felt like when all the students from big cities like Wuhan and Changsha played those foreign things like accordions, violins, clari-

nets, European flutes. I couldn't even have named those
instruments then, apart from the accordion and the fiddle.
What was my little bamboo flute compared with them?
When the M.C. announced me I couldn't play properly at
all, and I got hooted off the stage before I was even half way
through. I hid in a corner and cried my eyes out.

I lost both my parents when I was a kid, and my grandad
had to bring me up single-handed. There wasn't any money
to spare on musical instruments for me. My mother and
father both died in 1960. Say it was illness that killed them
if you like, but it wasn't very different from dying of starvation. Anyone who says nobody starved to death during the
three hard years* is talking crap. You writers stink: you
didn't say anything about deaths from starvation in the
sixties till 1981. What the hell were you all up to before
that? It took me a long time before I gradually realized that
writers had their problems too. Not many people have the
guts to speak up when it means putting their life on the line.
There are social factors and individual weaknesses, and they
interacted with each other. That's why I admire Liu Binyan
— he's not like that.

The M.C. at the concert, a girl in my class, came looking
for me afterwards. "What are you so upset about? We're all
medical students — this isn't a music college. The only
thing you should worry about is losing your battle." She
looked so sincere I fell in love with her there and then. I
didn't even know what she was called then and I'm not
telling you or your readers now. Why stir up trouble? I
found out the next day that I wouldn't have a chance with
her. Her old man was the deputy head of the faculty, and
the faculty's only assistant professor. I hear he's a full professor now, and on the committee of the Chinese Pharma-

* 1960-62.

cology Association. I warned myself against taking on more than I could handle, wasting my effort, and making us country boys look stupid, but it was no use. For a whole year I chased her with all the energy of a twenty-year-old.

I had to do it all very, very secretly. What? No way! I never even told her I loved her. Of course she knew: she could see right through me. It's only now that I realize that she knew exactly how I felt, while I didn't know the first thing about her. She didn't look down her nose at me, and she didn't encourage me either. There was no coldness and no passion either — she just drew a little closer.

We country folk are pig obstinate. For that whole year I got more and more drawn into my dream, but my work went to pieces. My only moments of peace were when I was with her. Dates? Impossible. I could only be with her in the classroom, with the rest of the class, for forty-five minutes at a time. I thought then that I'd never be able to live without her. But I had to do without her in the end, and it didn't kill me. On our first date we broke up. That was the first time we split up. Yes, there was a second time too. It's a long story.

Our first date was in the second year. We arranged to go to the botanical gardens to collect specimens. I was responsible for the buses, buying the tickets, and pinching some fruit. She hummed Deng Lijun * songs. Deng Lijun was all the rage then, and she hadn't been banned yet. We had breakfast on the grass. There was a spare cake that I deliberately left behind when we went. No reason, except that I'd got the idea from one of you lot. I'd read a story in which a girl broke with a boy because she despised him after he'd bought her an ice cream too few. You people do your readers a lot of harm. Fiction is just stories for kids.

---

*Deng Lijun (Teresa Teng), a Taiwan popular singer.

You have to buy a ticket to get into the botanical gardens, like going to a park. There were lots of young couples arm in arm, or even hugging. I'd just plucked up my courage to tell her I loved her when she suddenly greeted someone else — we'd run into the student who played the clarinet. Seeing how excited and happy she was to meet him brought home to me with a shock how little I mattered to her. So I didn't tell her how I felt— we just picked our specimens and went back to town. That story based on me said she and the clarinet-player got together later, but that's a load of nonsense. Neither of us were crazy. It couldn't possibly have happened. There was no need to run her down like that even if the author was praising me to the skies. The clarinet-player was just a spoilt boy from a rich home — he was as thick   as   two   planks.

Human relationships are uneven. To me she was a priceless treasure, but to her I was just a lump of dirt. I was completely depressed. I hated her and hated her family. I wished I could become really somebody overnight, so that she'd have to go down on her knees and beg me before I finally forgave her. I drank for the first time in my life. I didn't   get   plastered.

After my fury had died down I took my roommate's advice: "If you're going to be somebody the first things you need are the courage and ability to look reality in the face." That roommate was to be my friend for the next four years. There was no way I could forget the past. Even if those feelings had been ridiculous they'd been genuine, but once they'd died away there was no way of getting them back. I avoided her. She didn't understand what was happening at first, but later she made a joke of it. She didn't show any sign of relief: my wild fantasies hadn't bothered her at all.

Country people have a lot of homespun philosophy in their sayings, like, "Every boat has to change course in the end." By the third year we had a very heavy work load, which put a stop to all those so-called musicians and poets. It didn't matter what else you were good at — the only thing that counted was your marks. I'd been going out with my grandad on house calls since I was a kid and seen a lot of cases. I knew quite a lot about herbal medicine too. During the foundation courses in the first year I'd been preoccupied with my grand passion, but in the second and third years I got my nose to the grindstone and studied while they were into love and having a good time. So I came out on top: I was something special. I'd adapted to my environment and recovered my self-confidence. I felt fine.

I went back home to the village every summer vacation, but stayed in town reading during my winter vacations — I didn't want to travel in the crowded trains and buses around the Spring Festival. I couldn't wait to be back home, but once there I couldn't wait to get back to college. I felt at home in the village, but the college was my way forward. You feel at home in your village, but your village doesn't want you there. It wants you to be a success. It took me some time to realize that. Your home village isn't the whole country, and I'm not an exile away from it. In some ways there's no conflict between home and country, but in other ways they're opposed. There are things that China can accept but you can't get away with in the village. Anyhow, I reckon that people who make a go of things abroad and then come back do much better than people who only come back because they're failures. That's right, isn't it? But I'm talking off the top of my head. I don't know anything about what things are like abroad. I'm only guessing from my own experience.

Practically all my fellow students went home in the winter vacations. After the winter vacation in the fourth year the school's Communist Youth League committee got people to write essays on our home areas. It really put me on the spot. Where I come from is one of the most notoriously poor places in the whole of China, and there's not much to write about there. In the end I wrote a story about a fight between a tiger and a water buffalo. The buffalo won, but people killed it. I said it was a traditional story from where I came from. It didn't just get into the college magazine; the college got it published in a literary magazine too. That's another reason why I don't think much of writers: you're all just competing at making things up. It's not like that in pharmacology. You can't make a rhubarb potion out of ginseng.

I ended up doing well in my studies, and earning a bit of "artistic" or "literary" fame. Before I left to do an internship in my fifth year she gave me a book: *Love Must Not Be Forgotten.** Zhang Jie's a good writer. There was a note tucked in the book: "Let's carry on with the outing we didn't finish last time." It came as a complete shock. I was terrified of shattering the dream, of proving that it really was a dream. Only then did I realize that I hadn't yet won my independence from her. I quietly sounded out my roommate.

"Don't imagine that you're some kind of half-baked celebrity and that she fancies you because of your high marks and your story," he told me. "She's a lot craftier than you are. You're the darling of the whole faculty, and the student who's got the best chance of being assigned a job in a big hospital. Besides, traditional pharmacology tends to be even more of a family thing than Chinese medicine. A top professor would not be very likely to want you for a son-in-law." I didn't agree with him, and produced a whole list

*The title of a story published in 1979 by Zhang Jie.

of students from well-placed families whose work was good to show he was wrong. "They've all got powerful backers at home," he said in the end, "and urban residence rights. None of them would be willing to move in with the prof as a live-in son-in-law. But what about you? Students who come here from far away have to go all the way back when they graduate. So if he kept you here in town you'd be paying off your debt to him for the rest of your days. Besides, that family hasn't got much — he's just a hard-up professor who can't even run to a colour TV. Would a top cadre's son be interested in her? It might be on if the girl were pretty, but she isn't, just a bit pale, that's all. And even my mother would be paler than her if she stayed indoors for three months." My roommate was from the country too — the same county as me, in fact. He didn't mince his words at all, and he put everything in the worst possible light. The sad thing is, he was usually right.

But she was quite the opposite of what he made her out to be. She told me she'd gradually fallen in love with me after that disastrous performance. "It doesn't matter that you're a bit naive, and from the countryside too," she told me. "Love is mysterious, not just the mechanical reflection of superiority." Honestly, that really moved me. If you said that about why people love their native place you'd be dead right. And it probably goes for the way an overseas Chinese loves China. But do overseas Chinese manage not to have fathers as crafty as hers? He wasn't just crafty, he was a joke.

During the internship in the hospital we students of Chinese pharmacology practised in the clinic for Chinese medicine: no pharmacological research institutes offered facilities for getting practical experience. We had to eat in the hospital canteen, and my food allowance simply

wouldn't stretch that far. I had a scholarship of thirteen
yuan a month, and got ten yuan from home. This amount of
money was enough for me in the college, but not in the
hospital. The food was so expensive that I always wondered
if someone was making a profit on the canteen. She was
always helping me out on the quiet. She said poverty made
people pure and high-minded. That's the last thing poverty
does to you. All the poor people in the world are poor only
because they've got no option. I knew that perfectly well,
but I didn't like to say so.

When I was back to the college after my internship I was
always going round to her place. Her father was nice enough
to me — he came from a family of doctors of Chinese
medicine too. Her mother was a nit-picker, and as I didn't
have any good clothes I always felt a bit out of place, and
scared that they were going to send me packing. We two
were a lot closer by then — in fact, after we'd kissed I
started to feel a lot less constricted. Sometimes I even joked
with the professor and tried to make a fool of him. I'll give
you an example. "You've written articles attacking smoking," I'd say, "but is it really so bad for you?" Yes, it was,
he said: nicotine, sulphur dioxide, anoxia, anions, and all
that jargon. So then I asked, "Is smoking bad for
everyone?" Of course, he said: people's organisms are all
the same. Mind you, he knew I was just acting stupid, like
you're acting stupid with me. "So it is all right for Deng
Xiaoping to smoke?" I asked. "Did smoking shorten Chairman Mao's life?" He had nothing to say for himself. Of
course it's bad for Deng Xiaoping to smoke, and as we all
support him and hope he'll live to a ripe old age, the prof.
had a responsibility as a pharmacologist to say he shouldn't
smoke. At the very least he could have told his future son-
in-law in private that smoking is bad for Deng Xiaoping

too, couldn't he?

She wanted us to get engaged, and I was keen too. Her father said we should wait till the college decided to keep me on after graduation, and I agreed. By then all the other final-year students were rushing about to get fixed up with good jobs after they graduated. Nobody wanted to get sent to the countryside — of course that applied to students from the cities, but the ones from the countryside were even less keen than the city ones. My roommate wasn't rushing about. "I'm going to take the research students' exam, which'll give me the right to stay in town. When I've finished as a research student I'll have a master's degree, and I don't reckon anyone'll be chasing me back to the sticks then." He always did things straightforwardly, and charged in through the front door. He didn't go round to the back door — there weren't any back doors for him. He's a fighter, and he doesn't give up. He stands on his own two feet.

Just then my grandfather died. He was out on a call, and he fell over. It killed him — he was seventy-eight. It made me want to go back there and then. I decided to go and practise medicine back home. It didn't matter that I'd studied pharmacology — I knew how to treat most diseases. She took it very calmly — on the surface, at least. She certainly didn't try using love to blackmail me into not going, the way that story about me said she did. We knew each other well enough by then. Even if we'd slept together it wouldn't have held me back. Decorum and morality wouldn't have made the slightest difference — they couldn't have kept me there.

All she did was to stop me on the morning when we had to report our wishes for job assignments and ask me if I'd change my mind. When the girl you love pleads with you it has a magical power. I felt that this was the moment of fate.

All I had to do was say "I'm not going back", and the dreams I used to dream would have come true. What dreams? My fantasy in the first year of becoming a big shot, forcing her to beg for pity, and then forgiving her. But I wasn't the me I'd been in the first year any longer. I knew that if going home was fanaticism this was the only time in my life I'd ever be able to indulge in such fanaticism. There'd never be a second time.

I had a splendid reason for staying on, and a reason that I'd won by my own struggles: pharmacological theory is almost a complete blank in Chinese medicine. We Chinese are researching it now. So are the Japanese, and going at it hammer and tongs. I had my own speciality, my family traditions, and the professor's guidance, which added up to make me someone special. This was a way in which I could do something for China. Things would improve in the village as the national economy changed for the better. Besides, the village had already got better off in the last few years. For a talented student to be confining his attention to a little corner of the hills when the human race was advancing to the moon would have been putting my head in a bucket. Frankly, to be quite fair, even if only one graduate in the whole faculty was to be kept on in the college they'd probably have considered keeping me, to say nothing of my future father-in-law giving me a helping hand behind the scenes.

I stood there for quite a few minutes. I said nothing. I didn't even think anything. What I told you just now I'd thought hundreds and hundreds of times. In fact, if she'd only said a few more words I might well have given her the answer that would have made her happy. But my mind was on other things. My village is about eighteen kilometres by dirt road from the commune's clinic, and over thirty-five from the county hospital, half by dirt road and half by tarmac road. Since my grandfather's death there hadn't been a single doctor in the whole brigade. Pharmacological research could make up for my absence with other doctors and research workers, but the village couldn't manage without me: if I didn't go back, there'd be nobody to take my place. This wasn't an exaggeration: it was the literal truth. What the village needed wasn't me in particular but a doctor, but I was the only doctor who'd be willing to go there. The others wouldn't even go to the county town.

The only answer I could give her was, "I've got to go back." At the time I even thought of trying to persuade her to go back to the village with me, but then I remembered that she had the right to choose her own course in life. Besides, government policy guaranteed her the right to stay in the city. In the end we agreed to write often and give each other moral support. We did it too. She sent me scientific journals every month, sometimes with letters enclosed and sometimes not.

By volunteering to go home I "liberated" my roommate. The quota of assignments to our county was only one for the whole faculty, so that my going meant there was no need for him to. He also volunteered to go back to the county hospital, but he'd been very crafty: he put staying on at the college at the top of his list, and going back to the county town only fifth. When the heavens fall it's always someone tall who has to prop them up. I had to be the tall one. I was the only student in the whole faculty who volunteered to go back to his village, and a lot of the other students laughed at me for doing so. By then it made no difference what my marks had been like. Somebody even said, "If that's what you want, you should have volunteered for Qinghai or Tibet. You'd have done much better that way, making your

name and your fortune too." Crap! I just wanted to go
home. Qinghai and Tibet were nothing to do with me. What
would I have wanted to go there for? Other people said I'd
long had a wife back in the village and wanted to go back to
her, or that I was trying to use this as a roundabout way of
getting myself into the Party. You name it, they said it. My
roommate was beside himself with delight. He said I was a
real friend and that I'd done a very decent thing. In the end
he got himself a research studentship in Changsha. I got
commendations and a big send off. Some people really were
moved, like some of the teaching staff and the students
from lower years. But other students were just putting on a
show when they said I was a "model to be followed" and
expressed their "regrets". Inside I was boiling with fury.
The only thing to regret was that none of those stupid idiots
were willing to go. If just one of them had gone I could have
stayed in the city and got on with my pharmacology. The
local paper sent people to interview me, and hired the
author of that story about me. To put my motives at a fairly
basic level, my starting point was patriotism, love of my
village, and caring about the people. I didn't make any
fancy speeches. But they still insisted on turning me into
some kind of Lei Feng.*

There was plenty of trouble in store for me when I got
back home. When I got to the county town the public
health bureau insisted on keeping me. They said life would
be easier there. But could life in a county town have been
better than in the provincial capital? I turned them down
and went home. But the commune wanted to keep me in the
commune's clinic. They said I was the only regular graduate
in the whole hospital, and promised me promotion. Pro-

---

*The truck-driving soldier who since his death in an accident in 1962 has
been portrayed in the Chinese media as a kind of secular saint.

motion? To head of the clinic? Would someone who'd
thrown away a career as a specialist in pharmacology want to
be the boss of a pootling little clinic? I refused that too, and
insisted on going home. I wasn't being fanatical. Do you
think that I couldn't be sure of becoming a specialist in
pharmacology? I had even less certainty of being head of
that clinic. Never mind that I didn't actually want the job.
Even if I had wanted it, they'd never have stepped down for
me. The head of the clinic was very cocky. He was doing
very nicely everywhere: doctors have a lot more power in
the countryside than in the town — they're very big indeed
there. So I ended up as the only person in the village eating
state-supplied grain. In the cadre structure I came under
the county's public health bureau, but in my work I was
under the commune clinic.

When I got back to the village my people didn't give me a
warm welcome at all. Indeed, they were very cold. It wasn't
just that there was nothing like the firecrackers I'd been
sent on my way when I first went to college. They didn't
even give me eggs and hot soup noodles the way they had
when I'd gone home during my course. As far as they were
concerned I must have got myself into terrible trouble and
been sent back in disgrace. Why else would I have come
home? Who'd ever heard of a great scholar going back to his
village? In their eyes anyone who passed the college entrance exams is a great scholar. Their heads are still full of
mediaeval rubbish about "officials go away, men on the run
and bandits come home". I'd done nothing wrong, but the
story had somehow got about that I'd slept with a
professor's daughter — it was the professor's wife in another version — and been purged by the provincial Party
committee. To the people in my village the provincial Party
committee is the power centre that runs absolutely every-

thing, and everyone who works in the provincial capital works for the provincial committee — just as everyone who works in Beijing works for the central committee. What's even more sickening is that they call all foreigners Yankee devils, Japanese devils or "blackies". It's nothing to laugh about. That's what the people from my village are like, the people of our country. They don't want to be ignorant and stupid. In their eyes sleeping with another man's wife is a terrible crime. They'd gladly have stoned me to death, so as it was I got off very lightly indeed. In a moment I'll tell you about another great injustice caused by the ignorance of the people in my village.

A few days later there was a drastic change in the situation, not because of anything I did, but because my "deeds" were broadcast on the radio — and mind you put quote marks round "deeds" when you write this up because I made no great deeds, only the facts. "Even the wireless says our Shu Er's all right. He's something." Being "something" meant having some ability, being someone people could look up to. They were illiterate, but they really believed the wireless, as they called it.

I was able to get something done after going back to the village. Between October 1982 and February 1984 I saw a lot of patients and took some preventive measures against local endemic diseases. But it was nothing special — I was just an ordinary country doctor. Yes, I did go out in storms to see patients, and give transfusions of my own blood, but not often, only a few times. That's just a doctor's duty — it's nothing to make a fuss about. In the autumn of last year a branch of the commune clinic was set up in our village, and a graduate of a health-care college was sent to work there. It's quite like a real hospital; with her and me as doctors, and four nurses maintained by the commune. She was a "fixed direction student" who was enrolled from our county and sent back to the countryside after she graduated.

Once our village had the medical provision it had lacked before, the county hospital insisted on transferring me there. They said the girl was my replacement. So I've decided to get back to my pharmacology. I'm not staying in the county town. I had to apply a lot of times before they agreed to let me take the M.A. research student exams. If I pass I'll go on with my studies, and if I don't I'm going back home.

No, I don't care. The worst that'll happen will be the loss of some raw material for them. The worst they'll be able to say of me will be that I cleared off from the village, that I really did take a roundabout way to get ahead. I don't care. Let them say what they like. I do want to get ahead. If the village doesn't need me and I take the research student exams there's nothing wrong in that, is there? Is sticking in one place for the rest of your life the right thing to do? That's formalism.

Love? There's nobody just now. A lot of people wanted me to hit it off with the girl who came to work in the clinic, but I wasn't interested. If I get through these exams and become a research student I'll find someone in Beijing. I'm not going to look for a wife who can't live in the same place as me: that would be a lot of unnecessary trouble for myself and for the state too. I'm not going to run my life so as to provide good copy for people to write stories and plays. You can't live just to be in literature.

Yes, I'm in the Party, a probationary member. As a Party member I have to think about things like that even more and do as much as I can for the people. What I see now more clearly than ever is that I must make a go of things and beat the Japanese. My ideal now is: "Party member from the hills beats Japanese specialists in research into traditional Chinese pharmacology." That's my starting point now, and it's still very ordinary.

I had another reason for coming to Beijing: that case of injustice caused by ignorance and stupidity. There's a man in my village — let's call him Fourth Uncle — who built himself a house in 1969, he made up a couplet to paste on either side of the door:

Blessed Land chosen by Chairman Mao;

May the deputy supreme commander* come to this door.

Over the door was written

Stars of good omen shine on high.

Of course he was wrong to write that. But that was the era of "loyalty" and "adoration". Village people understand nothing. He'd taken a couplet that used to be about the Jade Emperor or the Eight Immortals or whatever and changed it to one about Chairman Mao. In the end he was arrested and flung into jail, for seven years. To start with he was accused of slandering the Great Supreme Commander and the Deputy Supreme Commander. Then when Lin died in 1971 he was accused of honouring him. He was only let out after the fall of the "gang of four". But by then he'd lost his family: his wife had remarried, and his son had died of disease. All they said to him was "Look to the future". Nobody said a word of apology, and the villagers didn't like him being treated like that, so they asked me to phone the offices that deal with such cases. They reckon that letters are no use as a way of contacting top officials: you've got to phone. They don't bother themselves over who you have to

---

*Lin Biao.

phone, or how. I want to write something up for the relevant authorities here and the people in the county so they can sort out Fourth Uncle's problems. Stupidity and ignorance! That goes both for the "criminal" and the people who handled his case. During the "cultural revolution" they said that if we didn't carry on with revolution then small-scale production would spontaneously give birth to capitalism. If we don't spread education and civilization a lot more widely now, "small-scale producers" will give the country a lot of trouble.

If I pass the exam I'll go to university, and if I fail I'll go home. I'll try again next year. If I fail then, that'll prove I'm not up to it. I'll behave myself properly and go home for good. Whether I go back to the village will depend on how far things have changed. If that former student who was sent back can cope by herself I might well return to the county. Even if I don't volunteer they can insist on transferring me. Besides, I'll have better conditions for research in the county.

Her? She's married. Why've you got to insist on asking me who to? What if I tell you I don't know? She married my old roommate. That's hardly surprising. They're both in Changsha now. It's a good place to be.

Translated by W. J. F. Jenner

"Vieux Paris"

The weather forecast is stuck at 39°C. Chongqing. We wanted to find a down streamer — from the lower reaches of the Yangtse — who had settled here during the Anti-Japanese War. An old actress who used to play the maid Sifeng advised us to go to the New Image Hairdressing Salon to see the master hairdresser Li Xuechu. Mr Li has retired now and he is an adviser to the salon. He took us straight away to see another retired hairdresser, Mr Xu.

In a covered vegetable market that is also a street, where peppers, aubergines and white gourds are piled up behind the stalls, are a number of old, black doorways within which staircases can be vaguely made out.

"Ah, it's you." "Yes, yes." In the presence of master hairdresser Xu Dexiang, who talks Chongqing with a north Jiangsu accent, Mr Li is happy to stand aside and join us as an enthusiastic listener.

ME? I don't feel a stranger here, no. I've been here for donkey's years. Back in my old home in Yangzhou my parents have both passed away. Besides, I reckon the weather's improving here. In winter the fog isn't as heavy as it used to be, and the summers aren't so hot. Or perhaps I've just got used to it. ("I expect it's because you've got used to it," added Mr Li with a smile.) Life's the same for us wherever we are.

Did you have your hair permed before it was cut? Was it layered? Did you get it done at Silian? In the old days Silian was three second-class salons and one first-class salon in Shanghai. They moved to Beijing, and charged the top prices there. That style's not bad. But the women here wouldn't have it. They don't think they're getting their money's worth unless their heads are covered in tight curls. The people here don't understand. They're narrow-minded. Can't be helped.

In the old days Chongqing wasn't as provincial as it is now. This was the temporary capital.* The wives of the Shanghai big shots all came here with their husbands. The work we did was the best in China. There were a lot more styles than there are now, ones you've never even seen. Of course we weren't trying for a natural effect, to bring out the feel of the hair itself as we do now. We went in for classical styles in those days, and that meant a lot of trouble. Times have changed, and lifestyles too. Who wants to go to the salon and spend all that money to have their hair done just for the one occasion? It's only good for a single day, and you have to go to the salon even to get it combed. Women will only do that for their weddings. There isn't much difference between people's incomes these days: the highest is only four or five times the lowest, if that. In the old days — well!.

I went to Shanghai when I was fourteen to start as an apprentice in a salon. Do you know what it meant, being an apprentice in the old society? When you signed your articles you signed your life away. First of all you had to act as a servant to the mistress, looking after the kids, emptying the chamber-pots, and cooking breakfast. Then you had to sweep up all the hair cuttings, hone the master's razors, and

---

* Of the Kuomintang government between 1938 and 1945.

wash and steam the towels. Only after that could you start learning your trade. When I'd stuck out three years of that — it wasn't easy — and served my articles, the Japanese started bombing Shanghai. It was utter chaos. Like everyone else, we ran away, and we kept on running till we got here.

Troubles or no troubles, when you got here you had to carry on with whatever you could do. I hadn't been here long when another downstreamer hairdresser got me into "Vieux Paris". In those days there were three groups of hair stylists in Chongqing: locals, Hubei people — they came here after the fall of Wuhan — and downstreamers from Shanghai and Nanjing. Of course, we downstreamers had all the classiest salons. "Vieux Paris" and "Nanjing" were both run by downstreamers in those days. When the Japanese bombed Chongqing we all split up and went round the villages carrying basic barber's equipment on carrying-poles. After the bombing was over we all came back to the salon. In the salon we always talked downstream and absolutely refused to learn Chongqing. We all ate at the salon too: the boss put up the money and docked it from our pay — we really did all eat out of the same pot then. We each worked on our own account, and the work we did was all terrific. If a newcomer joined us you could tell from his first move where he'd learnt his trade.... (Mr Li was nodding all the time, smiling nostalgically; "I came from Hefei in Anhui. I used to work in Nanjing, and I came here in 1938 too.") It's still true now. If you make enquiries about who the top class and really superior hairdressers round here are, they're nearly all downstreamers, and they've all retired. But there aren't many of us left here.

After the Japanese surrender in 1945 quite a few hairdressers went back to Shanghai and Nanjing. The ones who got back quickly enough did well. There were two currencies in circulation then, *fa bi* here, and the Japanese puppet government's money there. Right after victory the money here was worth many times more than the money there, so whatever you took with you multiplied in value. But how much money could people like us take back? I went back too, and worked in Shanghai and Nanjing. Then I came back here. You weren't free when you worked there: too many dos and don'ts. It didn't make any difference that I'd brought a whole lot of dos and don'ts with me in my head when I first came here, because once I was here they gradually got simplified and changed. But there the rules and regulations had got stricter than ever during the Japanese occupation. For example, hairdressers weren't allowed to wear watches or rings at work, but I didn't know. One of the hired hands in the salon came up to me and kept pointing at my wrist without letting anyone else see what he was doing. The penny didn't drop. Then the boss, who had been sitting up in the gallery, came over, snatched the watch off my wrist and thrust it into my pocket. Their idea was that if a hairdresser wore all sorts of things that made him look rich, no waiters, schoolteachers and the like would dare sit in your chair. You'd scare your customers off. There were too many of their stupid rules. I couldn't take it. I'm too quick-tempered. So I came back to work in Chongqing. (Yes, our Mr Xu is one of our really top hairdressers. His ladies' hairstyling is terrific. The only thing is that he's just a little bit difficult." So said Mr Li.)

Chongqing stopped being the capital after victory, but our business didn't slacken off. Even though it wasn't the capital any more there were a lot of funny customers left here. You name them, we had them. Yes, dance hostesses, girls on the game, they all did good business in Chongqing, so we did too.

No, trade didn't fall off after Liberation. Right after
Liberation everything looked good and everyone felt very
happy, so there were actually more people going to the
hairdressers than before. This building where we're living
now is where "Vieux Paris" used to be. We had a new salon
built after Liberation, and the old premises were divided up
for the staff to live in. This house isn't at all bad. You never
saw what houses used to be like in Chongqing, half underground, damp and stuffy. The dust from the street came in
through the windows — and so did the spit passers-by
hawked up. We were still doing a roaring trade in 1958. ("I
remember how people thought everything was possible in
those days — we invented any number of new styles," put
in Mr Li.) But once any political movement started our
business went through the floor. I tell you, nobody can beat
a hairdresser when it comes to detecting political changes.
Do you think that the campaign against Hu Feng didn't
have any effect on ordinary city people? But all the educated
people stopped coming to get their hair done right away.
They were all like rats, terrified of being noticed, remembered, and dragged into the case. If you ask me, that campaign started educated people on the downward slope.
Every time there was a movement our business fell off.
When it came to the "cultural revolution" in 1966, the only
women's style left for us in the trade was bobs. Weren't we
still doing some perms before that? But after it was made a
joint state-private business in 1956 I wasn't much bothered
about what sort of trade we were doing.

Back at the time of Liberation I took the lead among the
workers in making revolution. I was pretty thorough. We
chucked out our old tradition of all messing together at the
shop. I even nearly joined the Party, but my membership

was never confirmed. ("Mr Xu was too difficult," Mr Li repeated.) I just couldn't get on with our branch secretary. We never saw eye to eye about the salon: He didn't know anything about it. There were a lot of things I just couldn't take. I used to say what I thought, and I didn't have any control over what was happening, so I kept losing my temper over everything. And I lost my candidate membership of the Party too.

They have an easier time there now that I'm not bawling them out anymore. I've retired. I wasn't going to hang around in that salon any longer. If I'd stayed on as an adviser like our Mr Li they'd have made the money up to what I was earning before and I'd have got bonuses too. (Mr Li was still smiling.) But that wasn't for me. I value my freedom more than a few coppers. Could I see the disgraceful way those youngsters work and keep my mouth shut? If I kept quiet I'd be bursting inside and that'd make me feel ill. But if I spoke up I'd be asking for a row. The further away I stay from them, the better for everyone. I took a trip to Shanghai and Nanjing at my own expense, and went into "Violets" and the "Nanjing Road Number One Hair Salon" to have a look at how they work. It was fascinating, but you lay people wouldn't understand. Hairdressing's an art, with its scissor-cuts and razor-cuts. Your movements have to be rhythmic and regular — it looks nice, and it saves effort by cutting out a lot of unnecessary activity.

I really love this trade, but I absolutely refused to let any of my children take it up. I've got six kids, and I wouldn't let a single one of them follow in my footsteps. Yes, I couldn't take it easy like Mr Li, who's only got one. (Mr Li just smiles.) But I stuck it out. All of them are working now, apart from the youngest, who's still at senior middle school. I'd sooner they were hotel staff than in this trade. Hunh!

Just go out and take a look around: you'll soon see how far
behind Shanghai we are. It's not just the styles. We just
don't do the work as well as they do. Not that we're stupid.
We're just too cut off here.

Right or wrong, this is where I've made my life. Of the
hairdressers from downstream who came here some went
after the Japanese surrender and another lot left just before
Liberation. Some of them went to Hongkong and carried on
hairdressing there. But they all opened their own beauty
parlours and became their own bosses. Some of them have
been back in China on visits in the last couple of years.
They came to have a look round Chongqing and invited us
all out for a meal. Do you remember? They spent a hundred
yuan per table. Fantastic! The boss has to work there, and
harder than his employees: he's always the last to knock off.
It, isn't easy money. Of course I asked them about it.

Yes, I've got my opinion on that. We're no more stupid
than anyone else. But if you contract to run a hair salon, do
you get the right to fire people? In the old days the boss had
the right to hire and fire. If someone didn't work properly
you gave him his marching orders. That was the only way to
keep all your customers. But now! These youngsters, if you
give them a set quota of work to do they'll do it, but all they
care about is speed. They can do the work, but they cut all
the corners. If you're having your hair washed can you tell if
a little bit's been missed out? That's right, you couldn't say
which bit wasn't clean if asked. If you want to save yourself
trouble there are plenty of ways to do so. But if you want to
save yourself trouble this trade isn't for you. People come to
the hairdressers for a rest and a bit of luxury. If you don't
get their hair clean and you make them uncomfortable they
won't come back another time. If what people get paid is
much the same whatever they do nobody'll want to go there.
I wouldn't contract to run a salon unless I could fire people.

I'd sooner stay at home and make a bit less money. Everyone likes a happy life.

(As Mr Li came out with us he said very quietly in the road, "Do you think someone like Mr Xu could sit around doing nothing? For this trade the main thing you need is a hair-dryer. That costs a hundred or so and with that you're set up. You can make up your own cold perm lotion. So if he works at home and charges three yuan for a cold perm and styling it's cheaper than in a state-run salon and he makes a good profit. As an adviser to a salon I can't do any of my own work on the side. Last year he was asked to give classes and teach some students in Daxin, and he did some jobs too. He came back with over a thousand in his pocket." Mr Li gave another quiet chuckle.)

Translated by W.J.F. Jenner

Friends Old and New

She didn't want us to publish her name. She is now sixty-four, a retired worker on a pension of 52 yuan a month. She shares a two-room flat with her daughter in a newly-built housing block for workers. Some details of her account didn't accord with what we knew, due to the limitations of her own understanding rather than a deliberate attempt to hide anything. Because of this we have put in a few extra authors' notes

I am from Fenghua County in Zhejiang Province, like Chiang Kai-shek. My father was a peasant. He rented his land from a landlord. When I was thirteen my father sold me as a maid. The landlord took me in lieu of rent. When I was fourteen, he raped me. Few pretty maids avoided this fate.

I was very ignorant then. I only knew that a girl who had lost her chastity would never find a husband, or if she did that he would ill-treat her. I was ruined.

The landlord's house was on the outskirts of town not far from the centre. One day I heard that a labour contractor had come from Shanghai, so I sneaked off to put my name down with him. It hadn't occured to me that he would ask for a guarantor. I had no one to vouch for me so I went quietly back. I only wanted to become a worker to escape from the landlord's house, although I had heard that it was easy to earn a living in big cities like Shanghai, and that men there didn't mind about their wives being virgins, if only they could work and earn money. I knew that I was a good worker. Of course I wanted to get married. In Fenghua girls married at twelve and often had a baby by the time they were thirteen.

That autumn a girl who lived nearby told me that another labour contractor had come to look for girls to work in a silk mill. He wasn't asking for guarantors. I stole into town again. I was told that I would earn three dollars a month. I made my mark agreeing to go that very day. Then I sneaked off to Shanghai with the man.

When we reached Shanghai, the man took me with three other girls to a two-storied house where he and a woman examined us minutely. I was the last one to be looked at. "I won't keep her if you have slept with her," said the woman. I thought as the factory was so strict it was lucky they didn't know about the business with the landlord. I made my mark again and the labour contractor went off with the other girls.

"From now on I am your Marha and you must behave yourself," the woman said.

I thought these must be the rules so I just nodded. She took out a cheongsam and a pair of embroidered slippers and told me to put them on.

"It is no good me getting dressed up like that," I said. "I've come to work."

"I've bought you," answered the woman with a strange smile. "As to work, what work would there be here?"

I had been sold into a brothel. It was in Fourth Avenue in a well-known red light district. This was in 1933. I was fourteen.

For the first three days I didn't have to receive any clients. They were waiting for someone who was prepared to pay a lot for "the first time". My first client was a Master Something. I ended up getting a terrible beating from him. He didn't pay a penny, which meant the Mama went for me too. I had never claimed to be a virgin; it was the contractor who had tricked them. The gentleman simply beat me but the Mama jabbed my calves all over with a needle. Afterwards, nothing showed and I had to receive more guests.

The brothel was a hell on earth. Every day I had to receive at least a dozen guests. At most it could be twenty or more. The charges were fixed according to how long they wanted. When time was up the Mama used to bang on the door shouting, "Send him out."

We had to receive men just the same when we had periods, only then we took those who wanted to "penetrate the red" as it was called. I got pregnant twice. We had to start work again on the third day after the abortion. I don't know how many men I've been with altogether. Between when I was fourteen and when I was thirty there must have been tens of thousands of them.

No, in all the tens of thousands, there was never one who wanted to marry me. That only happens in novels. In the brothel there was a saying, "The stream of men is like an endless flow of water." My body was riddled with disease. I had syphilis and I was addicted to heroin. No one would have wanted to take me for a wife.

I had been sold to the brothel, so unlike the girls who were working there on their own account, I had no right to refuse a client. I should have got thirty percent of what men paid for me, but I never did. Apart from that first outfit which the Mama paid for, I had to buy everything for myself.

How many prostitutes were there in Shanghai? About

30,000. (This is not an accurate figure. The total for prostitutes in Chengdu in 1949 was 29,800. There must have been more than 30,000 in Shanghai. In addition to the prostitutes in brothels licensed by the government, large numbers of bar girls, hostesses, masseuses and guides engaged in clandestine or casual prostitution. — authors' note)

Those who contracted syphilis got what they deserved. Even when I had the sores I had to receive clients just the same. They had given me the pox and I gave it back to them. Of course it is curable, but we couldn't afford the treatment. After the Japanese left, the new American medicine came in. (This was probably penicillin.— authors' note) But we didn't have the money for it. (Figures from after Liberation show that over half of all prostitutes were infected with venereal disease. — authors' note)

Women became prostitutes for the money. Many were from very poor backgrounds like mine, but some had previously mixed with the wealthy. There was a woman who had been a film star in a "Flower House" not far from our brothel. She had gone from starlet to dance hostess, then she started to sell herself. She said she had been cheated by men so now she was going to cheat them.

You are right. You have got to have some idea in your head to keep you going. Otherwise you just couldn't sleep with all those thousands of men. At first I just felt there was nothing to be done. It was my fate. Later I believed what the other girls said. The most absurd idea was that although people usually considered that men were playing around with us, we were also playing around with them. Furthermore when they had had their fun, they had to pay good money for it, money which we got, so that we were the ones who gained.

It's true that men did sometimes give me tips. Still, I was very surprised when I saw the Japanese film *Looking Towards Home*. I don't think a prostitute could ever really have got hold of all that jewellery as it was described in the film. I just don't believe it. (Some prostitutes did in fact become very wealthy women. — authors' note)

When you asked me about "going straight" you show that you are not very well up on this sort of thing. We never used that expression. After all, we weren't thieves. We talked about "getting out", or "coming off the game". I finished with it on National Day in 1952. I was one of the last. (Shanghai was liberated on 27 May, 1949. The new municipal government began to close the remaining brothels on 25 February, 1951. They rounded up over 500 prostitutes for rehabilitation. On 25 September, 1952, another order was issued under which clandestine prostitutes were to be dealt with and the last group of nearly one thousand prostitutes was taken in. Finally, in July 1953, the Security Bureau banned bar girls, dance hostesses, etc. — authors' note)

I was hardly conscious of the setting up of New China. I'd seen so much already. The Kuomintang, then the Japanese, the Americans, then the Kuomintang back again. Now it was the Communist Party but I was still selling my flesh. A lot of the girls were coming off the game. The government found jobs for those who left of their own accord. But I didn't follow them. I didn't really believe they'd be able to support themselves. I still wanted to wait for a good man who would free me from that life by marrying me. People said the Communists were good. All right. I would wait for a good Communist to marry me. It never occurred to me that a Communist wouldn't go to a brothel. I thought that all cats ate fish.

Then I heard that the Communists were going to close the brothels, force us to shave our heads and make us into communal wives. I was frightened. Just as life had been getting a bit easier, more problems appeared.

Why do I say life had got easier? Well, in the campaign against counter-revolutionaries in 1950, the government executed a lot of gangsters who ran girls. That meant there was much less pressure on us. What's more, the government didn't collect any tax on what we made. With the Kuomintang, we used to say, "Each of them wants our bodies, and together they want our money." So afterwards we did feel life had got easier and that we had the Communist Party to thank for it.

All the brothels in Shanghai were closed in the 1951 campaign. I stayed on the game secretly, working from a coffee bar. I couldn't have gone to a dance hall. You need the skills to work as a dance hostess. Whatever I earned went on heroin, for my addiction was getting worse. Often I couldn't draw any custom and lived in fear of being found out. On the eve of National Day 1952, just as I was expecting a bit of extra business with the holiday, I was detained by the Security Bureau. They put me in a labour reform school.

Over a thousand of us were taken that night. We cried and yelled. People like me made specially hard cases. I'd been on the game so long and heard so much reactionary propaganda. Then they didn't allow heroin in the camp. When the craving came on, I didn't want to cry but I couldn't stop the tears. The school cadres used to claim that they were helping us to escape from hell but I felt that they were thrusting me into it.

In the first years after Liberation there was still trouble in Shanghai. About two weeks after National Day the school was surrounded by gangsters — several hundreds of them. They wanted to get us out. We were also trying to force an escape. We started to struggle with the school cadres. Under the rules they weren't allowed to strike us or even to swear at us. They just stood their ground, barring the door. Some of the girls who had already been in the school nearly a year helped them. Then those girls realized that we might actually kill someone, so they started snatching the kitchen knives we were carrying and real fighting broke out between us.

Lots of police arrived outside and arrested the gangsters. We saw that there was no point in going on. However tough they are, prostitutes always fear the police. In the old society they really used to bully us.

Yes, you are right. We didn't take much notice of the cadres. In fact we rather despised them. In the old society it was poor people who were mocked, not prostitutes. When we saw the army uniforms the women cadres wore we would think to ourselves that they didn't look like men and they didn't look like women. We felt superior to them. The school governor was a spinster a couple of years older than myself. Her name was Yang. "Knows fuck all about anything," we used to say in private. "How can they put her in charge of us?" Actually she turned out to be a much better person than us.

True, we were a noisy lot. As soon as we got to know someone we wanted to find out all about them. Well, you writers are like that too, aren't you? Don't keep interrupting or I'll forget where I've got to in my story!

When I first went to the reform school, nothing put me to shame. Nothing seemed too foul for me to stoop to. We were supposed to study for half the day and work the other half, but as I was an addict, I didn't have to join in. Some of the others just messed about instead of working too.

Half our study period was devoted to politics and in the other half we were supposed to "remember the bitter past". The girls who had been there longest took the lead when we discussed the past, then some of the others joined in. I thought it was all a waste of breath. Everyone knew about the past. What was real bitterness anyway? The school cadres kept telling us that the government just wanted us to start new lives. The girls who had been some time at the school talked this way too.

Suddenly a new rumour sprang up. The wounded soldiers needed blood transfusions. The government wanted us to give blood. In those days I was so naive, I believed everything I heard. Just a few days later, some people really did come to take blood. I made a great fuss and managed to break one of the flasks, but in the end I let the doctor draw out just a little. I said to myself that they must want to find out what group I was.

After a while the doctor came back with the cadres.

"The tests show that you have syphilis," said the doctor. "You can move into sick bay while you have treatment." I was struck dumb. What the girls said was true. The Communists did want to save me.

So I moved into the sick bay. I weighed less than seventy-three catties before I was treated, now I am about one hundred and ten catties. You can see I'm not fat now, so think what a skeleton I must have been then.

When I was better, I started my new life. We had lessons and I learnt to read at the school. I can read newspapers now and I get the gist, although there are characters I can't recognize. We worked too. Each of us learnt some skill. I was taught to knit socks on a machine.

Actually, people like me were quite easy to reform,

because our origins were humble. Once we saw the light, we knew what was right and what was wrong. The difficult ones were the "good-time girls". They claimed to have "sold their smiles, not their bodies". That was nonsense of course. Silly liars. Their heads were full of stupid notions. They were vicious too. One of them asked a cadre if she had ever been to Shanghai's theatreland, Bailemen, or eaten in one of the grand restaurants.

"Why are you so proud of the very things you should be ashamed about?" asked the cadre. But in those days you just couldn't put that girl down. She started to curse and break things. The reform worked in the end though. She's a good worker today. She couldn't hold out against the People's Government. No indeed!

There were some infuriating things about the reform school. The cadres treated us like members of their own families but we did a lot of quarrelling among ourselves. The "good-time girls" bullied us. They thought they were clean and we were dirty and vulgar. Some of them didn't even allow us to touch their beds.

"You slept with officials and yet you're so fucking clean," I used to yell at them. The reform school had a slogan about seeing who could be first to wash off the filth of the old society and start afresh. It was quite catchy but I can't remember it properly now.

Have you ever seen the film *Stand up Sisters?* It's a pity it hasn't been shown for 20 years. It tells our story. Such a realistic film.

I wept when I got my first wages at the reform school. The first clean money I had ever earned! I left that place in 1956. You had to satisfy certain conditions before you could go. Firstly your political attitude had to be good. Secondly you had to be completely clear of syphilis and thirdly you had to have a skill which would enable you to support yourself outside. (In fact the second condition was that the woman should be clear of all venereal disease and that she should have no bad habits. — authors' note)

I went to work in a clothing factory. The labour bureau found me the job. The sock-making that I had already learnt was no use to me there, but thanks to the reform school I was now able to support myself. If the government hadn't cured my diseased body and changed my outlook, I would never have lived to do that.

You writers really want to know everything, don't you? That is a good question. Yes, I do have to fill in details about my life on forms sometimes. I used to hate answering the question about employment before Liberation. So I went to ask the factory director's advice and he said it would be all right to put "no regular employment". That was a great weight off my mind. I was ashamed to put down that I had been a prostitute, and yet it would have been untrue to claim that I had been unemployed. Everyone needs to keep face. I never wore a red armband during the "cultural revolution" and I didn't join any rebels either. Why? Because I couldn't have attacked such a good director. One should have gratitude. As to filling in my class background on forms, it should be "lumpen proletariat", but during the socialist education movement in 1964, I was told that I could just put "urban poor".

I got married in 1958. My husband was a pedicab driver. Our go-between had told him all about me and he said he would decide when he had seen me. I was quite straightforward with him at our first meeting. "Although the government has re-educated me I have been woman to ten thousand men," I said. "That's something that can't be changed. I feel guilty towards you. If you can accept this that's fine, but I can't demand it of you." "Let the past rest," he replied. "As long as things are all right now that is all that matters." Things were arranged very quickly after that. Just before we were married, I asked him if he despised me.

"I'm lucky to find a wife at my age," he answered. "You must have a son for me so that we will have descendants." I told him that couldn't be guaranteed because I had had two abortions.

"We'll get married anyway," he replied after a little thought. "We like each other and we are both from poor families." His attitudes were less progressive than mine — I had been through the reform school.

We had a good life together. He was a nice man, kind and honest. Very caring. He passed away last year, a month before our daughter was due to graduate from university. He didn't live to see it.

"Was your life so clean in the old society?" I asked him once. He reddened and said nothing for a bit. "We pedicab drivers couldn't afford to marry," he replied at last. "If we had a bit of money we went off to a brothel." We never spoke of it again. No, that's right. You can't dwell on the past. Perhaps we had even been together before. There was no way we could have recognized each other. The new society allowed us to be human beings.

I never did have a son. I got seriously ill during my pregnancy in 1959 and had to spend three months in hospital. It was a difficult birth and afterwards they found a growth on my womb. They had to operate. So I couldn't have any more children.

I hardly met any discrimination at work. Many of my workmates really tried to help me and treated me like a sister. From time to time I still see some of the girls from the reform school. Some of them became workers, some shop assistants, some nurses and some peasants. It closed in 1958. In all, it had saved several thousand women. (We understand that women who left the school also became cadres, kindergarten teachers and actresses. A small number went back to their old profession and had to be taken in again. Former officials from the school say that before 1953 women became prostitutes due to the historical circùmstances. The women who they had to take back again later had broken the law and were treated differently. — authors' note)

My daughter didn't know about my past until she had just started middle school. She quarrelled with a neighbour and the woman started abusing me. "Your mother is a...." she screamed.

I explained to my girl that I had been forced into a living hell in the old society and the new society had released me. I had done my best to help build up New China. I was better than someone who had been an ignorant housewife all her life and didn't know how to work. Afterwards I ran out and had a big fight with that woman. I didn't feel guilty. She was the one who should have felt guilty.

What a lot of questions you ask! Since you ask them what can I do but answer? In the old society I wasn't a high-class prostitute but I wasn't one of the lowest either. But of course we prostitutes were at the bottom of society anyway. In New China I have learnt I am equal with everyone else. The best of my sisters have joined the Communist Party and others have been chosen as model workers. Not all of us have done so well. Not all of them earn as much as I do, some have smaller homes, some no children, some never married. We all have our own disadvantages. Anyway we owe everything we have to the People's Government. In terms of income and standard of living I am in the middle of the best-off group.

Translated by Delia Davin and Cheng Lingfang

A Roadside Mathematician

*A crowd of men with a sprinkling of women have formed a
semi-circle outside a public toilet. He stands inside that
semi-circle pointing at a big chart hanging on the wall and
expounding his "Eleven Short-cuts in Calculation."*

*Someone squeezes in, then squeezes out again. "Bah! A
charlatan!" Someone else glares at this speaker. "Rubbish, he's a mathematician." A youngster chortles, "He
likes holding forth, he's a roadside Ph.D., the Hua
Luogeng* outside the lavatory, who comes here every day
to lecture on his short-cuts in calculation...."*

HEY, no photographs! What are you up to?

No one can interview me here. What d'you think you're
doing? (We have to assure him we're not going to steal his
patent and have no intention of accusing him of disturbing
public order. — authors' note.)

My mistake, sorry. You see, they're a mixed lot here.
Some of these young rascals are out to debunk me, they
want to spoil my business. One youngster sent a photo of
me teaching to a newspaper along with other pictures of
venders of oil-stain removers, showmen with performing
monkeys, pedlars of rat poison, and people posting up ads
for swapping housing. Said we should all be "mopped up".
But I'm not like those others, I'm popularizing short-cuts in

---

* A distinguished mathematician.

calculation, that's a science. Wait till I've cleared up and we'll find somewhere quiet to talk. "Well, comrades, something has cropped up, so I'll stop here for today. If you've any problems we'll talk about them tomorrow. See you then."

See how many people there are with time on their hands. When they've nothing to do they'll crowd round to watch anything. It's taken us five minutes to break through that cordon!

My name's Zhao Shipu, I'm forty-one, a worker. Maths is my hobby. I'm really sold on it. I know eleven short-cuts in calculation for all the fundamental operations: addition, subtraction, multiplication, division. Faster than an abacus! If you memorize my formulas and use an abacus too, that's even faster. Calculators? I can't compare with them, but how many people have calculators? My formulas are for accountants, students and shop assistants who don't have calculators.

Actually these methods aren't my own invention. I've just synthesized different principles and logarithms. But I like passing them on.

My parents are dead. I had a wife but we divorced, she took the kid. We got on each other's nerves. I couldn't stand her!

I finished middle school in '63. As I couldn't get into senior middle school, I waited to be assigned work. In those days they didn't talk of young people waiting for jobs, they called us young people at large. There was no private enterprise either, so all you could do was drift. Things weren't so free and easy in those days. Not to say American films, you seldom had a chance to see films from Hongkong. I remember clearly how I queued up all night to see the Hongkong film *A Dream of Red Mansions*. In the cinema I discovered they were all mainland opera singers using the Shanghai dialect, which I couldn't understand! I left in less than ten minutes and re-sold my ticket. It had cost fifty cents; after watching for a bit I got one yuan for it! It struck me that this wasn't a bad deal. So I found out which films were popular, then queued up at three or four a.m. to buy tickets. I hadn't much money; I'd buy a dozen tickets and sell them at higher prices. When I'd doubled my capital I bought more, and did pretty well out of it. In one month I made dozens of yuan. That was quite a big sum in those days when you could eat out for one yuan. A portion of roast duck for eighty cents, plus pancakes, scallions and soup came to one yuan six cents. Nowadays a meal like that would cost ten yuan.

But I got caught out. A policeman nabbed me at the cinema entrance, and I was detained for questioning for a week before they let me go home. In those days to be nabbed like that was a real disgrace — your family felt they'd never live it down. And I felt I'd lost face completely. It wasn't like nowadays when juvenile delinquents think nothing of being locked up for half a month, and even boast about it, then go on swilling beer, dancing and shouting abuse in the street.

It wasn't all that hard then to find work, and you were encouraged to go to the countryside, but that was up to you. I joined an electrical appliances factory. It was under collective ownership, not up to a state-owned one. I could perfectly well have waited, but a state-run works might not have suited me either, and this place was near home, so I signed on for two years' apprenticeship spraying on paint. I only took two weeks to learn that job, and in less than half a year I was fully qualified. But I got paid much less than a master worker doing the same job. Our workshop head was a menace, who'd been a housewife before '58 when she joined the factory. She was forever boasting, "A dozen of us women started this factory, it was really tough." Always blowing her own trumpet. And she never did a stroke of work, just finding excuses to run to the Party secretary to inform against other people. Much later, when I saw her pay her Party membership dues, I realized the bitch was a Communist! Later still I heard she'd used her Party card to get herself transferred to town from the country, so I'd even less use for her.

In the "cultural revolution" we all revolted, and I organized a rebel group of nine mates called the "Revolt-to-the-End Brigade". We gunned for our shop head, and joined in the attack on Liu Shaoqi. Looking back now, it was all wrong. But the whole country had gone haywire, how many were there who didn't go overboard? A few maybe, but most of us were so befuddled we made complete fools of ourselves. Later a rival group gunned for me too. My "crime" was profiteering during the hard years, the evidence being the self-criticism I'd written during detention. They'd broken into the archives and gone through everyone's file. Before that I'd had no idea that business had been written up in my file. Of course, our country's economic crisis was in '61, and I re-sold film tickets in '64; but since they insisted on lumping the two things together there was nothing I could do about it. They pounced on me, and that was really the end of our Revolt-to-the-End Brigade. It broke up!

That was why my wife divorced me. She sold vegetables and had no guts, the bitch! I send her postal orders, ten yuan a month for the kid, but we don't meet.

After that rival group seized power, they locked me up in a small dark room with some other "bad elements" in our factory. And there we squatted all day, never seeing the sun except at struggle meetings. So someone often said, "Why don't they haul us out as side-kicks in a struggle meeting?" To be a side-kick was easy, it just meant standing next to the main target, so for us that was a treat. We weren't even allowed to read the works of Chairman Mao, for fear we might learn tactics to fight back. All we could study were the three standard articles, and later not even those, because "Serving the People" said, "These battalions of ours are wholly dedicated to the liberation of the people." What battalion did we belong to? A battalion of reactionaries! So we couldn't read it aloud, only to ourselves.

A technician in that small dark room asked me, "Do you know about optimization, Old Zhao?" Of course I did. From that he went on to tell me all sorts of dodges for working sums out quickly. I was keen to learn, found it most interesting. By the time I was let out of that little room I was crazy about maths. I'd learned that society is so cramped, if you elbow or knock into someone you'll get cursed. But maths gives you plenty of scope. I studied a little higher mathematics until I'd mastered integral calculus, which was enough, I found, for quick calculation.

Yes, I'm crazy about quick calculation. I've summarized the experience of other people, summarized it into eleven rules, highly effective. It's no use, but I have fun with my mates by getting someone to set problems in multiplication or division of figures up to one thousand. By the time he's stated the problem I've got the answer worked out. That's fun. One of my mates suggested, "Since you've nothing much to do, why not go to publicize this in the street?" I thought that was a good idea and I'd enjoy doing it. So I went ahead.

Afterwards I discovered that apart from having fun I

could make a bit of money. It costs seven cents to produce one of these booklets, and I can get them printed without any introduction from my unit. The publishers' rule is that introductions are needed for works of literature or politics, which they will only print for organizations; but for scientific or technical works all you need do is pay them. I sell these for ten cents each, making thirty cents on ten copies. After work while I enjoy myself this way I can earn eighty cents, no problem. Besides, you learn a lot. There's nothing phoney about quick calculation. I'm not selling ox bones passed off as tiger bones.

I get no kick out of my work: That woman is still our head, and though she and I are "classmates" — like all of us shut up in that small dark room — she thinks I lifted a rock to drop on my own feet. Says, "If Zhao Shipu hadn't organized that Revolt-to-the-End Brigade, no one would have gunned for him. Serves him right!" Hell, I can't be bothered with her. Women and low characters are hard to cope with. Anyway, she can't dock my pay.

Some people think I'm crazy; I ignore them. They're not doctors, that's for sure. It's a form of escapism for me, that's all.

No one's introduced me to any girls, who'd have me? Didn't you hear someone call me "the Hua Luogeng outside the lavatory"? What does he know about Hua Luogeng? He learned about him from TV.

Yes, I'm pretty cynical, not a proper Beijinger. But I enjoy living like this, and objectively it helps our modernization, so the government won't stop me. The police don't interfere either, they know me, I come here so often. One fellow said he was from a publishing house and asked for a copy of my booklet so that he could help circulate it. Later he came back and said my stuff was worthless — it had all been discovered already. Yes, he was right, but why shouldn't I spread other people's discoveries if I want to? I didn't ask him to publish me! I do this mainly for fun, I enjoy it.

You can say whatever you like. Lots of people try to talk me out of this. No way! Some praise me for doing my bit for our country in my time off; some criticize what they call my hocus-pocus. Let them say whatever they like.

Wait a bit, I've something to add. Quite frankly, it's the honest truth I've told you, not a word of it made up. But I haven't given you the name of our factory or my own real name, although my surname *is* Zhao. It's not that I want to fool you, but to save trouble I'd rather you didn't know where I work.

Oh, wait a second, let me give you a copy of "Eleven Short-cuts in Calculation"....

Translated by Gladys Yang

The Road to an Ideal

Tall young Cao, aged twenty, is a learner driver. On the road from Guangzhou to Shenzhen and back he is cheerful and serious by turns, not too talkative.

His ideal hasn't yet been realized, but he cuts quite a dash. "Next time I'll be driving you!" So saying he ducks under the coach to tinker with it, leaving on his seat his sole purchase in Shenzhen — a pound package of sweet plumcake.

MY mandarin's no good, so I'll speak Cantonese, OK? All right, I'll say whatever comes into my head.

I started this job last year when I'd passed the exam. After finishing high school I joined a food store set up by our neighbourhood committee near Gaodi Street. There I sold sausage-rolls. The pay wasn't bad but I didn't like it there, wanted to be a driver. Ever since I was a kid I've wanted to be a driver, because drivers have special kudos, able to drive big coaches all over the place. So when the transport company took on more workers I went for a test, but I flunked it. I'm weak in physics and didn't pass in the principles of mechanics. That was two years ago.

My family said, "Forget it, driving's dangerous. Soon you can take a test to get into a big shop run with Chinese and foreign capital. They pay well." I thought: Everyone has his ideal, and mine's not overambitious, so surely I can pull it off. I'll sit the exam again. At my own expense I studied in a night school for drivers and in a truck maintenance class. As I used my own savings my family couldn't stop me. My elder brother had a friend who was a driver. He told me, "What you're learning won't be of any use when it comes to driving, no use at all." But what else could I do? He'd been assigned by the state to be a driver; nowadays the policy's changed, everyone has to pass a test, there's no other way. One of my classmates said, "Everyone else is out to profiteer; why insist on learning to drive? There's no future in driving." He was right in a way, a driver can't make much money; but not everyone can profiteer — it's against the law. I'm too dumb. If someone smart gets into trouble he can wriggle out of it, but not me.

The next year, last year, I took the exam again and came 29th — I passed. Now I'm a learner driver, his assistant (He points to the driver. — authors' note). They'll check up on us later on, and those who have worked well will be sent to the Public Security Bureau and issued with licences as regular drivers. The others will have to go into service trades. No, this is a bad stretch of road; when the road improves he'll let me drive for a spell.

We're passing Dongguan now, where many overseas Chinese live. Many of the earliest Chinese Americans came from here. We call them the settlers in the Golden Mountain because they went to America to pan for gold. Dongguan's also known for weight-lifting. Quite a few world champions come from Stone Dragon Town here. Chen Weiqiang and Zeng Guoqiang, gold-medallists in the Olympics, came from here.

You're not the only ones. Lots of people mistake me for a tour guide, though actually I don't know the first thing about it. That's something else again. Of course, I'll look

after you, presently I'll get everyone's passes checked at the
border, and this evening I'll find you all somewhere to stay
— I've already contacted a hotel and I'm pretty sure they'll
let me have rooms. I've plenty of pull, got you moved from
the back of the coach to sit beside me. I'm quite someone,
yes, my say goes! (He laughs, then sobers down again. —
authors' note) Yes, drivers have more kudos than other
people, I think. That's the check post in front, you won't
have to get down, just hold up your passes. I often make
this trip, so they know me here, and after a casual look
they'll let us through. But when we start back from
Shatoujiao I must check that no one's missing. If some of
you run away I'll be in trouble! (He laughs again. Once the
coach has pulled up he runs into the border check post.
Sure enough, the inspectors just look at us from the door,
then wave us on without asking to see our passes. —
authors' note) There you are! What did I say?

No there haven't. None of our passengers has skedad-
dled. It's like this: the better off the mainland becomes, the
fewer people want to run off to Hongkong. If some do go,
the Hongkong authorities extradite them. When we get to
Shatoujiao you'll be able to see for yourselves, many things
are more expensive, a whole lot more expensive, than in
Guangzhou. No, electrical appliances aren't all that cheap
either.... Look, another traffic accident, that's a Hongkong
car. Gourmet powder's a reasonable price, you can buy
some to take back, and their good confectionery is
popular.... (As the road is narrow and it is raining, we pass
five vehicles that have crashed. At most he points them out,
remarking, "A poor driver". Sometimes he seems oblivious
both of the overturned vehicles by the roadside and of our
shocked amazement. — authors' note) No, I buy cake in
Shenzhen.

Oh, so you've been to Foshan? Then you must have taken one of our company's coaches. Must have. I've been making regular runs to Shenzhen for four months now. As soon as we started this route I got a permit to cross the border and joined this fleet of coaches. The regular driver and I were in the first batch. It's tough all right, much tougher than in Guangzhou. Only people who don't know us imagine that coming to the special zone is a cushy job. The places where visitors go in the special zone charge high prices: Xiangmi Lake, Xili Lake, or the amusement parks, going with you we lose out!

We get charged preferential prices, just half what you pay for a meal, but even so we have to choose the cheapest dishes. Otherwise on the pay we get in Guangzhou, eating fifty meals a month in Shenzhen we'd be broke. What with a subsidy for each trip I make about eighty yuan a month, not too little. A bit less than selling sausage-rolls, still I prefer it.

Once we've rounded this corner you'll see Shenzhen's high-rise buildings. The first time I came there was quite a forest of them, but each trip I make there's something new to see. The special zone's showing the way for the whole country, it's our greatest hope! No, I'm sure you'll agree with me that there's nothing wrong with the open door policy. Look — Shenzhen! I bet you'll find plenty to write about here.

First we'll drive through the city to give you a general picture, then I'll take you to your first stop — Shatoujiao. When we started making these runs, there were as many signboards and arrows by the road as there are now, all indicating some work site. Now a lot of those signboards have gone — the building's finished; but new signboards and arrows have appeared. Look there — in a few months this new signboard will be another huge building. That's how fast things are done in Shenzhen! (He keeps pointing out signboards and arrows to us, as if they interest him more than completed buildings. The driver puts in, "It's only in Shenzhen that Young Cao rattles away like this, sounding like a poet!" — authors' note) So what? What's wrong with sounding like a poet? Each time I come here I feel carried away. In the special zone everyone can think big, work to make his dream come true. All those arrows aren't just pointing to work sites, they're pointing to an ideal.... ("Hear that?" puts in the driver. "No wonder he got top marks in composition and failed in physics, eh?" — authors' note) A master shouldn't make fun of his apprentice....

Here we are, we'll park here. Just ahead is Shatoujiao and the Sino-British Street. On the left is Three Family Shop, a bit farther on you come to the free market.... No, I'm going to see to the coach, besides we two don't have any Hongkong dollars.

Translated by Gladys Yang

At Your Service

Sun Jingkui, male, works in a crematorium — No, he corrects us, saying: I'm a mortician.

DON'T imagine that we blurt out the truth to everyone: I burn stiffs. Certainly not! I'm in the Public Utilities Bureau. That's no lie, we do come under the Public Utilities Bureau. The Public Utilities Bureau and the Public Security Bureau have this in common: they're both in charge of people, one of the dead, the other of the living. And people are more afraid of us than of cops, as if we were zombies ourselves. In fact there's nothing scary about corpses, but people are scared of us, thinking we're the last stop on the way to the nether regions. So much the better. "I'm from the crematorium!" Scare you to death, all the better to burn you up.

Don't laugh. My mates and I, we keep up our spirits, never pull long faces. You think it funny that we should crack jokes because you don't understand our job — hell, who'd trouble to investigate us, you all imagine us working grimly away. Fact is, we don't wait for the end of the memorial meeting, we've perked up while you're still mourning in silence. We make wise-cracks; "We're the King of Hell's gatekeepers", "We've a contract with the hospitals", "Next item, 'at your service'".... What a laugh! Because we're looked down on, does that mean we can't have fun? Of course people look down on us, thinking we're below par and must have flunked life's test, or we wouldn't be doing this job. In fact, there's more to it than meets the eye. We've got what it takes! Some time ago we were at Nine Women's Mound (the grave of some women martyrs near the East Lake in Wuchang, now a pleasure-ground— authors' note). We were having a swell time when an old fellow asked us, "Are you students in Wuhan University?" I told him, "No, we're from the Public Utilities Bureau." He had to ask what it did. I told him, "We see to everyone. More specifically, our unit is much the same as this gravemound." His eyes nearly popped out of his head. Why? Did he expect us to have waxen complexions, with tunic suits buttoned up to our necks and flowers all around us? That's the dead!

You think we're abnormal? We're not. We take our work seriously. Do our best for the dead and treat'em all equally well with no sloppiness about it. This is mainly for the living, to set their minds at rest. We often joke: If we cremate them well, one good deed deserves another and when we're dead their shades will lend us a helping hand. Introduce us to girls, for instance, or change us some funny money.* Foreigners, those who die in China, have to be cremated too!

All right, let's get down to brass tacks.

I was born in Beijing, in Dongsi. My father had been transferred there, and I go wherever he does. After high school I flunked the college entrance exam. I waited for a job but didn't get one. When I was fed up waiting I had a row with our district committee, the section in charge of "educated youth". They said, "There's a job in the

---

* Notes issued in exchange for foreign currency, with a higher purchasing value than the equivalent Chinese currency.

crematorium, will you take that?" Ugh! I really didn't want to! Right?

My mistake was I told my old man. He said, "All jobs are alike. They all need doing, don't they?" Went on to preach at me. I kept my mouth shut. Didn't want to go, so why should I agree? After that he kept on at me for turning down work, just loafing. Made me so mad that I had a row with him too. Then I signed on, fuming, for the crematorium. Before doing that I swore at him, "Don't worry. I shan't quit till I've cremated you!" Quick as a flash he said, "That's fine, just fine." Honestly, it's my father you should write up, he's quite a character, honest, good-hearted, broad-minded — all the old Confucian virtues. He joined the revolution in '46, but he's still only deputy chairman of his factory's trade union. Sometimes I kid him, "How long have you worked for the revolution? Thirty-odd years? Nearly forty? Where has it got you? Men who didn't join the Party till '64 are already ministers. You, you've messed about for nothing all your life." He couldn't care less. "I'm no good, no education; this job suits me fine, can't compare with those brainy fellows!" And with that he goes on to talk about piddling household chores, or bustles off on his "business". There aren't many people with his sense of duty. You know, all units are alike: a man quarrels with his missus, a kid falls ill, someone's short of money, they all turn to the trade union. It's become a liaison post between government organizations and the people. The most it can do is issue subsidies.

No, that's not the way it is, there's no question of passing any test. Stick it out for a few days and you get used to it. There's no "test". Stories like that are made up. If you're mentally prepared you won't find this job too scary. Besides, we're materialists. Death is like a light going out.

Talk about spirits or ghosts is just twaddle. People killed in car crashes, explosions or fires are a gruesome sight, that's true, enough to make you throw up, but they're not ghosts; you can get used to them. The hardest thing if you talk about "tests" is not getting an inferiority complex; in other words you must build up your self-respect. First let's. not talk about loving your job, the main thing is to love your life, to be sure that what you're doing is worthwhile, and if you're doing our job it's worth doing for life. What do you say to that?

It's easier said than done.

To start with I was a porter, loading the hearse, calling from house to house to fetch the old folk. Why call them old folk? Because it's mostly the old who die at home in their beds; and talk of "dying" doesn't sound good, better say they "passed away". We're a civilized country, China, we don't talk crudely, we prefer euphemisms. In three and a half years on this job, I've seen all·sorts of people. Some relatives laugh, others cry; plenty put on a show of mourning. It's husbands and wives who weep with real feeling. If colleagues weep, that's genuine too. As for the rest, we have a doggerel:

When sons cry the earth starts quaking;
The daughters' hearts seem breaking;
Daughters-in-law fake tears over this parting,
And sons-in-law sound like a donkey farting.

Of course, I'm talking in a general way.

I'll say there are! When we start carrying the stretcher out, some relative who thinks he knows what's what will say, "Turn east and carry him out head first." When we're in the yard or the street, some of them bring a plank to put over the dead man's head, to make it seem he's in a coffin!

Goodness knows how many of them are Party members or Youth Leaguers, but I can assure you there are superstitious Party members too. In the villages it's even worse, they want all the frills, right? We're an old country but a young one too, a mixture of old and new. I know, I've gone into the history of funerals and interments. Most people know perfectly well that there's no Heaven, no Hell, no future life, but they still go in for all that mumbo jumbo. May not believe in it, but they still do it, as if it's wrong not to burn paper money, letting down the dead and against their sense of what's right. I've often wondered which counts more, when it comes to a funeral, common sense or conscience? We don't like to interfere, except maybe to say, "Are you ready now? We must get moving." That's as far as we go.

Sometimes there are painful scenes: the father has died and his wife asks their son: This money, are you giving it or not? Sounds as if they've been arguing about this for hours. The son is nearly fifty. He looks at us, then at the rest of the family, and makes up his mind, "I'll burn it!" Takes off his army uniform and kneels down to burn the paper money. By the time we've loaded the body on to the hearse, he's put his uniform on again, ready to go to the crematorium to fix up the memorial meeting. I feel sorry for him and offer him a lift. We don't normally do that, only allowing two of the family to come with us to go through the formalities. We take the dead, not relatives. But he sends a young soldier with us to handle things, he has his own car! Shocked, are you? Well, it stands to reason. It's right to uproot superstition, but you have to make allowances for human nature too. Anyway, in three and a half years I've seen a lot, it's too bad I can't write a book. If I did, I'd have first-rate material, writing about the things I've been telling you. People don't always practise what they preach, don't act on their convictions, and that's excusable, especially in our time. Lots of strange things happen when people are beside themselves with grief. Don't you agree?

So many of the living go through the back door, of course there's a back door too for burning the dead. In other words the living must pull strings to get them cremated. Everyone has relatives and friends, right? Some use the back door to speed up the cremation, jump the queue; others want it delayed, want the body refrigerated. They're generally waiting for relatives from far away. My father too asked me to open the back door. "Kui'er, I've something to ask you...." I said, "Give me the name and address." Made it snappy and drove straight off.

I count as not bad at this job. In summer, decomposing corpses stink! When it rains or snows we get covered with mud and slush. But this is our job, isn't it? Each year I've been commended for my good work. In a unit like ours that's not hard. Other people, trying to put themselves in our place, feel it's tough on us. In any other profession you might claim to have done well, and they'd say I could do even better; but not when it comes to us. Yet there are no stories, films or TV programmes especially about us. Everyone has to die, but no one wants to be in at the death. Death is going home, but who wants to switch on the TV and see what it's like? Besides, whether a crematorium counts as the last stop on the way home or the first stop is hard to say. Look upon death as going home, they say, but you're not yet home when you're dead, still taking up space on earth, depending on us to turn you into ashes.

Take pride in your work, please people and be polite — that's our motto. Taking pride in your work is very hard — it means doing an honest job. We have our professional ethics! How can you offend a family in mourning? The dead don't know what's going on, but the family sees it and if you rough handle the dead they'll think you too callous. Treat the dead well to comfort the living, isn't that what I said just now? But sometimes we're really put out by the things they do, dressing the dead in good clothes, wearing a wrist-watch and with whole sets of bedding. What use are those to the dead? These last few years it's been better, most corpses don't wear watches; I've heard some people are afraid we'd steal them! In a forest you get birds of every kind. When I die I don't care if I'm cremated naked; better save money for the living! Why burn it up?

In the "cultural revolution" many people died unjustly, struggled against, beaten to death, or driven to suicide. Whole families, men and women, old and young, or husband and wife were so hounded, all they asked was to die together. I missed out on that, though, I'm only twenty-four. I wasn't even a "little red soldier"* then. We still have suicides, mostly for love, more girls than men. "Here's an 'unnatural death'" — everyone understands. Most of those suicides are too narrow-minded. Those girls are all so pretty, it's painful seeing how their families sob. They shouldn't do themselves in when crossed in love, should take a broader view, not commit suicide. When you're dead, meat loses its flavour, you can make yourself up and no one will see you, right? The relatives are crying over spilt milk — why didn't they do something for the girl earlier? Should have looked after her better when she was alive.

When you've seen a lot you grow callous. But I still can't bear to watch old folks mourning their children; that goes against human nature, against objective laws. Though old and young alike go down to the Yellow Springs, it's still heart-breaking; especially now that we have family plan-

---

* Children too young to be Red Guards.

ning, one child to a family. Most young people and children die of illness or accidents. Medicine is racing with Death; it often wins, but sparring with Death it can lose. It's not as if the devil were one foot tall and doctors ten feet — there's a limit to what they can do. So this law can't be broken. Though cancer needn't be fatal, once it's spread it's hard to cure; and what about other diseases? Life is short, each day brings you closer to the grave.

Yes. More die in spring and late autumn. Or round about festivals, especially the Spring Festival. My old colleagues say that in the past most people died in winter, but not any more. This of itself shows how good socialism is. No more frozen corpses in the streets. No, my political level's very low, but you learn certain things in this job. Certainly some people look down on us, some are afraid of us. When I knock off I read all sorts of books, literature, philosophy, history. Another thing is I meet all kinds of people, in every walk of life, who come to us when there's a death in the family; so that gives us an insight into society. Life's vertical, it comes to an end here; society's horizontal, part of it is scattered here. Yes, sometimes it comes to a scrap. One says, "Go ahead and cremate him." Another says, "No!" When they get het-up one threatens, "I'll lam into anyone who dares to burn him." They want to keep the corpse as material evidence, so as to get hold of some money or property, or to have the dead man's name cleared. Nothing we can do, we've our instructions. Without an order from the Public Security Bureau to keep the corpse, we have to cremate it. For instance after a car crash or death during an operation, the family can be most unreasonable, may come here to raise a rumpus. Maybe the trouble-makers miscalculated, got too little compensation. Not all of them make a row, by no means all. Do you mind me maundering like this? Since the economic reforms the crematorium hasn't made any contracts — too many technical problems. If I were to make contracts I'd put up a couplet on my gate: "All men on earth must die." "Don't leave ill-will behind you." And over the lintel I'd write "Look ahead". That would be meant for the living, naturally. I don't want them to be cursed after they've died, don't want them just out for money.

It's drivers and electricians who aren't satisfied with their jobs. Well, if you're browned off why not sit the exam to be a research student or go to teach in college? Fact is, they're not up to it. Most people doing our job are forced to it because there's nothing else they can do. Don't you agree? And if no one did it, the fields would be strewn with corpses. Besides, this takes some doing.

The last two years I've cleaned and made up the corpses. I learned how from books on cosmetics and barbering, applying skills used by the living to the dead. It's usually very simple, you powder them, rouge them and comb their hair for their families to see when they pay their last respects.

It's harder with traffic accidents or accidents at work, when the skull's smashed in or the nose and mouth are missing. With accidents like that, the family and friends insist on holding a memorial meeting and viewing the remains. I use whatever I can: cottonwool, paper pulp, plaster, grease paint, artificial hair. Whether the result is like or not's hard to say; so long as half the face is left I can usually manage. If the whole face is smashed in that's too bad, I have to work from a photo, and it's not so good. A photo's a single shot, a single flat view, and how am I to tidy up a flat surface? Can't expect people to close one eye when bidding farewell. So that's a big headache, and it may be a flop. But people have set ideas and expect the dead to look different, so that helps. Then there are those old revolutionaries, who've worked hard all their lives. When they die many of their old comrades-in-arms come to view the remains, veterans who were their buddies on the battlefield. I make sure that they leave the world all spruced up, I feel I owe it to them. There are fewer and fewer of these old comrades now, so my heart aches laying them out. They made a big contribution to our country, at least to one region, in one field, so we must see to it that they're well cremated.

That goes without saying, the family's very grateful. Laying out's an art, isn't it? But the final product only lasts a few hours before it goes into the furnace — don't nod, I've not finished yet. The artistic effect lives on in people's hearts. Right?

That's simple. Something missing in the middle? You show the head and the feet and put a cardboard dummy in between, with clothes on, under a sheet. That does the trick. After all, you come out of the womb dripping with blood, if you get run over by a truck you peg out dripping with blood; but how can I send a bloody corpse into the furnace? Some cases are hopeless though, they come in plastic bags all smashed to pieces. The memorial meeting's held after cremation. Here's one case I heard about. Some troops or sappers, I can't remember which, were testing a plane or warship, when something went wrong and two of them were killed. They tried to salvage them from the sea, but could find only part of one, I forget whether it was his stomach or his legs. After cremation the ashes were put in two caskets, because no one knew whose they were. Those were better than any remains, they died in a good cause, deserved to be buried in the Martyrs' Cemetery in Beijing, didn't they?

Are you tired? I've talked so long. Any questions to ask?

Rubbish. People who don't understand us talk nonsense like that. How could we? It would be against the law.

A lot of people's ideas about crematories come from that film. It's given a completely false impression! If I were the head of that crematorium, I'd never have allowed them to shoot that scene.

I bathe and wash my hands. If we're run off our feet I may forget, but in any case we use spoons, don't eat with our hands. However, if someone's died of illness, we make sure to use disinfectants. Traffic accidents are different; a day before he was healthier than me! My wife's always afraid I won't wash thoroughly, she doesn't realize we have much better welfare facilities than her Transport Bureau. Oh yes, my pay and perks are above average.

My wife's nothing special. I've read in novels and stories of women doctors, university graduates, marrying morticians; but that wouldn't be reportage, would it?

Do you ask everyone you interview that question? All right, I'll tell you. I'm a cut above my colleagues in my work, living conditions and education. I think I compare favourably with the rest of my age group.

I think of a whole lot of questions, regarding my work, life and various other things. Including whether or not, when my father retires, to ask his factory to take me on as a worker. Sometimes I reach conclusions. For instance, I'm certainly not going to transfer to his factory. Sometimes I reach no conclusion, and may not have by the time I'm incinerated. I often think...often think: We've a little girl, nearly a year and a half; when she's bigger will she be ashamed to tell her classmates, colleagues and friends that her dad works in a crematorium? Will she tell them? This is quite a problem I think. No, I can't go by my old colleagues' experience, it doesn't apply to me.

If you use my name, don't give the name of this place. If you name this place, write that I'm so and so from that crematorium, don't give my name. Anyway that's how I want it, OK? I've my own point of view, my own ideas, right? I don't want to make a name.

Come home with me for a look, come on, never mind!

Translated by Gladys Yang

"A Fly in a Bottle", That's Me

Jinling Hotel, Nanjing's first-class hotel, has just been completed and is still practically empty. It is ten in the evening and the attendant is sleepy. "If you want to chat, try the Victory; its coffee bar is open to the public." A smile lights up her tired face. "Go on, you'll find honest-to-goodness Nanjingers there!"

The Victory Hotel Coffee bar sells beer too. People are dancing between the tables. The admission charge is one yuan.

Luo Bin, male, nineteen, is holding a glass of beer and smoking a good brand of cigarette.

YOU'RE not a Nanjinger? That's why you don't understand. The coffee bar in the Jinling Hotel is top-notch, it even revolves, but they won't let us in there! In the whole of Nanjing, dammit, this is the only place where we can kill time. The Friendship Store is just not friendly to us, Chinese aren't allowed inside! The Jinling Hotel is the same, it's maddening. Should be smashed!

I know all that, we're still short of funds, need foreign currency, must safeguard foreign visitors — you don't have to tell me. You and I have different standards, we're not birds of a feather. If you've any guts, record what I say and print it! Let people judge for themselves. In China, in Nanjing, why can't Chinese go to places where foreigners go? The Dingshan Hotel, the Shuangmenlou, and the Jinling you spoke of just now all keep us out; even the bloody curio shop serves foreigners only. We can't go into the shop for overseas Chinese, and those who can can't go into the Friendship Store; yet foreigners who go there can get into any hotel! It doesn't make sense. My dad's a Party member. I ask him, "Is this in line with the Marxism-Leninism you believe in?" He acts dumb.

Yes, quite right, some places are out of bounds to foreigners, but I'm not allowed in those restricted zones either. Foreigners coming down the Yangtse aren't allowed to photograph Nanjing Bridge, but neither am I. Besides, I've no camera.

I'm waiting for a job. I don't mean what you would by that. I don't count keeping a stall, with a trading licence, as waiting for a job — those people have something to do. I don't do a thing, sponge on my family. Some time ago a foreigner, a woman, came here and asked me, "Waiting for a job, does that mean unemployed?" Ha, she spoke damn fluent Chinese, with no farting foreign accent. I knew she was having me on — she understood. I told her, "Unemployed means you've lost a job; waiting for a job means waiting for work. They're not the same." That floored her. She said, "You're good at repartee." I retorted, "You're good at firing off questions!" I couldn't be bothered with her, was thinking, "You're not my wife, to waste my time talking rubbish." But I kept a smile on my face to look friendly. Hell, I know some foreigners come here to make friends, some come as spies to pick up secret intelligence. Most of them come for fun, and when they've had enough fun they ask all sorts of questions. Then they go home and publish articles to recoup the cost of their plane fares. That way the trip costs them nothing and they make a name. Right? That's how it is. But whatever seems right to me you say is wrong. We can't see eye to eye. You're a writer, can make money. Don't say what you think. We don't see eye to eye. No, anyone who can scribble a few damn lines is a writer, a cut above us. But I despise the lot of them because they're out to fool people. As I see it, Liu Binyan is about the only honest writer there is. Don't get het up, I'm not getting at you. Didn't you tell me to suit myself what I said? What's so special about "suit yourself" — that's a phrase I picked up by watching TV ads. So it slips out, dammit, from habit.

Swearing's a habit I have. Everyone likes cussing. Depends how you look at it. In our country the worst off are the youngsters waiting for jobs. Me? Hell, I'm one of the worst of the lot, I've reached a dead end. Some of the better ones study and learn skills to serve society, but not me! In this life it doesn't pay to be too good, or even fairly good. You only lose out. You mustn't break the law either, it's not worth it, squatting in prison is no fun at all. So I've bloody well chosen to drift. Haha, you're right. I'm a backward element among the youth waiting for employment.

I'd like to work. I honestly don't want to go on drifting. But nowhere wants me. If anywhere wanted me I wouldn't be at a loose end like this. But, dammit, they all want college graduates, who wants someone like me? I've not even got a high-school certificate, failed six out of seven exams. Passed in sports, but that's not worth a fart! How can I enjoy life? At a loose end with nothing to do, I've nowhere even to let off steam, that's why I come here. To dance, to blether and drink with people I know or with strangers. It's become a habit I can't break, I have to come even if it means borrowing money. You think, my dad gives me just ten yuan a month, not even enough for fags let alone to come here. Don't worry, I don't steal it, I'm no thief. I know how to buy cheap and sell dear — savvy? It's not smuggling. Take jeans for instance, locally made but passed off as foreign goods, four yuan a pair in Guangzhou, my mates and I bring back several dozen pairs and can flog each for ten yuan. If people want to be suckers that's their look-out! Speculating? In a way. I do it on the sly, don't let my dad know. He's a Party member, works like an ox for the people. I'd like to be an ox, but where the hell is the cart? Or the land? Huh, I'm a wild bull.

I? Of course I believe in communism. The mess I'm in is one thing, but there's nothing wrong with communism. And I'm all for Old Deng. If not for him, hell, we'd long ago have had to go down to the countryside. With these reforms the old peasants have divided up all the land, so there's no more "going to the countryside". I may look down and out, but I'll be damned if I'd go and live in a village! Besides, these last few years our country's really picked up and restrictions have been lifted, all thanks to Deng the Great and the Third Plenary Session of the Party.

My name's Luo. I was born in 1964. I'll be twenty this year, next month is my birthday. At school I was run-of-the-mill, nothing special. I've been waiting for a job since September '82, nearly two years now, damn futile. The residents' committee sent me last year as a casual labourer to boil water. I quit after two months — it was futile; I made little more than fifty yuan a month. Besides, you don't understand, there was no chance in that job of becoming a regular worker. And everybody looked down on me for doing it, so it's better to wait for a job. I've asked people to find me work, no use, I've no pull and no money. My dad's a grade-20 cadre, not even a section chief, who's going to help me? Hell, I've had a rotten deal, born into such a shitty family — when factory workers retire their sons or daughters can step into their shoes, but that doesn't go for cadres. With my dad a piddling cadre I'm at a dead end!

Self-reliance, yes. But how many people get anywhere on their own? Everyone depends on connections. There you go again, you disagree. We look at things differently.

> It's pull counts most, then money;
> Doctors and drivers get whatever they please;
> Train attendants and shop assistants have their perks,
> And it's useful to have parents overseas.

Have you never heard that? Such people get along all right. They're top-drawer, dammit. Me, I'm the bottom of the barrel! Worse off than a girl at the bottom, because she may take someone's fancy and marry a top-drawer fellow, shooting up overnight. Me? I haven't a hope.

Look for a girl? She'd have to be blind to take me. I've figured it out. If I can find work next year, after three years as an apprentice, by the end of '87 or the start of '88 I'll be earning 38 yuan a month. No one is going to marry me before that.

What makes me think I can find work next year? Because the state's finding jobs for us all in batches. Next year's bound to be my turn. But I've no graduation certificate, after three years' study I flunked the final exams; so maybe no one will take me. (A girl invites him to dance — authors' note.) Go and find someone else. Can't you see we're talking business? (She looks at him and swears, then moves away — authors' note) You don't know, she's a tramp! Expelled from her school. That's how it is in Nanjing, it's always the girls who ask the men to dance, damn peculiar. I? I'm not afraid of her! I'm a buddy of her brute of a man. I've learned bad ways here, that's why I don't let my kid sister come to pick up bad ways too.

OK, I've no hope, I just hope the country will grow rich, then I can live a bit better. The one thing I'm proud of is — I'm Chinese. I've a right to vote, I'm a citizen. So it disgusts me when Chinese suck up to foreigners! Look at places like the Friendship Store, they're the limit! If I were a big shot, first thing I'd do, I'd kick out the men guarding the gate of the Friendship Store and Jinling Hotel, then I'd close down this coffee bar — few decent people come here. I count as one of the best! But I'll never be a farting official, can't even get myself taken on as an apprentice.

Yes, as a kid I had damn crazy ideals, longed to be a tankman. Idiotic. Now I'd still like to fight in the next fucking world war, off to the battlefield to risk my neck defending home and country. I know, I know, everyone wants peace, why should I want a war? I'm fed up, bored to death. Besides, my life's worth nothing. If worthwhile types like scientists and engineers die, they're a big loss to the country; my death would be a good thing. As it is, I've not done anything worth a dog's fart.

I often think I'm a fly in a glass bottle, with light but without any future, and I can't take out the cork to let myself out. Dammit, I often doubt, with the bad habits I've picked up these last two years, whether I could do an honest job of work in a factory. It's a good thing there aren't many people like me, or the country'd be in a bad way.

Translated by Gladys Yang

A Shadow

Zhou Wei, twenty-nine. His daughter Zhou Xiaoxuan is very like her grandmother, but he is thinner and darker.

ACTUALLY, I've nothing to tell you. My life's been too run-of-the-mill. The only difference between me and my contemporaries is that I'm Zhou Xuan's son.

I don't know much about my mother. That in itself creates an invisible gap, makes me feel there's a break in my history. When a colleague told me that a paper was serializing the life of Zhou Xuan, I wrote to the editorial office, but for some reason or other they didn't forward my letter to the writer. Later, during my home leave, I went to see the editor. The policeman's uniform that I was wearing nearly caused a misunderstanding! The editor couldn't believe that Zhou Xuan's son was a policeman. That was in '82 when I was a policeman in Inner Mongolia.

How do I remember my mother? As someone full of fun. She was a film star and singer driven out of her mind by the reactionary forces in the old society, a woman with a loving heart.

I was five the last time I saw her. She had encephalitis, and Shanghai doctors were trying to save her life. I was taken to the hospital and ran up to her bed calling "Mum!" She woke up, slowly opening her eyes, and whispered, "Wei — little son." Then her eyes closed again. I said softly,

"Mum's gone to sleep." But a doctor thundered, "Take that child out, quick!" I struggled in the nurse's arms sobbing, "I want my mum!" That was our final parting. I never saw her again.

After she died I was sent to an orphanage, started living in a collective. We were well looked after there, could eat as much as we liked. Once I ate four bowls of rice fried with egg, scaring the nurse in charge out of her wits! I was too full to move! We had thin clothes in summer, padded clothes in winter, and were issued underclothes too. Got a new outfit pretty well once a year, just as they do in the army. Next to the orphanage was an old people's home, and the old folk used to give us sweets and cakes. I learned to climb trees there, still can.

Once I ran away from the orphanage, wanting to find my old home, thinking there I could find my mum. I'd no idea who my father was. I don't know whether that orphanage still exists or not, I've heard that it was disbanded or merged with another.

In the orphanage Huang Zongying, the wife of Zhao Dan, sent me sweets and drawing-books, because what I liked best as a child was eating sweets and drawing pictures. Later Mama Huang took me out to live with a couple called Bi, then to board in a kindergarten. I was the tallest child in that kindergarten, I've kept a photo in which I'm the first in the line. It's a photo of us playing. Since I went to Inner Mongolia in '68 I've never had a chance to go back to that kindergarten to visit our teachers, but I often think of all those kindly "aunties". As for the other children in that picture, I can't remember the name of a single one.

In the first form at school I had a sudden craze for playing the flute. By then my elder brother Zhou Min and I had been adopted by Zhao Dan and Huang Zongying. This new family was fine, but we children were a strange lot. In Mama Huang's words we none of us turned out the way they'd expected. Our elder sister Zhao Qing was keen on music when she was small, but later took up dancing. Our elder brother Zhao Mao learned the piano, but in school he played basketball and later he went in for films. I played the flute for some years, but now I catalogue films.

When I was in the fourth form I transferred to the primary school attached to the Shanghai Conservatory of Music, and went on later to its middle school, learning to play traditional instruments. I took part in the Shanghai music festivals, performing as a soloist when I was ten. I thought I was getting along swimmingly, till the "cultural revolution" upset everything. That happened when I was twelve.

Only once did I put up a big-character poster. The school told us to put up posters, so I wrote one. It was aimed at our form mistress, Chen. Whenever I go to Shanghai I call on her. That was my only poster. Our school broke up, and the others went off to "make revolution", but I didn't go. I was a target by then. Zhou Xuan, Zhao Dan, Huang Zongying and even Zhao Qing were all "baddies", and as I belonged to the "five black categories"* how could I be a rebel?

Once our school held a struggle meeting against our head-mistress Jiang Ruishi, the wife of He Luting. After the meeting they beat her with a leather belt which had an iron buckle, so that the first lash drew blood. I went to cover her, wouldn't let my classmates beat her. In '77 she sent her daughter to see me, to express her gratitude. Actually she'd no reason to thank me; I'd been afraid that iron buckle, if it struck her head, might kill her.

---

* Landlords, rich peasants, counter-revolutionaries, bad elements and Rightists.

In '68 school-leavers were called upon to go to the countryside, and my whole class went down, lock, stock and barrel, to be educated by the villagers. I went to Inner Mongolia. At first I was very happy, feeling I'd discovered a new continent. Gradually that feeling wore off and I grew very homesick. This isn't worth talking about, so many stories have been written on the subject.

After two years there they made me cashier for our production brigade, and at one time we were so broke, all the money our brigade had was one cent! Yes, honestly. So doing the accounts was very easy; the brigade leader didn't worry about me embezzling money. Poor as we were we still fooled about — though we had five hundred *mu* of fertile land, we had to turn seven hundred *mu* of wasteland into "Dazhai fields".* As each *mu* yielded only thirty catties, we didn't even get back our seeds. I also worked as assistant to the vet, helping him to deliver foals. Foals can stand as soon as they're born, and they soon start walking.

My first year in the country my pay was fifteen yuan sixty cents. A year's pay was only enough for two weeks' food! I figured it out: some school-leavers had to pay money to the brigade!

In '71 I was sent as an apprentice to the research institute of the Ministry of Space Industry. The first year I earned eighteen yuan a month, later getting twenty-one and twenty-three yuan. When I finished my apprenticeship I worked at the heat-treatment furnace. A tiring job. But I put my heart into it, found it interesting. I read lots of books on the subject. At the same time some classmates and I ran a propaganda team in our spare time. We had quite a few

---

* Under the influence of the ultra-Left line, Dazhai, a poor brigade which terraced its barren hillsides, was held up as a model for the whole country regardless of the different local conditions.

talents in our brigade, musicians, dancers, stage designers — the lot.

In the research institute I fell in love, but it didn't work out. The girl thought that as my mother had been a film star she must have left me a lot of property, and as my foster parents were famous actors and writers I must have money. When she discovered that I was a poor bachelor with only thirty yuan a month she ditched me. Other girls felt that my family was politically suspect and were afraid to get involved.

In the summer of '82 I was made a policeman. Why? I think probably because I had a clean record, couldn't drink without turning red in the face, and didn't even smoke. And our leadership was concerned because my health had been bad for some years, and work at the heat-treatment furnace was so heavy. Of course, I was keen myself to be a detective.

In '81 I married. My wife was still studying in college, now she's working in Beijing. It wasn't easy for a nobody like me, a policeman in Inner Mongolia, to marry a Beijing girl. My colleagues joked that my luck must be changing.

My father-in-law's a practitioner of Chinese medicine, with quite a name. He's been written up in the press, on the front page too. My wife is his only daughter, she's a few months older than me. Our little girl's one year old, we're saving up now to buy her a piano, so that she can become a genuine Zhou Xuan Junior.

In May '83 I was transferred from Inner Mongolia to Beijing. First I worked with a newspaper for three months, then was loaned to the Chinese Film Archives to proof-read captions. As I haven't got my residence permit yet — it's fearfully hard to get one for Beijing — I'm not on the Archives' payroll. So at present I'm working for nothing, but our chief says they'll reimburse me later. It was quite an achievement solving the problem of husband and wife living apart. We only managed it with the help of a lot of senior comrades.

I'm a bastard. But I've never felt discriminated against. That's due to our socialist system, and maybe partly because I'm Zhou Xuan's son. In new China, no matter what size family they come from, I feel orphans aren't isolated but well treated. I want to do something worthwhile — I owe it to our people and our country. I'd like to study film theory and write plays.

Compared with the rest of my age group, of course I'm nobody special. Still, compared with many classmates who have settled down in Inner Mongolia, I may count as a cut above them. But I've changed jobs so often I've not achieved anything professionally. This puts a pressure, a heavy pressure on me. Materially we count as well off, we have a colour TV set, a fridge, a radio and tape recorder. Things that many people my age haven't yet got. But I didn't earn them myself, they were mostly given us by my father-in-law. Some people live on past gains, some on their old man. I don't like doing this though, it worries me.

What I feel most strongly is this: In our socialist motherland orphans aren't neglected but cared for. My mother's old friends Wang Renmei, Li Lili and other "aunties" have all shown concern for me. Uncle Yan Hua, my mother's former husband, writes to me. He was a popular singer who later went into business and is now an industrialist.

Translated by Gladys Yang

Where Apes Howl Endlessly

A clear tributary at the mouth of Wu Gorge is marked on the map as the River Daning. Having sheer cliffs on both sides, it is known locally as the Small Gorges.

A motor-boat chugs upstream through the narrow gorges. He is standing in the prow watching out for rapids. The crew call him Captain Zhang.

WHERE do you expect to find towmen? Ha, comrade, we're all towmen. We've been towing boats all our lives here, like our fathers and their fathers before us. In '71 we switched to a motor-boat. In tricky stretches we still have to punt. In places like this with sheer, slippery cliffs you couldn't tow the boat, had to stick close to the cliff and punt it along. See all those little holes chiselled in the rock? They were for the old plank towpath along the precipice dating back to the Three Kingdoms.* How was it made? Stone masons were roped round the middle and lowered from the top of the cliff to chisel those holes. All the way to Wuxi, wherever there are sheer cliffs you'll find a plank towpath. And from Wuxi all the way to Shennongjia. A motor-boat takes half a day to reach Wuxi, for towmen it used to take five days upstream. Sit tight! If you don't want to get wet sit in the cabin. There are several rapids like this; it's not the worst. In one place there was a big rock in midstream which

---

* The third century AD.

disappeared when the river was in spate. A boat knocking into it would be smashed to pieces. Each time a man with a rope had to swim to that rock and haul the boat along, while the crew used poles to ward it off the rock — if it got sucked over you'd had it! Now that rock's been blasted away.

At four or five I played about on a boat; at eleven or twelve I started towing; at eighteen I became a "skipper" in charge of a boat. My dad didn't have to teach me, it's not hard to manage a boat if you know the river and have guts. Helps if you drink and eat meat.

This river used to be busy, not any more. There's a highway now on the other side of that hill to Wushan County, used by trucks and motor-coaches. In the past all goods had to be shipped in or out. By Wuxi there are mountains, very wild, getting wilder the farther you go. They produce rare herbs as well as local products, and some strange people too — some live just on grass. What's sent in from outside is mostly coal. In the past not many people travelled by boat, only merchants and KMT troops. Not many people lived here, but lots of troops were stationed here: KMT troops, local troops and other units. We dreaded soldiers using our boats to ship guns and ammunition. They made us carry it ashore, beat us if we weren't quick enough for them, and paid us with mouldy rice. Today it's a different world. Isn't that right? (He questions one of the passengers behind us, one of the district propaganda committee who looks something of a scholar. "Yes, indeed. Wu Gorge is the longest of East Sichuan's three gorges. Apes gibber above it." — authors' note) Those were the days with boats plying to and fro when the river was really busy. We all grabbed at business, buying goods one trip for the next. For a skipper, knowing the river wasn't hard; the tricky thing was grabbing business. One trip you might make several dozen strings of cash, enough for a bushel of good rice. At Wushan waiting for a cargo you had your fling. Of course there were prostitutes, that was in the old days. Wushan County town was lively then. The dockyard bosses, those devils, stung you for each day you moored, and the damn shipping bureau taxed you too, whether you'd made money or not. Where I lived there was a swine. When KMT troops came he collected taxes; and when the power changed hands and other troops came he went right on collecting taxes! After Liberation he was still in charge but I paid no attention to him. In the "cultural revolution" they gunned for him, such a piddling little official! I felt sorry for him and said a few words to him, but now that he's in the clear again I ignore him. The prostitutes weren't so bad, everyone has to eat; the worst people are those who throw their weight about no matter who's in power.

In those days, yes of course, we were superstitious, sacrificed on the boat to the Dragon King, and burned incense and let off fire-crackers when we landed. When we'd eat meat we first offered a bowl to the Dragon King. Boatmen had a special jargon, special names handed down from the past. We never liked women passengers, had all kinds of taboos. If they broke one we fined them red cloth or fire-crackers; oh yes we were strict about it, because we didn't want the boat to capsize. No one believes that stuff any more, we've got rid of superstition. It's odd how many strange things used to happen on the river, but rarely nowadays. We say the Communist Party has driven away most ghosts — maybe the Dragon King's fled?

My home's in Dazhang, the first big town after the Gorges. I've four sons, lucky aren't I? Ha! This woman back here bore me three, and brought one with her. My first wife was no good, I divorced her. At first I thought nothing of it when my mother quarrelled with her daughter-in-law. That's the way women are. When I went home I gave them a talking-to. Then I discovered that my wife wasn't treating my mother right. That was during the hard years, and if the old lady ate an extra bite she'd curse: Drown yourself, drat you, when you cross the river! My mother lived on the bank opposite Dazhang. I told her off for cursing the old lady, told her off time after time and beat her up, then lost patience and divorced her. We had a daughter, she took off with her. I hear she's since married someone in the hills. My present wife's first husband was a skipper too, drowned in an accident. When she was introduced to me I liked the look of her, so I took her and her son. We've never had a row, and she's good to my mother. Actually my mother, how should I describe her? After my dad died she remarried, then she died, and my step-father took another wife, then he died. But she's an old lady, isn't she? We have to show her respect. If there's anything good to eat, she gets helped first. We have to set an example for the young ones. Put yourself in her place, how do you want to be treated when you're old? Do as you would be done by.

See that wooden boat being towed there? Now the policy's changed, private citizens can own boats. In a stretch like this boats can only be towed where there's a beach on the bank. You could do it yourself if you were strong enough. You strip to the skin, just wearing shoes, otherwise your feet would be burned by the sun on the pebbles, no matter how thick your soles are. When the going's hard you get down on your hands and knees.

Bah, this doesn't count as a chanty. You don't need to sing rousingly on a motor-boat. When you reach a rapid, a couple of shouts, all punting together, and you're over it....In our town we've a fine singer, a big strapping fellow.

When he bellows out a chanty it re-echoes through the gorges! Want to hear one! Next rapid we come to, I'll get the crew to sing at the top of their voices.

Just before Liberation I managed to get myself a wooden boat. I'd saved up seven strings of cash after several trips, and half-way home found a man in a hurry to get his old boat off his hands, so I bought it and shipped a load of stuff to Wuxi, delivered my cargo and sold the boat then built myself a new one to take home. My mother couldn't believe it! When I joined the co-op they reckoned its cost but never paid me the money, gave me some grain later on. In '71 we switched to motor-boats. I was still in the three-in-one group (a combination of old, middle-aged and young in the "cultural revolution" — authors' note). We didn't get up the rapids till the fifth go — the horsepower wasn't enough.

Look back, stand up. See those coffins hanging in that cave up on the cliff?

We have a contract now, four men to a boat, each month we pay our collective one thousand yuan, and each of us can make over a hundred. A lot?! It's not easily earned. Nowadays we take passengers. People going into the hills on business, but mostly tourists, especially in summer, not in winter. Last year a lot of foreigners from different countries came, to help open up tourism in Sichuan they said. They went back this way and all opted for this place to invest in. We helped ship those foreigners. It pays when they book a boat. So much per boat, not so much per head. Last time we had retired Red Army veterans and old workers. We stopped whenever we came to something worth seeing and let them have a good look, sometimes helped them ashore. Our country owes them so much.

There's another company in Wuxi which competes with us for passengers, seeing who can give the best service, whose boats are smartest and most comfortable. After this trip we'll overhaul the boat, not that I want to, but it belongs to our company and what they say goes. With the boat in dry dock we can't earn a cent. During this overhauling we've decided to fix up a removable awning that can be rolled up on both sides, so that passengers in the cabin will be able to see the top of the cliffs and the clouds above the gorges.

Do I think it a lovely landscape? Ha, after all these years on the river I'm used to it. Anyway these gorges are natural, not man-made. In April the hillsides are a mass of flowers, red, yellow and the water's really clear then, clearer than now. If you watch it from the bank you can make out distinct currents of brown and green. It's a fine sight, even after all these years.

I'm fifty-eight, we boatmen retire at sixty. I've two sons at home waiting for jobs, waiting to take over from me. Oh, young fellows in a small town have nothing to do when they leave school but kick their heels. What jobs are there for them? They've no land to farm. My elder son doesn't want to be a boatman, my second boy's dead keen. Not unless I retired early, but I'm still strong. I can't spend a single day idle at home. Each trip missed out on would mean so much less money. Taking passengers you can't count on a steady income, so our company's thinking of buying a big boat to ship goods along the Yangtse. I shall stick to this stretch of river though. My Number Two ought to make out all right. All my life? I've just plied this stretch from Wu Gorge to Wuxi, where boats can't pass. I've never sailed right down the Yangtse.

Monkeys? Yes. Sometimes troops of them come down to drink. It's said there used to be black monkeys on this cliff and brown monkeys on the other side. They never crossed the river but gibbered at each other across it every day, scaring people with their row. When boats passed they all chucked down stones. There aren't many left now. Henanese like performing monkeys. They used to come up through Shennongjia to trap them here, but later they weren't allowed to. If they were caught they'd be fined. Monkeys are really smart. See that bare cliff going sheer up? They can swarm up it. Once one of them slipped and fell, fell into the river. We punted over and picked it up, but it died before we got home.

Can you see them now? Yes, with any luck you can....

Translated by Gladys Yang

Sideline

Wang Meng is twenty-nine. He is cheerful, always laughing, and chubby. The way he talks and behaves reminds you of a big-bellied Maitreya Buddha in a temple. He tells us that the work he now has in hand is designing the office that Monkey would have had when he was Protector of the Horses in heaven for the Jade Emperor.*

I'M a stage designer with the professional drama company of the Guangxi Autonomous Region. But I haven't done any serious work for the company: there's no work to do. Hardly anyone wants to see spoken plays in Guangxi nowadays. There's nothing new, incisive or profound. What I'm concerned with is putting something on the stage that'll make the audience sit up. But it's not worth all the trouble: it can't be done. What people want to see is Cantonese opera. When the Cantonese opera troupes go to the villages peasants who've had a good harvest will spend money like crazy to get operas — any operas — performed, and for nights on end. As long as there's plenty of noise they're happy. What if the troupe has only brought a couple of sets of costumes and props? No problem. Doesn't matter what the period is or which opera it is — just sing! They're even doing operas that have been banned for ages. And if you don't know the opera, just fake it up. The audience don't

---

*An episode in chapter two of the sixteenth-century fantasy novel *Journey to the West.*

care what it is — they're enjoying themselves. But with our spoken plays the more performances we give, the more money we lose. The best thing is for us not to perform at all. Every province in the country has a provincial spoken drama company, and on top of that some central government departments have got their own, as well as the armed forces and the Trade Union Federation. Below that there's a whole load of companies run by prefectures, cities and counties. If you ask me they all ought to be closed down, apart from a few really good ones.

I studied stage design at university, though I'd never been interested in that sort of thing when I was a kid. What I really liked was painting. I've planted rubber on Hainan Island. What happened to all us school-leavers· who went down to the countryside was the same. You rode in a lorry across mountain after mountain for days on end without knowing where you were. Then they tell you to get out and suddenly a horde of bare-chested men in patterned shorts come rushing out to welcome you with drums, gongs and slogans on red banners. That was the state farm. What did I feel about this later on? I remember lying in my thatched hut looking out through the window at a piece of clothing that had been hung out to dry as it blew in the wind. It looked just like a person. That's when I decided to take up painting again and get out of there.

I got out and became a dancer in a theatre company. Can you imagine it? Someone like me learning ballet and doing the splits! I learnt how to do the model ballets and performed in *The White-Haired Girl*.* I took the university en-

---

*During the "cultural revolution" years there were only a handful of officially approved "model" stage shows, of which two were ballets, *The White-Haired Girl* being one of them. This was based on an earlier and much better folksong-style opera of the same title.

trance exams in 1977. That year stage design was the only speciality on offer that had anything to do with art. After the exams I waited for days and days until finally someone told me there was a letter for me at the gate. I could see it. was an official letter from the college. The people round me all said, "If you've passed you've got to stand us a meal." "Nothing doing," I said. "It's bound to be a rejection notice." I took the letter without showing any expression and without even letting my heart beat any faster, walked slowly back to my dormitory, climbed on the bed, pulled my quilt over me, tore the envelope open, and lifted the quilt up to have a look: "Admitted." I let out a great sigh of relief and took it out in the sunlight to have another look at it. I really was in, damn it! Only then did I get happy. If you know what despair really feels like you'd do best not to bring it on yourself. I learnt how to avoid that a long time ago. It's very easy: don't have any premature illusions.

I wasn't a very well-behaved student. I didn't reckon the college's teaching methods were up to much. They issued the students with the texts of the lectures in advance, then the teachers read the lectures out. Was that teaching? There was one teacher they brought in from another province who knew nothing. He was really vicious. You had to paint with the colours he wanted. When he walked past he'd put his hand out and change one of my brushstrokes. As soon as he'd gone I'd change it back again. Then he'd change it again, and I'd change it back again until he got fed up with me and told me to clear out. That suited me fine. If he was running a private school he could teach his students to hold their brushes upside down for all I cared. Colour sense is an artistic question. In the end that teacher cleared off and stopped teaching. There are too many restrictions in stage design: you're like a woman with bound feet. There's the script, the director, technical considerations, and other things too. I got good marks in my speciality: apart from one 4 in my first year from a teacher I quarrelled with I got 5 in all the other years.* My graduation design was for the Indian play *Sakuntala*. I set it in a theatre like a sports stadium with spectators all around, layer upon layer of them, three-dimensional. But we haven't got any theatres like that in China. It set the teachers quarrelling among themselves. Some of them liked it and some of them thought it was a load of rubbish. One of the teachers went to England for a conference not long ago. He took my designs with him and people had nice things to say about them. I'll tell you a funny thing about the college. One of the teachers had the nickname Mr England and we called another one Mr America — they sound just like real names. That was because they always talked about England and America.

Because the teachers quarrelled I ended up being assigned a job back in Guangxi. My girlfriend said she wanted to break up with me, so we got married. The best assignment you can get after graduating is being kept on at the college: you can get to see all sorts of new and interesting things, and you've got a chance of being sent abroad for further study. But I'm not one of those. I had no chance of being kept on at the college as a teacher. The only students the staff like are the ones who know that $1+1=2$ and not 3.

Nanning's not so bad: you can make a lot of money. I've switched to traditional Chinese painting, and I turn them out in batches. I pin a whole row of sheets of Chinese paper up on the wall, fill my brush with watery ink, and give each one a dab in turn. Then it's thick ink and the same stroke on each of them. That way I can do a whole batch of identical Gods of Longevity, cats, landscapes or whatever it

---

*In this system of marking 5 is the highest mark.

is. Of course they sell. I have my paintings on show in a gallery in Guilin, and in the busy season I pull in several hundred yuan. Outside the tourist season is my time for following my own interests and doing my own work. I do illustrations and comic books too. When I'm doing illustrations I read the beginning of the story and the last few lines, then start drawing. Eight yuan a picture. It doesn't matter if I get the picture wrong and it's nothing to do with the story. If they ask questions I can always find an explanation that'll keep everyone happy. Most fiction's no good: a silly story and rubbishy pictures to match. The plot's usually much worse than the lines in my drawings. The main thing in comic books is to make the characters good-looking, especially the men — they've got to be handsome. It's mostly women who read that sort of stuff when they're telling the story to children and amusing themselves at the same time. I've done some work for films and television too, but the scripts weren't up to much. I made a bit of money, but only a bit. And I've got my own students as well. Lots of people want to learn how to paint. I don't know what they're after. Do they think there's a future in it? Is it to get into university? For education? I've never gone into it. I set up a plaster cast or a still life and let them get on with it. I don't correct them much. Most of them would never have a clue even if you held their hands while they were painting for the rest of their lives. I charge them twenty yuan a month each. There are so many people wanting to learn that I can take my pick. I set my own standards, and take the students who'll be useful to me in future. There are even a few with real talent. I don't take money from them.

University graduates get fifty-four yuan a month in Guangxi. That's nowhere near enough to bring up a kid on. They're saying some people ought to get rich first now,

aren't they? Well, I'm getting rich. We intellectuals ought
to be making decent money and living well. But don't think
of me as making good money, absolutely not. If you really
wanted to pull it in there are some pretty shameless ways of
doing it, like pestering foreign tourists with a bundle of
scroll paintings and not leaving them alone till they've
bought one. I've even seen a tourist buy one and tear it up
on the spot.

I've got a son, and when he came I really didn't want him.
When I was waiting for him to be born I was sitting outside
the delivery room doing the designs for a television play.
When they called me in I tore a strip of paper off the
bottom of the picture I was doing, put a bit of red paint on
his tiny feet and took his footprints. His first step in life!
The little devil's just like me, always laughing. When we're
bathing him or dressing him we always make a game of it,
and he laughs as though he'd never stop. I sing him lullabies to get him to sleep. I know lullabies from a lot of
different places — Guangdong, Shanxi, Jiangsu, Anhui.
Don't you believe me? Then listen.... (He sang the first lines
of a whole string of songs in different dialects, like in an all-
star singing programme on television.—authors' note) The
longer you sing to him, the more awake he is. He just gazes
at you with wide open eyes to see what interesting thing
you're going to do next. I've discovered that there's only
one sound that'll get him to sleep — a low monotone like
this, "mmm". When I was teaching him to say "Pa" to me I
kept saying, "Pa, pa, pa" over and over again. He opened
his eyes wide, held his breath for a long time, and then
suddenly burst out with it: "Pa." I was so pleased I almost
fainted. Whenever I've played with him since then he's kept
on saying it over and over again. I'm his dad, but he's my
boss: he costs me eighty yuan a month.

I do all right in Nanning. I'm quite well-known in the local art world. I've joined the Zhi Gong Party* and pay twenty cents a month for my membership dues. You can test me on the party history if you like, but you won't catch me out. It used to be the Hong Bang,** but the party's constitution now says it "accepts the leadership of the Communist Party ... and works for the Four Modernizations". It specializes in overseas Chinese work, and all our members come from overseas Chinese and intellectual circles. Think I've got it all off too pat? I could tell you a lot more than this.

Don't get the idea that just because I'm a bit of a joker all I'm interested in is food and bed. In the last few years my interest in painting has jumped from Impressionism to Picasso. I've been searching like hell through masses of Chinese and foreign stuff to find my own style. You get the feeling that people have trodden all paths they can find, and yet a lot of places are left untouched. You've got to make money, but you never stop experimenting and exploring. A lot of us painters are like that, probably because the really admirable great masters of the past were poor and crazy. A year and a half after graduating I visited the college again. I found that the top students who'd been kept on there were just painting the same old stuff. That made me feel a lot better. I may be stuck there out in the south, but I don't feel at all backward: my thoughts go a lot deeper. If everything were just right I'd find it dead boring. "Is that all there is to life?" I'd be asking myself. The thing that really counts is

---

* Founded in 1925 by an overseas Chinese group in America, the Zhi Gong Party is one of the democratic parties which co-exist with the Communist Party in China today. Its members are mostly returned overseas Chinese.

** A secret society.

being able to see good art exhibitions from abroad. Of course, the only place they'll take any notice of is the National Art Gallery, but I'll go even though I have to pay for my own train tickets. Of course you often have to stand all the way to Beijing and all the way back to Nanning, but so what?

People are funny creatures. You can't live without money, but when you've got a bit of money it's not worth the trouble of earning even more. When life gets too comfortable you start trying to make things hard for yourself. That's why the moment my old teacher sent for me I came back here. I've worked it out, and I know I can't earn much here: it all has to be split seventy/thirty. Seventy per cent of what I make goes to the Guangxi authorities, and all I get is thirty or so yuan a month as an allowance for being away from home. But say what you will, this is the real thing for me, and I can get on with my painting and see what happens. There's a chance I may get a big exhibition. But if they mess it all up I'll say "bye bye".*I'll go back to Nanning with a single somersault, like Monkey.

A few days ago I went back to Nanning to see my wife and the kid. I got quite a shock, I can tell you, when one of my painting students came to see me. I asked him what he was painting. He told me he wasn't now, then asked me how much a year's advanced study at the Central Academy would set him back. A thousand, I told him. OK, he said: he was planning to buy himself a place to live in Beijing and take an advanced course. The way he talked really made me sit up. He told me he'd given up painting for trade. How much had he made? I can't tell you straight out, but ... but he's already a ten-thousander. How true the saying is, "After a few more days in your cave you find a thousand

---

*The speaker used the English words.

years have passed outside." I'd only been away for about six months and I could hardly recognize the place any more. I got the impression in the theatre company that half the staff had become deputy managers or board members of some company or other. The moment you meet them they whip out their cards. Even when everyone was celebrating a wedding at a reception they were all talking business. But here I am, still talking about art and complaining about how this is wrong, and I'm fed up with that. Basically, I'm fed up with myself. Why bother? I'd do much better sitting in a café and talking business like those people. If you make a go of it you can pull money in by the handful, and for no effort at all. Art will never make you a ten-thousander, not even if you flog your guts out. If they can all make money, I reckon that I could do just as well as a lot of them by really having a go at it. But I still don't want to go in for business — I'm not that broke yet.

Translated by W.J.F. Jenner

Wings

She was making pickles when we went to her house. Her hands were covered in red chilli powder. She is a member of the Chinese People's Political Consultative Conference. Today, China's millions of young people wouldn't know that; indeed, even her name might not be familiar to them and yet they have all sung her songs.

Gu Jianfen. 48 years old. Born in Japan.

I have composed a thousand songs? Surely not? I think about 300 have been issued. It only really counts as a song if someone has performed it and a music magazine publishes it. Li Guyi and Zhu Fengbo are the best singers for my songs. Although Zhu Fengbo has been singing my songs for four years, I still haven't met her. Whenever Li Guyi comes over to my house, she carries off a stack of music with her and then chooses what she wants from it. What you can hear now are all things I wrote last year and the year before. I don't have my own group of singers to try things out with, so I can never hear my work as it is written. That is a real problem. Of the pieces I wrote in 1983 only the "Marathon Song" was recorded in the same year. It was commissioned for the international marathon race in Beijing so they wanted something with a slow steady tempo to make it right for long-distance running. But the song itself took a very fast course. It was recorded only a couple of weeks after I'd written it. Do you want to hear it?

When I was little, we lived in Japan. My father was
involved in business there. I still remember the Japanese
folksongs I used to sing to amuse myself as a child. There
was one which went:

> There is a little kitty
> Who lives near my house.
> She doesn't wash her face
> Before she eats.
> Dirty little kitty, dirty little kitty.

I used to sing and sing. No wonder I went to the Northeast
China Arts Academy.

I was in the Northeast all the time from 1942, the year in
which we returned to China. I first came to Beijing in 1955.
I stood in the great Tiananmen Square and thought how
wonderful any song, however simple, would sound here.
This was the heart of the nation. I made a wish that a song of
mine might be sung there at the celebrations of the 10th
anniversary of the People's Republic.

My wish didn't come true. Before the tenth anniversary
in 1958 I was branded as a Rightist. I was sent away from the
Central Song and Dance Ensemble to Liuhe County in
Jiangsu Province. It didn't seem so terrible. We had a great
send-off with drums and gongs. At the time, I felt that I did
come from a bourgeois family and did have some rightist
ideas, so I needed to reform. In Jiangsu with some
colleagues, I set up a music school. We had wind, string and
percussion, singing all sorts of things.

Then came the "New Spirit". Our whole family was to be
sent to become peasants in a national minority area in Guizhou Province. We didn't go. We would have been finished
if we had. Small fry like us would have counted as big

villains in such a small place, wouldn't we? We would have been killed in some struggle in the "cultural revolution". At the time our director threatened to hand us over to the Public Security Bureau if we wouldn't go. I don't know what charge would have been made.

Not knowing where to turn, I got in touch with the Jiangsu Provincial Song and Dance Ensemble. They were willing to take me on, but my director wouldn't agree. He said that we had to be sent somewhere tough to be reformed — life in Jiangsu wasn't hard enough. No, this wasn't a matter of a personal grudge. Absolutely not. It's just the way things were at that time. It was quite fair and reasonable. Oh yes, that's right. My husband was the choreography director. His mother was Japanese and this counted as another of our crimes.

In the end, my husband was sent to Inner Mongolia to gain experience of life there while I went to collect folksongs in Yunnan Province. The dance troupe which my husband directed had won a silver medal at an International Youth Festival in 1959. That was why they would never let us go. If we had left the Central Ensemble, the silver medal would have gone with us. So the decision was made to retain us under supervision, and not to allow us to appear in public. A collection of my songs was put together in Shanghai — even the typesetting was done — but the leader refused his permission for it to be printed and so I lost the work of several years. I made enquiries about it recently. Someone from the publishing house told me that even the compiler had not survived so I could hardly expect that the proofs would have done. It made me more grateful than ever that I'd been lucky enough to survive.

My success came after the smashing of the "gang of four". At the age of 42 of course, I couldn't compare with some of the younger song-writers. They had talent and prospects. I was just glad that I hadn't been killed or gone mad or soft in the head during the "cultural revolution". In those years I was without a care. I wrote a lot. My songs just flowed. I would never have thought so many people would like them. I got so many letters. Perhaps it was because not many songs were coming out at that time. And there were fewer still that people wanted to sing. I just kept writing. It was my reply to my public.

I thought that the young school-leavers must have things that they wanted to sing about and that the young people in reform schools should have a voice too, so besides writing, I went to teach them to sing. I felt that I understood them and they understood me.

A group of unemployed young people in Tongxian County put their money together to send a representative to see me. When we met he bowed deeply and said, "I've come to thank you on behalf of all my friends. Your songs are the first ones we've heard sung about us." An army coastal communications company had one lookout post every ten miles. Each one consisted of a hut with a telephone guarded by a single soldier. On New Year's Eve, at the stroke of midnight, the company commander sent out a telephone order that each of them should sing my song, *Come Gather Together, Young Friends*. They couldn't gather together because they were serving China. Such admirable soldiers!

Some people have said that I write vulgar songs. Perhaps they mean popular songs or perhaps not. I don't know. Others say I've become rich and famous. Whenever there is a problem about one of my songs they come to me, not to the lyricist. For example, in 1980, when the Taiwan singer Deng Lijun was becoming very popular here, there was a lot of criticism of her sentimental style. It was said that I produced the same kind of stuff. This isn't true. (In the same year Gu Jianfen received an award from the United Nations for *Come Gather Together, Young Friends*. It was chosen as the outstanding song from the Asia-Pacific Region. — authors' note) But of course there may be something in it. Why else would I have chosen to call a piece "Wings"?

I wrote a song called *Moving House*. It's about a woman of thirty who had registered her marriage five years earlier, but was still unable to live with her husband because they hadn't got a flat. Everyone in her family was really worried. It's a humorous song. In the end she was allocated a flat by the factory she worked for. Everyone was delighted and came to help her move. The ensemble sang and mimed moving house at the same time. When it was performed in the sports stadium an audience ten thousand strong laughed so loudly they nearly lifted the roof off. In the theatre the audience crowded up to the orchestra pit clapping and singing. There was some criticism of using a song to expose social problems. In fact it does the opposite. It is a song of praise. After all she got her place in the end. These days do people in their twenties get their own flats? Precious few.

We ought to find out what sort of songs people want. I did a survey in eleven universities. I sang 16 songs accompanying myself on the piano. Then I talked about how I had come to compose them. Finally I asked for written comments. Some of the students gave me marks; others wrote about their reactions. One put down, "16=1". Could he have meant that they all sounded the same? I had been very careful to make sure that I chose a variety. Could they have still been too alike?

So my output has slowed in the past year because I am trying to think how I can write better. I visited South

America — my only trip abroad since we came back from Japan. In those three months I heard a lot of songs. They certainly do sing over there. We Chinese can be even more emotional; how many songs do we have in our hearts? So now I am thinking about the relationship between music and life. I am in my forties, but I still have to think about this because the source of our music has been harmed. I hate slogans like "High, fast, hard and loud" which governed our compositions for so many years, but what is my own work like?

I have two daughters. The elder one is married. Recently I invited my elder sister to move in with me to help with the housework. I can't cook and compose at the same time. I just mess up the food. I'm a song writer, but I was reduced to using my spare moments to write my music.

Now I will answer your questions.

I earned my first fee when I was still at university. I spent it on a pair of leather shoes. I was a poor student but life was fun. Compared with other composers of my generation I'm doing well. I have a certain political status, and materially I'm quite well off. I earn 110 yuan a month and my husband is on about a hundred. If one of my songs appears in a magazine I get about 10 yuan; if one is recorded about twenty— a bit more if I conduct myself. I've earned over 3,000 yuan in fees in the last few years. That's not such a lot. I don't get as much as people who do the music for films. They can use a few simple bars so many times over. I'll never match them. But my songs have been very successful. Some people's music is forgotten as soon as it is written.

Come Gather Together, Young Friends got the national award for the best song of 1980 and the UN award for the best song in the Asian and Pacific region. *That Was Me* got the national award for 1982. I've had a few other awards as well.

I am a member of the Zhi Gong Party. I joined not long ago. I first applied to join the Communist Party in 1960. That was at the time of economic difficulties. I used to save my grain to give to my husband and my children. My husband needed a lot because he was a dancer. I volunteered to reduce my ration to 27 *jin* per month and I applied to join the Communist Party at the same time. I have always been loyal to the Communist Party. It is something concrete, not abstract. In the twenty years since I applied to join the Communist Party I have never changed. I joined the Zhi Gong Party because I wanted to feel closer to the Communist Party. Every month we have a meeting to discuss documents, organize activities or talk about the problems of overseas Chinese people.

Party dues are ten cents a month. I only found out about the party's links with overseas Chinese groups in the United States after I joined it. Some of the old members taught us its history. Recently someone went to lodge a complaint with the Ministry of Culture, accusing me of having joined the Zhi Gong Party instead of the Communist Party. He was told to go away and make a proper study of the matter before he presumed to make judgements about me.

What was my most difficult time? When the "gang of four" was in power, of course. Luckily, because I was writing songs for ordinary folk, I knew all sorts of people, waiters in restaurants, soldiers, workers, kindergarten nurses and the children themselves. They all helped me. In fact I'm still in touch with them. Our friendship was forged in hard times. Even now, colleagues who can't get their children into kindergarten come to me for help. Not that the nurses will oblige me for nothing. They always make me write them a song.

My most painful memory? ... It is of my piano.

We lived in Dalian at the time of the Japanese surrender in 1945. The tanks of the Soviet Red Army trundled about, demolishing Japanese houses. Tins of food lay in the street alongside steelyards that had been used to weigh things in shops. We still use one of those Japanese steelyards for rolling out dough at home. The Japanese just wanted to sell up and go home, so everything was very cheap. There were heaps of pianos in our street — so many I could have played them from our house all the way to school. I asked my father to buy me one.

"How could we afford anything so expensive?" he asked.

"Go and have a look anyway," I begged. "The whole street is full of them." He took a bit of money for ordinary shopping and came back with a Yamahano No.I—the very best Japanese model.

That piano went with me everywhere. In the sixties, when my mother was very seriously ill, we had to spend a lot of money on her treatment. Later, when both my parents died, their funerals cost a lot. At the most difficult time we only had thirty yuan left for our family of four to live on, We sold everything except the piano. That piano was my life.

By 1966, we had cleared our debts with great difficulty. Then the "cultural revolution" began and I couldn't play the piano again until 1973. Don't be so naive. No, of course I couldn't write songs. I just had to concentrate on reforming myself. If you had been heard playing the piano, a charge could have been brought against you, and it's impossible to play without making a noise. In 1971, after Lin Biao's death, I "liberated myself". I exchanged recipe books for sheet music and was regarded as a first rate cook.

Later I took up knitting and spent hours poring over patterns.

I could see the piano all the time. I dusted it every day. Then I think I got a bit deranged. I couldn't bear the sight of it any more and I kept thinking about selling it. My husband warned me that I would regret it, but I sold it. Yes, I did.

I wanted it to be taken a long way away and we arranged that I shouldn't know who had bought it. But I do know now, I know where it is. I do regret it. It was my fault. I wasn't tough enough.

I couldn't bear life without a piano, so my husband got hold of one which had been covered in big character posters. It's the one I have now. It is state property; it doesn't belong to us, but anyway it has been allocated for us to use.

That is a question only a woman would ask. No, I hate quarrelling. I can't do it. I just sulk. My health isn't very good. My circulation is poor and I am anaemic. All the same, recently I still had to make a trip to record some of my own songs for the Pacific Recording Company. I had to have an injection on the plane but I couldn't change the appointment because they had already booked the recording room. I've got the tape. Would you like to hear it? I don't know where I've put it. I'm not very keen on their elaborate accompaniment, but they said they had to consider the market. Anyway, I want to find a better lyricist. There are so many things I want to do, we'd better hurry up and finish this.

Oh good, I've found it. I was short of breath you know, so my singing is not very good. Let me put it on for you.

"Sorrow and happiness both flow along the same course,

Everyone has a share of each."

"I wander through a wood of poplars.
The leaves change from green to yellow.
They flutter down all around me."

I am one of new China's composers. I owe all my success
to the country and the people. I've achieved quite a lot in
the last few years, so my debt to the people is very great.

Translated by Delia Davin and Cheng Lingfang

A Parade

There has not been a National Day parade since 1971. This year, 1984, marks the 35th anniversary of the founding of the People's Republic, and a large parade and ceremony is planned to take place on Beijing's Tiananmen Square.

On the 13th of July, at the foot of the Monument to the People's Heroes, the "Public Transportation Parade Squad" has just finished rehearsal.

Jin Jingyi, male, 43, Manchu nationality.

THAT'S right, our squad is preparing for the big celebrations on the 35th anniversary. We've practiced more than ten times, mostly using time outside of work. Only when the entire squad practices together do we use work time, and even then we don't dare use much. Surely you don't think it's like those years, when at the drop of a hat it was "political work takes precedence over everything else!" and we'd be off shouting slogans instead of working?

Which work unit are you two from? Shouldn't I go and notify the leaders before you interview me? Well, all right, I won't go stirring up trouble for myself. Anyway, it's not like a few years ago; now there's free speech, us common folk can have our say.

My surname's Jin, meaning gold or money as in "trade and finance". What's this "Mr. Jin"? Just call me Old Jin, that's better. Don't laugh! Take Old Deng for example: his official title is Chairman Deng Xiaoping of the Advisory Committee, but don't all of us common folk call him Old Deng? It's more intimate. I'm a Bannerman,* a Manchu, one of the five nationalities they used to say made up the Republic of China: Han, Manchu, Mongol, Hui and Tibetan. Now it's the great unity of the 57 nationalities, all of them equal. Talking about this reminds me of a story: The year before last on the second day of the Lunar New Year, all four of us in the family went to eat a meal at the Fangshan Restaurant in Beihai Park. This restaurant serves dishes based on recipes from the Qing court; they're very good but also extremely expensive. Usually the place is filled with foreigners and people from elsewhere in China; everyone crowds each other and you have to wait forever for a seat. But since it was the New Year, there weren't very many people. On the first day of the year, everyone's busy wishing their elders a happy New Year, and on the second, everyone eats a meal for the peace and harmony of the family. In the restaurant, we ran into a guy from Hongkong who was there all by himself. This guy, hm — you couldn't say he was rotten to the core, but he was, well, devilish. He told me he'd come to Beijing on a business trip; I thought him quite industrious not to take a break at the New Year. After hearing I was a Bannerman, he asked me if I was related to the imperial family. I told him that Bannermen surnamed Jin themselves belong to a branch of the Aisin-Gioro clan,**and that most of them were related in some way to the imperial family. Then he asked me if I supported the present political system. I answered, "Of course I support it." Then he said, "But don't you belong to the

---

* A Banner was originally a military unit of the Manchus, distinguished by the colour of its banner. It later became an administrative and social unit as well.

** Ruling clan of the Qing Dynasty (1644—1911).

imperial clan? Why should you support a republic?" I told him, "If I don't support the Communist Party, who am I supposed to support — Queen Elizabeth of the English Concession?" This guy! Wasn't he just asking for a lecture when he asked me that question? It's no problem if you don't support the Communist Party, but you should at least admit the facts. And although Chiang Kai-shek's government was also a "republic", its accomplishments in those several decades simply couldn't compare with those of the Communist Party, so what's the big idea of resisting it? Of course we must look at the whole picture; Taiwan's economy is not bad, in fact that gadget at my house is from Taiwan. What gadget? The television.

This imperial relative has come a long way from his roots! To this day, I've never seen what the emperor looked like, only seen him in films. He's dead now, but even if he weren't, I would know him and he wouldn't know me. A couple generations back we were doing all right, eating grain from the imperial stores, but by my father's time none of this glory reflected on our home — he was a rickshaw puller. If it hadn't been for Liberation, if things hadn't gone well I might have become a beggar. So would it be decent of me not to support the Communist Party? But I don't support fake Communists like Lin Biao, Jiang Qing and others of their ilk. Even before they fell from power I hated them, hated their guts. I have a very simple addiction: I love to eat meat, any and every kind. But I can't stand "textured vegetable protein". I really don't understand why they make the stuff when pork can be got so easily. In the advertisements and on TV they even say it's tastier than meat. What absolute rot! Fake meat is not meat, and a fake Communist is not a Communist. In my opinion, fake Communists like Lin Biao and Jiang Qing are not even as good as the Kuomintang! At least the Kuomintang has capitalists and landlords supporting it; Lin Biao and those others made enemies of everybody! When they were criticized a few years ago, it was said they had tried to restore capitalism, but I don't think that's right; the only thing they wanted to be was emperors — they wouldn't have known how to restore capitalism! It's quite clear to me: in today's China, nobody should think of trying to become emperor — if you dream like that, you're certain to fall from power! Yuan Shikai, Lin Biao, Jiang Qing — all of them were careerists. Jiang Jingguo has some pretty big ideas too: "Unite China under the Three People's Principles " — doesn't he realize how futile that sounds? After the reunification of Taiwan with the mainland, it's fine if he wants to have his "Three People's Principles" over there, but if you tried it with all of China it just wouldn't work. Then there's "China Spring "* — that's an even bigger load of damn nonsense; do they think they can put their mixed-up views to use to govern China? Pretty ambitious bastards!

That's right, I like to pay attention to state affairs, like to read the papers, like to talk. What's wrong with it? It's a hell of a lot better than raising flowers and goldfish at home.

The liberation of Beijing happened in the spring of '49 after the Kuomintang general Fu Zuoyi came over to the Communist side. The Liberation Army entered the city to take over its defence. I was eight that year, poor; I'd never been to school. After the ceremony welcoming the troops into the city, the citizens of Beijing held a parade to welcome the Liberation Army and celebrate liberation. I ran after the troops, too. On the street, a woman of the performing ensembles was teaching songs: "The Sky Is Bright Over the Liberated Areas" and "Without the

---

* A Chinese dissident group.

Communist Party There Would Be No New China". She would sing a line, and us cityfolk would sing it back, studying it very earnestly. By now she's probably a big cadre somewhere. I also learned the songs at that time, but try as I might I could never understand why "the sky was bright over the Liberation Army". Was there another sky over the Liberation Army? Only after I became literate did I realize the words were "liberated areas", not "Liberation Army". At liberation, us poor folk were so happy we could hardly stand it. Suffering people are always hoping for a change of dynasties, if for nothing else.

Before Liberation, there were some parades in Beiping, mostly demonstrations by students expressing their opposition to the civil war and hunger. My parents said, "Don't go running around with those students! Watch out for the 'black dogs' and the guys with iron helmets — they'll shoot you!" The "black dogs" were the police; the guys in the black helmets, the military police. They were vicious bastards. The Kuomintang and the Three People's Principles Youth League also held some parades for the Double Tenth* and to "suppress rebellion"; the common folk never took part, just looked askance at the proceedings. But I used to run along just for the fun of it. If you took part in the parade, you could turn in the little flag they gave you for a hunk of steamed bread to fill up your stomach. This was to get the beggars to join. The steamed bread was made of mixed-grain flour; if you ate it, you'd never get beriberi! *Me?* No, they never gave me any. Remember, I was only six or seven at the time.

On the first of October, 1949, I attended the ceremony marking the establishment of the People's Republic. I was just a squirt of a kid, no parade squad wanted me, so I hid in

---

* Anniversary of the founding of the Republic of China (1911).

Sanzuomen to watch. When Chairman Mao proclaimed, "The People's Republic of China is hereby established!" I heard it. Actually, I couldn't understand the mandarin Chairman Mao spoke with his heavy Hunan accent, but I understood that, anyway. During the "cultural revolution", when my son was seven, he was forever going on about "Chairman Mao teaches us...." It finally got to the point where I couldn't stand the monotony of it, so I lectured him: "Chairman Mao has a strong accent. If he actually were to speak to you, you wouldn't understand a thing, you little squirt!" My wife got frantic: "Be careful! That's reactionary!" That gave me a fright — if anyone outside had heard, I would have been material for a "struggle session".

After I finished primary school, I went to work as an apprentice in the public transportation company. At the big celebration for the tenth anniversary of the founding of the People's Republic, I took part in the parade. At that time there were no rehearsals — they would just make an estimate of the number of people there were to be, and everyone would put on his best clothes and parade past Tiananmen Gate dancing, singing and shouting, "Long li e the motherland! Long live Chairman Mao!" At that time the leaders of the Party Central Committee were Mao Zedong, Liu Shaoqi, Zhou Enlai, Zhu De, Chen Yun, Lin Biao and Deng Xiaoping; come the "cultural revolution", a whole bunch of them fell from power at once: Liu Shaoqi, Premier Zhou, Marshal Zhu, Qld Deng, Chen Yun — all of them got into trouble. I'm not counting Lin Biao; that bastard reaped just what he sowed. Thinking back on the 50s, people's hearts were really in tune with each other; the whole country was happy as clams.

From August to October of 1966, Chairman Mao reviewed the Red Guards eight times, and I was there two of

the times. One of the times, Tiananmen Square was packed
with people waiting, lying on the muddy ground. Every
once in a while they would stand up to see if Chairman Mao
had come out yet. When he finally did, everyone went wild,
the orderly formations disappeared; everyone was only
thinking about how exciting it was! To tell you the truth, I
didn't see a thing. I could tell you that I saw the great
commander, but actually all the figures standing on the
Tiananmen rostrum were wearing army drabs and were only
as big as the tip of your little fingernail. To be honest, the
only thing I got was a full day in the blazing sun. The other
time, Chairman Mao was to come by in a car. Several
hundred thousand Red Guards were waiting by the side of
the road, waiting and waiting, just for Chairman Mao. But
this time I didn't see him clearly either, because as soon as
Chairman Mao's car came by I was shoved to the very back
row of spectators by some of the more powerful Red
Guards. Before this, I had also been in parades to "Support
Cuba and Oppose American Imperialism" and to "Support
Vietnam and Resist America". My work unit sent me to
participate in these. After August 18, 1966, Red Guards
appeared all over the country, and I joined a "rebel group".
"People's Bus Rebel Group" was short for "People's Bus
Company Workers' Revolutionary Rebel Group". By that
time, "public" had become a "bad word"; public telephones were called "people's telephones" and public buses
"people's buses". The reason was simple: the idea was to
serve the people, not the public. Didn't "the public"
include landlords, rich peasants, reactionaries, bad elements and Rightists? However, they did not change the
name "public toilet"; even landlords have to piss! At that
time, I had already become a cadre in the bus company.

During the "cultural revolution" there were lots of

parades. Down with this, up with that, here a victory, there an alarum; there were parades for everything, and each parade meant a great crowd of people milling in Tiananmen Square. Eventually, every time the paper published "Chairman Mao's newest directive", we'd go out and parade around. Singing songs of quotations from Chairman Mao, dancing the "loyal dance", hopping and prancing we'd come to Tiananmen. And we never felt tired — it was almost sinister. We couldn't figure out where all that energy came from. When the "East Is Red No. 1" satellite was launched, we had another parade. When the launch was reported, there was yet another "newest directive": "We also must launch satellites"; goodness knows when and to whom· Chairman Mao made this speech. As a result, everyone on the street was shouting:"We also must launch satellites!" But if you think about it, it's really quite a joke. A billion people all launching satellites?

In 1969, at the celebration of the 20th anniversary of the People's Republic, we ceased production for a month to drill our parade teams. We marched exactly in step, more army than the army itself. Our mustering-place on the first of October was at Dongdan, which is a good distance from Tiananmen. At ten o'clock in the morning, we listened to Lin Biao's speech. Lin Biao had the voice of a real tobacco addict; his voice was always breaking off in mid-pitch. Let me do an imitation for you: "Com — rades: This is the twen — tieth anniver-sary of our gre-eat People's Republic of Chi-na." But at the time, no one dared laugh. Laugh? "Counter-revolutionary element!" Boy, did they spend a lot of money on that parade! We got up in the middle of the night, put on our cotton padded overcoats and went to wait on the street. After a wait of 7 or 8 hours it was our turn to march, so we cast off our overcoats, revealing our sparkling white shirts and blue trousers, and took up our "little red books". On that day, it was impossible to count even the toilets: Chang'an Boulevard was lined with temporary toilets walled with grass matting or sailcloth, while at major intersections there were buses that had been converted into toilets — what a lot of money they spent! That year, my wife was a member of the "flower-waving team". They didn't march but stayed in front of Tiananmen Gate with a gaily patterned ball in each hand. These balls could be manipulated to reveal five separate colours. Several hundred thousand people practiced for a month and a half to be able to make words with the coloured balls while standing in formation. How much money did the state spend for each of those balls? A few years before, people had waved little paper flags they had pasted themselves; suddenly, parades became all fancy like this. On that day, Tiananmen Gate was also certainly "well-decorated"! Chairman Mao, Premier Zhou, Marshal Zhu, Lin Biao, Jiang Qing, Kang Sheng and Zhang Chunqiao were all there, as well as that scoundrel Chen Boda. No, Wang Hongwen was not there; remember, this was '69; he wasn't on the scene yet. It was only after Lin Biao got his just deserts that Wang came in to be his "replacement".

There was no parade at the Tiananmen Incident in April, 1976; people were just commemorating Premier Zhou. The hearts of all the nation's people were heavy with grief and apprehension. Only after measures were taken by the police to suppress the Tiananmen Incident was a parade organized. Ten years of disorder had come to this, and this was about as far as things could go — everything had been scattered, turned upside-down.

When the "gang of four" was smashed, everyone was insane with joy. No organization was needed; everyone paraded for three days. I shouted my throat raw, although my wife said it was from drinking so much. I did drink a lot, but that was only to let the happiness pour out of my heart! Since then, there have basically been no parades. Oh, come on — I said *basically*. You people are certainly picky about language! There have been a few so-called parades; in '77 and '78, there were a bunch of people who made a fuss a few times about "rehabilitation", "democracy" and "human rights". They didn't think too hard about the state of the times — with things the way they were, could the government have possibly let them run things any old way? Later, the "democracy wall" was abolished, and that group's act was finished. Once, one of their parades blocked the passage of the public buses, and the driver called in to report: "There's a parade blocking the route; I can't get through." I told the driver: "Drive right through! Do you think they would dare wreck the bus?" Sure they had the right to parade, but what were they blocking the buses for? Perhaps they didn't get their fill of parades during the "cultural revolution". When the Chinese football team beat Kuwait, several tens of thousands of youths came out on the night streets to celebrate, all of their own accord. Besides "Stream out of Asia into the whole world", their slogans included "Increase Rong Zhihang's pay!" and "Give the football team a bonus!" Too bad that later the football team lost its edge by losing a couple of games and along with them the possibility of competing in the World Cup and the Olympic Games.

I volunteered to take part in this year's parade celebrating the 35th anniversary of the People's Republic. I'm getting old; in another five years, when it's time to celebrate the 40th anniversary, I don't think I'll be able to get up the energy.

Translated by Stephen Fleming

Living in Widowhood

Xi'an city.
She is a 41-year-old pattern designer, with "worker" status, currently holding a cadre-level position.

I know. Of course I know why you want to talk to me. My only request is that you don't publish my name, and also that when you've finished writing the piece, you send me a copy.

It's fifteen years now since my husband and I parted. I dreamt of him last night, perhaps because your visit today has been constantly on my mind. He, he still looked the same, he hadn't changed at all. After I woke up, I broke out in a sweat, and I wept.

Fifteen years ago, he went off to Sichuan on official business. We had heard that there was fighting in Sichuan but that the Design Institute was still operating, so he was sent there. As he was leaving he said he would return as soon as possible. At that time the baby was just one month old and I was on maternity leave.

As it turned out he never came back. After he got off the train he walked right into the town-wide fighting. A stray bullet.... (She was crying and the rest of her sentence was inaudible. — authors' note) First there was a telegram, and then later on his work card and money were returned. It was the railway authorities who dealt with it — he died in front of the railway station. A year later I went to collect his ashes and I asked them: "Are these my husband's?" They said "Yes", and pointed out the spot where he had died. Later on the leaders of the two opposing gangs were caught, but they didn't know who had killed my husband either. He was killed in the mêlée, nobody admitted responsibility. I sobbed as I watched the trial of the "gang of four" on televison; executing Jiang Qing ten times over still wouldn't appease me.

I kept the home going single-handedly, being both mother and father to my children. Ting Ting is already employed as a worker, and Fan Fan is attending senior middle school. She was originally called Wei Hong but later on her name was changed — the character "Fan" appeared in my husband's name. We haven't had any great financial problems. I received 30 yuan in widow's entitlement, a sum which was reduced to 15 yuan after Ting Ting started working. My husband's death was considered to have occurred "in the course of official duties". No, I don't know whether or not the families of those involved in the fighting who died qualify for welfare benefits, I don't know.

I've always had the courage to carry on with life; there's the children to consider! Many people are sympathetic towards me. The Party branch secretary and various friends at work all express their concern about me. There are also some who really understand me, for example there's him.

I'm sorry, I don't want to mention his name. I'm afraid of starting rumours. He's a technician, and in fact we work in the same factory. When Fan Fan was little and got measles he was the one who carried her to the hospital. However, my two daughters were arguing with me just a few days ago, saying that if I married him they would leave home and have nothing more to do with me. But, in reality, how could

I possibly marry him?

At first I used to cry all the time, feeling down-hearted all day long. We shared an office when he was sent to work in our factory; he was in charge of designing and I was responsible for pattern materials. He would often advise me that crying was futile and that one had to find a way of distracting oneself. He suggested that I study design with him, claiming that the kind of patterns designed by our factory didn't necessarily require the skills of a university graduate.

When my spirits improved a little, and my daily life had settled down, I really did start to study drawing. In 1973, a textile handicrafts exhibition was held in Beijing and a pattern which we had jointly designed was exhibited. During those years, the name of the factory, or the words "collectively designed" or something similar was all that identified exhibits. On this occasion, however, since they were to be shown to foreign buyers, all the designers signed their names, and we too signed our names.

Rumours immediately spread around the factory about how Xiao Jianqiu had taken a fancy to the young widow. The whole factory had seen the film *Early Spring* which had been criticized in the early years and consequently they all said that you could already see the evil influence it was having.

Of course I was utterly disappointed. And very hurt. I felt it was unfair to him for although he was completely innocent he now, along with me, became a target of unjust accusations. I went and told him: "In future don't come to my house anymore." As a result, he created a big fuss and his shouts were overheard. In fact I know that he was really in love with me.

What was he shouting? Oh, "It's not only love, there's

also our friendship," and such like. All in all, that's what he was getting at. He's really stubborn, as stubborn as a mule. He continued coming to my home in the same manner as before.

Consequently, the rumours became even more fanciful. I didn't know what to do for the best. I said to him: "If you continue to visit it will only create trouble for me." From that point in time, not only did he not come to my house, he even avoided me at work. But on that day, he said as he left: "Don't think that just because I don't come everything will be fine; it's more complicated than that!"

I really just wanted a quiet life. If I never achieve anything great in life I don't mind, but what I do mind is people gossiping about me. Do you have any idea how difficult it is for me? People are always making jokes at my expense. Such people have in the past expressed concern for me but they also talk about me behind my back. If I wore any new clothes people would say I was flighty or vain or worse.

To this day he still hasn't married. If he had had it out with me a few years ago then I actually would have married him. But now I'm old and don't think about such things. I'll soon be starting menopause, how could I consider marriage! Moreover, my daughters are against it. I've struggled through innumerable hardships to bring them up; what is to be gained by upsetting them now?

I've read the book you're referring to. In my opinion authors constantly write on the subject of love that's out of reach; why don't they write about my kind, where it is reached only to be lost again? Those, for example, who are a generation younger than me, are in a complete daze without ever having reached anything. I have held everything in my hands only to lose it all. My experience is more tragic than that described in *Love Must Not Be Forgotten*. I've lost both love and friendship in my lifetime, and moreover, I've harmed him.

Some things are impossible to explain. You just wouldn't understand. I'll tell you a story: I read it in a book.

There was a widow who scattered a hundred copper coins on the floor of her house every evening. She would then blow out the lamp and grope around in the dark until she had picked all of them up, following which she would fall into bed, completely exhausted. After her death the one hundred glistening copper coins left behind were evidence of how she had endured the hardships of widowhood throughout her lifetime. What age are we living in now? Surely I can't be expected to behave in such a way! I surely can't use the coins bearing the emblem of our People's Republic as "chastity coins", can I? But when will these prejudices ever disappear?

I'm no talker; if you have any questions just go ahead and ask.

Of course my life is quite full, I don't feel it is empty, it's just that I have more worries on my mind than other people. At least I have in the end succeeded in bringing up my children and I've also done my bit for the country. The patterned material worn by foreigners might just include some of my designs.

No, to date he hasn't brought up the subject of marriage.

Of course the person I love the most is my husband, how could it possibly be anyone else? Next come my daughters.

Many people have tried to matchmake and introduce possible partners to me. And some still do. But, without exception, I have refused them all. They say: "Take one step forward and your life will become complete," but I'm not convinced. Ever since I stopped him from coming to my house I have known that nothing in this world can be made complete in just one go.

I earn 60 yuan a month, with bonus about 82 yuan altogether. It's quite sufficient. However we don't have as good a life as the majority of households because how many others have husbands who only bring in 30 yuan? If he were still alive he would be an engineer; he graduated in 1963.

I can't compare myself with others in the same situation. Do you mean other widows when you refer to "others in the same situation"? There's no way of making a comparison. I very rarely go out; widows don't make a habit of getting together either. It's best just to let the days pass uneventfully.

Of course, the person who has moved me most deeply is him. But the matter that has most moved me was not of his doing. Last autumn, the factory sent quite a few groups of people to various places to hold seminars to promote the exchange of information — actually their real aim was to find out what our rivals were up to. As part of the reform measures each factory had to find ways of creating new designs. One afternoon, I was informed that I would be going to Sichuan, but the following morning the head of the factory came to my home looking for me and said: "It would be better if you went to Shanghai and Suzhou. I've only just taken up the job here and there are some things which I'm not completely aware of." I immediately burst into tears and the head of the factory said: "Oh, don't cry, it's precisely because we are worried about upsetting you that the change has been made...."

I really don't believe that there are people who would want to read about such things. Do you think you might be writing all this in vain?

Translated by Elizabeth Campbell

Drinks and Smokes

A Beijing-Baotou express train. Hard sleeper. Five minutes after departure.

WHERE are you going? Same here. Been there before? Got somewhere to stay? Me? Been there lots of times. My factory does business there.

Have a smoke. One of mine, I insist. Not up to your standards? Drinks and smokes are for everyone. OK, if you have one of mine, I'll have one of yours.

How old do you think I am? No, thirty-six. Born in the Year of the Rat.* I'm from Zhuoxian.** I'm a purchaser and salesman — always on the road. We've got quite a lot of factories in Zhuoxian, all sizes. Mostly they make parts for Beijing, Tianjin and Shijiazhuang. My factory does quite a lot of different lines. Mostly plastic mouldings: polyvinyl, polystyrene and fibreglass-reinforced plastics. We've never stopped working for a single day since we were set up in the "cultural revolution". There's always a rush on this or a shortage of that. If a commune-run factory's going to make a go of things it's got to be able to cover what's in demand all over the country. All the reforms and competition keep us busier than ever. We've got to bust a gut to get business. And we've had to adjust to all the big changes going on. It

---

* 1948.
** A county just south of Beijing.

used to be buyers that had to go down on bended knee. Now it's the sales people who get treated like dirt.

All that entertaining. All that flattery you have to lay on with a shovel. You two wouldn't have the faintest idea what hard work it is. When it comes to sweet-talking and getting on with someone from your own neck of the woods, "three endorsed letters of introduction are no match for the friendship of someone from your home town," as the saying goes. The man in charge of the procurement and sales department in the factory I'm going to in Baotou is a Zhuoxian man. Name of Zhang. So I spun him a yarn: "According to the present division of area Zhang Fei* was from the same commune as me You are also called Zhang, so you must be descended from Zhang Fei. No doubt about it. Goes without saying." I laid it on with a trowel, he lapped it up, and I had the contract with his official stamp on it. I told him he was right to be backing commune-run industry and getting the economy moving. "It's good for the country, good for the factory and good for our home. Could you do with some sesame oil? Good stuff — from home." Then he says no because he's scared of getting into trouble for breaking the rules. "Go on," I say, "try a couple of pints." I went out and bought a couple of bottles there in Baotou. He was none the wiser.

Entertaining? Loads of it. They're a crafty lot of so-and-sos, goes without saying. I'll give them everything except the "four don'ts". I've even taken people to the Dasanyuan Restaurant in Beijing: a meal for four cost 239 yuan 50, and that didn't include the cigarettes and booze. The "four don'ts"? It's a saying we have. The only soft things we don't eat are "flowers", which is what we call cotton bolls in Hebei; the only hard things we don't eat are lumps of dry

---

* A legendary hero of the second century AD.

earth; the only things with four legs we don't chew are
tables; and the only things with two legs we don't get our
teeth into are our parents. You've only got to mention
negotiations and they'll come straight out with suggestions
about a nice quiet restaurant — and quiet restaurants don't
come cheap.

Of course our socialism would be done for if everyone
acted like that. But if nobody did little factories like ours
wouldn't stand a chance. You wouldn't understand. We just
can't compete. We're no match for state factories in quality,
efficiency or anything else. There's only one thing we're
good at: providing booze and cigs. Whatever you want we'll
give you. Can state factories do that? No. That's why people
buy our stuff, even though it's more expensive. Raise your
glasses and forget about policy; once the chopsticks start
moving everything's possible. It's not their own money
they're spending when they place an order. There's no long-
term future in doing things this way; but it keeps us going
for the time being. You won't get far trying to stop
corruption single-handed. And where would the factory be
without orders?

Do you think I enjoy it? Crap! I have to eat quite a lot
before every banquet — I'd be sunk if the drink got to my
head. I sit there looking at the spread, all stuff that her at
home — the wife — has never seen in her life, and I have to
coolly tell the waiters to take it all away and feed it to the
pigs. It's like Monkey filling his belly with cold water to try
and look like a fat man.

As for Party rules and national laws, there's no way we
can keep the rules, but we can't break the law. Can't have
anything to do with crooks. At most we do things that are a
bit bent and go against your conscience. I'll give you an
example. Say the factory's just made a trial prototype of

something we can't mass produce yet, and we've got to go out and sell it. If we don't clinch a deal, it's the old story: big brother gets the noodles, second brother drinks the soup, third brother has the dishwater and little brother goes hungry because he's left with nothing. So what are we to do? We buy other people's products and use them as our samples to get the orders. It's trickery and deception — criminal fraud. When I was down south on a buying mission for a few days back I heard a recorded speech over the loudspeakers — must have been Bu Xinsheng* or someone. It said, "If we're going to have reforms we'll have to get some people on something. We won't shoot 'em, but they may get arrested. I don't know what the charges will be, but we've got people who can cook them up. But nobody's going to change the spirit of the Third Plenum." **It was a good speech and it made you feel terrific. Then I thought about myself and what I do. Is that reform? No need to cook up a charge: it really is criminal. And nobody would have to blow it out of proportion — it's big enough as it is.

Well, we're at Badaling.*** Aren't you two getting out to have a look? Persimmons are several cents a half kilo cheaper here than in Beijing.

What do you want me to talk about my childhood for? It was very boring. I've never had the makings of a real farmer. My old man was a farm hand, and farm hands were even worse off than the poor peasants. At least poor peasants had a bit of their own land, but farm hands were just landlord's hired labour. We were liberated early and had land reform early.****That was when I was born, so they

* A member of the Communist Party Central Committee since 1984.

** The Central Committee meeting in December 1978 at which Deng Xiaoping's reforms were launched.

*** Where the railway line crosses the Great Wall.

**** His county came under Communist control and went through the redivision of land before 1949.

called me Baotian — "Landkeeper". I was to keep the land we were allocated in land reform. When I finished senior primary school I went home to be a commune member. It was a disaster year then.* There were big floods, and I got together with other people from the village to go begging in Beijing. We begged for a year until we were arrested there and sent home. Later I took up slope-pulling. Don't you know what that is? You got a length of rope, tied it to an iron hook, and stood at the bottom of a slope. When you saw a pedicab or pedicart wanting to go up you hooked it and pulled it up to the top, and they gave you a cent or two. It cost me quite a few fights to pull things up that slope. Once I pulled my brother-in-law's ear half off. To this day his ear still flaps. Mind you, I had no idea then I'd marry his sister. I had no way of knowing what she was like.

When the "cultural revolution" came along I was in a "Peasants' Rebel Regiment". We went to stay in Beijing and ate for free at the reception centres for Red Guards who were travelling round the country then. We ate there every day, and nobody interfered. Who'd have dared? We were the "revolutionary young warriors invited by Chairman Mao". I went to six of Chairman Mao's eight rallies for the Red Guards. When it wasn't on to stay in Beijing any longer because the "revolutionary young warriors from outside the capital" had to "go back to their own units to struggle, repudiate and reform" I went to Tianjin. And when they chucked people out of Tianjin I went to Baoding. Baoding was chaos — armed fighting. Were there? Of course there were! Lots of "reception centres" and "supply bases". One day you ate at the "Three Reds" reception centre, and you agreed with them. The next day the Jinggangshan Army**

* Around 1960-61.

**Rival coalitions in the factional wars in Baoding.

supply base fed you, and you were for Jinggangshan. I was for whoever fed me — I got by. When the 38th Army intervened to stop the fighting and didn't pull out I took repatriation expenses and went home. I'd seen the world, and so when I got back I became a buyer.

Tricks of the trade? Plenty! I don't rely on a notebook. If you put everything in a notebook and it gets lost you're sunk. I keep it all in my head — what Zhang and Li and Scarface Wang do, what they like eating, what they want, what I can get from them. When I go to a new place the most important thing is to get an accurate picture. You've got to find out what they're short of — it's scarcity that makes things valuable. Isn't that what the national economy and the people's livelihood is all about? They look after the national economy with their state plans, and I sort out the people's livelihood — food, clothes, consumer goods, entertainment. Do you think I'd make myself look stupid talking to you like this if I didn't mean it?

You two have got a fair bit of education. Where do you work? You expect me to guess? Tricky. You don't look old enough to be officials, section heads. You're certainly not workers, peasants or soldiers. Students? No, too old. I give up.

What? That's done it. If you write this up and my bosses hear about it I've had it. Better not write about it. Don't write about it. But I'm not worried if you do. The problem is mine, but the roots are with the "gang of four". It's true, isn't it? It's all their fault.

You ought to realize that we're all bullshitters. We get on the train like gentlemen and get off like blind men. We do our job like children, and go home like con-men. It's a hard life. And what's in store for us? Tongues worn out, shoes worn through for no good reason, a whole basketful of crimes to our name, and the black house. The black house? Clink. Don't believe everything I tell you — we travellers like spinning a line.

The economy? It's doing fine. It's done very well since the Third Plenum. In 1960 more than half the people in the village, men and women, young and old, got "balloon sickness" — distended bellies. My dad died then. In 1970 the factional struggles were so bad that the harvest was ruined, but radio and TV lied and said it was a good one. In 1980 the contract system had started and things looked up. Honestly, commune members are better off than factory workers these days. But I can't leave. If I did the factory would be one man short. Now you can see TV aerials going up over every house, and people can eat good-quality rice and white flour. Of course it's a good thing. But there's too much corruption about. That's why the Party's being rectified. That's right, isn't it?

Have another cig. I can claim for it on expenses. Let's have a meal — I can claim for that too. Is it true, what they say about it being possible to contract for commune-run enterprises? I'd love to do it — I could make it more profitable than it is now. If I contracted for it I wouldn't have a single buyer or sales rep. I'd let anyone who wanted to do the job for a short spell. I'd make them an allowance of so much a day to cover everything. I wouldn't give them entertainment expenses.

No, I'm not a good one — I'm a lousy salesman. But if an honest man tried to do this job it'd be too much for him. He'd get nowhere. Do you know the people in the Baotou Industry Bureau? Or the Beijing one? Tell me how it's done and I'll pay you for the information. Everything's called "information" these days. But what is this information? It's beyond me.

Don't be so sure. My basic wage is thirty yuan, but the main thing is the commission rate's good. They repay what I actually spend when I'm away from home. Don't be fooled because I eat and dress well — I don't make as much hard cash as my old woman. No, no kids. She was married to another bloke, had a son by him then got herself sterilized. The bloke died, and she married me. But she had to leave the boy behind with the other family to keep it going. Fine. So my family dies out. She had a couple of operations, but they couldn't join the tubes up again. That's that. Let's not talk about my family. Why don't you two tell me about yourselves? I've heard that authors can earn two or three hundred yuan for a night's writing. Is it true? Tell us about it....

Zhangjiakou. Let's get out and stretch our legs.

Translated by W. J. F. Jenner

The Kid

One night, this tall lanky guy was kind enough to give me a ride on the back of his bicycle, since we happened to be heading in the same direction. In order to avoid getting fined by a traffic cop, we stuck to the little lanes and alleys that you find all over Beijing. Weaving through the crooked backstreets of the city with amazing dexterity, he never stopped talking.

I'M nineteen years old, never had a job, never been to college, never sat around home waiting for somebody to give me a job either. Last spring I took the entrance examination for the Central Academy of Fine Arts. (In China, students apply for admission to arts colleges earlier than to normal institutions. — authors' note) My scores on the painting, colouring and modelling tests had to be some of the highest among the huge number of people who applied. But that goddam school wouldn't take me. They got uptight when they saw that I had "three years of reeducation through labour" on my record.

Remember back in 1980 when a gang broke into the Foreign Trade Centre? I was one of them.

None of us had any specific idea in mind when we did that, nor was anyone involved out to get anybody's goat. We were all really frustrated about something, though I can't tell you what it was. It was like we were all bored out of our wits or something. That's all there was to it. Do you know what I mean?

I grew up in relatively comfortable surroundings, a hell of a lot better than most people. My grandfather was a scholar who specialized in the study of ancient architecture. He had already retired when I was a kid. My father is an artist with a pretty decent reputation. Since I was an only child, I grew up with just about everything a boy could want. In my school there were a lot of kids whose fathers were officials with ranks like department or bureau chiefs. Whenever we did things together, I always felt I was under some sort of pressure. Even though I was always the best in everything I did, the truth is that they and their families were a lot better off than we were. They also had this arrogance that was buried so deep in their bones, there was no way I could ever match them. Maybe this was some kind of jealousy on my part, but in any case, I wasn't going to play second fiddle to anyone. Then again, maybe I was too sensitive. The kids in my school came from a wide range of backgrounds, some of them very complex. There were even kids in my class whose fathers hauled things around on tricycle trucks for a living, but it looked to me as if they were a lot happier than I was. If you had a skill you could at least take care of yourself. But if you didn't, you could blow your top and it wouldn't get you anywhere; you were about as helpless as a heap of rubbish. This is a lesson I learned for myself when I was in the labour camp.

There was no political motivation behind that incident. A bunch of guys got together, broke into the building and smashed the place up a bit. We broke windows and destroyed some of the things inside. Those kids I was talking about took part in it too, but they certainly weren't out to get anybody in particular. There wasn't any real reason for what we did, except that we were all bored out of our wits. That's the only reason I can think of.

In those days I was still something of a show-off. After the incident took place, the cops were out to arrest us. I could have gotten away then, since I wasn't living at home.

But I was worried about my paintings, so I went back home in order to put them away so the police wouldn't mess them up when they showed up to search the house. When I got home the cops were there waiting for me. The way I figured it, no matter what happened, they were going to arrest a bunch of people, so the best thing for me to do was to take responsibility for the whole thing. So when they took me to the police station, the first thing I did was to confess that I had organized the whole break-in, so they didn't have to go after anyone else.

I was a minor then, so they gave me three years of reeducation through labour at a camp near Zhongtiao Mountain in Shanxi.

It was there that I learned how the world really worked. That place was full of every sort of criminal you could imagine. When a new arrival showed up the other guys in the cell made you undergo an initiation rite. The first day I went to work, a couple of guys tried to take advantage of me, but I just ignored them. But that night, the moment I lay my head on the pillow, someone forced my quilt down over my head and a whole bunch of them started beating me up. The same thing happened the second night. At this point I had to think of something, since if this went on any longer they would have ended up beating the living brains out of me. So the next day, I picked a fight with a guy, pinned him to the ground and aimed the point of my hoe right at his face. I told him, "I don't care which one of you started it the other night, the point of this hoe can't tell you bastards apart anyway!" I was stuck in the camps now, so whatever happened things couldn't get much worse. At this point, that guy cooled it. I mean he gave in to me. That night, I went to bed only pretended to be asleep. The moment I felt someone tugging at my quilt I turned over and hopped out of bed. The whole bunch of them were standing there about to jump on me, but I had them scared shitless. "Hey! You little bastards still looking for trouble?" They started coming closer, so I picked up a thermos flask and "opened" it in the direction of the guy who had tried to suffocate me with my quilt two nights before. Those glass fragments and hot water "blossomed" all over him. You can imagine how that guy looked. At that moment, every one of those bastards "cooled it". Sure, we had thermos flasks in our rooms. We were there to be reeducated; that's very different from the guys who were serving sentences. We could turn out the lights in the room at night, but they had to keep theirs on. The difference is like night and day you know. We were there since we'd made some mistakes; we were part of some sort of contradiction between the people. The guys who were serving time were real criminals. That's an entirely different kettle of fish. You don't know what "opened" means? When you use it as an adjective, it means "broken". For instance, "who got their head 'opened'" means "who got their head busted open". When you use it as a verb, it means "throw". That's what I meant when I said "opened" before. That's slang, you'll never find it in a dictionary. Some of the words in the dictionary are really poetic, you know, like "the flowers blossomed" or somebody opened his present". But in slang it means that somebody was all splattered with blood. You like the way I know the difference between a verb and an adjective?

   I learned that when I was studying for the college entrance   examinations.

As a result of what happened that night, I became their leader. That was nothing to be proud of, really since it had nothing to do with any skill or achievement on my part. After experiencing the incredible monotony of life in a labour camp, I suddenly came to the realization that my entire life up to that point had been a waste, and wrote letters to all those guys who had been involved in breaking into the Foreign Trade Centre, explaining this to them. But those bastards in the camp who I now had under my thumb made fun of me for it. I responded by ignoring them. I knew that if I wanted to carve out a niche for myself in society, I'd have to do it through my own efforts. So I started studying junior middle school textbooks. By the time my three-year stay was over, I thought, I'd be ready to take the college entrance exams.

Fortunately, at that time they weren't making city people in labour camps give up their urban residence permits, so when my three years were up, I went back to Beijing. Be-lieve it or not, all those guys whom I'd been real tight with in the past were still scrounging around, fooling around with cute chicks and selling stuff on the black market. Goddammit, it took me all those years to realize what an idiot I'd been all along. I spent three years of my life in that godforsaken place on account of that bunch of creeps; what a f— waste of time.

Now I'm taking third-year senior middle school classes. I joined a class in the middle of the course and I have to pay tuition, but I didn't have to register. I'm taking Chinese, mathematics, English and history; I need these courses if I want to apply to any of the arts academies in the future. I have a lot of trouble writing essays. I've got plenty of expe-riences to write about. Problem is, I can't make use of them in the kind of papers they want you to write in middle school. You know, things like "My Most Unforgettable Experience" or "My Favourite Teacher". They've got this very rigid form you have to follow. It's like wearing a pair of pants that are too tight for you. I know a lot of middle school students who do nothing but study all day long. They're a bunch of dumb idiots, but they really think they're hot shit. Actually, except for all the crap they learn from textbooks, their minds are complete blanks. I'm not at all impressd by their straight A's. Sometimes, though, I feel inadequate and sorry for myself. When class is over I pack up and leave, and never say anything to anybody. Going to school really leaves me feeling depressed.

I get along quite well with my grandmother. You know the way old people can dote on you. But my father and I hardly talk to each other. When I was sent away to the labour camp, he became real self-righteous and said: "Didn't we go out of our way to raise you right?" I had made a big mistake for sure, but I still didn't agree with him. When our arguments became intolerable, I left. I just ran away from home.

I'd hang around the streets, and sometimes I'd stay overnight at a friend's house. It got worst in the middle of winter, but I couldn't go to my grandmother's house; that wouldn't be running away. I didn't have any money, I couldn't change my clothing, and I couldn't get anything to eat. One time the cops were about to stick me in a holding pen since they thought I was some unemployed hayseed trying to sneak into the city. When one cop finally realized what I was he said to me, "Get out of here, get out of here. Go home and take care of yourself. You'll freeze your ass off walking around the streets in the middle of winter."

There is one place in Beijing I really like. It's really fantastic. Can you guess?

It's the Yuanmingyuan Garden. I love the way the weeds grow wild there, and the ruins. I love the open spaces, and the fact that there's never anybody there. I know how the colours and the scenery change with the seasons there. That place is like my own private nest. I'll take you there some day. I clear a little space in the middle of a field and make a little nest for myself. It's surrounded by a thick wall of tall weeds. There's a little patch of sky above my head, and when I lie back I can hear the wind rustling through the grasses. I like to read there, and paint. If a couple comes by, I always make a point of getting out of their way. When it snows, the sky turns grey and the earth is covered with a beautiful white blanket. When I look up at the black branches without any leaves on them, I feel like I'm the only person in the whole wide world.

Does my father still support me? Yeah, I'm afraid so.

I'm still planning to go to university. That's all I want to do now, and I don't care what school I get in to. There must be some school somewhere that will accept me. You know me, if I go to college, I'll do as well as any of those stupid bookworms, even though I won't win any academic prizes. I'm sure some school's going to take me some day.

Translated by Don J. Cohn

Schoolfriends

It's a commemorative celebration. About three thousand women and a scattering of men have gathered in the old-style school courtyard. It is the 120th anniversary of the founding of the Bridgman Academy for Girls, now known as the No. 166 Middle School. A cluster of old schoolfriends, all upwards of 50 years of age, are singing together on the platform.

Cao Shizhi, dressed in a dark green Western-style suit, stands at the very back of the meeting in a group of four or five other women of indeterminate age.

THIS gathering reminds me of the film *Long Live Youth*. Don't you think it's like that? Were you at the Bridgman Academy too? No? What a pity. You wouldn't feel the same excitement then. You do? Well, perhaps you are easily excited. It's a pity Bing Xin isn't here. I heard that they phoned her yesterday and she said then that she intended to come. She was in the class of 1914. Later she came back to the school to do some teaching. Quite a few famous people were produced in this school.

What about me? I finished junior middle school here in 1965. These were my friends at school. We've just found each other.

This is the daughter of Zhou Ruchang, the expert on the

Dream of Red Mansions.* She was in the year above me. As
soon as we got here we went to look for the classroom our
year was meant to meet in. Each room was labelled to say
which classes should meet in it. We looked all over the place
before we found ours. Several hundred people must have
gone through the school between 1964 and 1968 but we
were all supposed to be in the one room. The girls of the
1930s and the 1940s had a room for each year. There were
only a few people in each room. At least we were better than
the later classes. About 2,000 people must have been here
between 1969 and 1984 yet they were only given one room.
Just a minute! — Miss Zhao!

She used to be our class tutor. She was an old girl too. She
went on to the Central Academy of Fine Arts from here and
was sent back to teach at this school when she graduated.
Have you noticed that the women on the platform sing like
professionals? That's Bao Huiqiao playing the piano. No, she
hasn't divorced Zhuang Zedong. I've heard they've tried to
persuade her not to.

I work in the Number One Department Store as an accountant. Yes, you recognize this suit because it is our
company uniform. That's right, we two both work in the
same place. I suddenly realized that she was an old classmate when I was transferred there two years ago. (Her colleague says, "I went to a handicrafts training school after I
left middle school. Then I was sent to a factory to be a
worker. Ten years later there was a change of policy and I
was transferred to the Department Store to work as a
window dresser. The woman writer Yu Luojin was a classmate of mine at the handicrafts school."—authors' note)
No, we all wear uniforms, but they are not all the same. The
managers wear wool, department heads wear a woolen mix-

---

* A famous 18th-century novel, one of the great masterpieces of Chinese
literature.

ture and we wear this man-made fibre. We are the same grade as the shop assistants.

I didn't do senior middle school here. I went to technical school.

Is it a good thing to go to senior middle school? That depends on whether you have a chance of getting into university. I thought it over and decided that technical school would be better for me. For one thing my marks were nothing special. Then there was the problem of my family's political status. My father was a clerk in the Shanghai Bank. He started work there before Liberation and stayed on until he retired in the 1970s. No, there was no problem with him. He wasn't the sort of person who gets involved in politics. It was my mother. She had been a housewife but after Liberation she began to teach in a night-school. In the anti-Rightist campaign of 1957, Zhang Naiqi, the leader of the China Democratic National Construction Association, was labelled the country's biggest Rightist. She was a member of that group, and small fry or petty intellectuals like her who didn't keep their mouths shut were all made Rightists too. She was sent to a labour reform camp outside Beijing. They rehabilitated her a few years ago. My brother couldn't get into university because of her. He suffered from depression and became mentally ill a few years back. There were four of us in my family. He was the only boy. I'm the youngest. My two sisters went to university but I wasn't as clever as they were. No one at home gave me any advice when I was deciding what school to try for, so I made the choice myself. The women of our family are all alike. We don't bother about domestic matters much; it is outside affairs which interest us. We take after my mother. The technical schools advertised for students in the papers. At first, I planned to go to the Liming Petroleum School but it moved to Daqing that year. I applied to quite a few technical schools; all of them were linked with heavy industry. The specializations were engineering, metallurgy and power. I didn't think I would make a good nurse. The technical school I ended up at was my sixth choice. It simply trained purchasing agents. I thought that would be all right. It would give me the chance to travel and I could be involved with heavy industry. I didn't realize that school had no links at all with industry. It was the Beijing Commercial School. My teacher told me I had filled in my form well because I had applied to schools in Dalian, Qingdao and Qiqihar. When they saw I was the sort of person who was willing to go anywhere they would want to have me. That was Miss Zhao whom you saw just now.

I spent ten years as a shop assistant in a mountain area near Beijing. I wasn't allocated the job, I got it as a result of the policy of sending people to the countryside in 1968. I only had one year at the technical school. I spent four years at a village supply and marketing co-op. Then I worked in the commune shop for six years. All that time I was in the village. In that little shop we sold everything from silk to garlic. The hardware department sold tyres for carts, door hinges.... We bought all sorts of things too: timber, medicinal herbs, red mountain haws, scorpions, eggs, nuts and pork. When we bought a pig it had to be butchered and then the meat was sold in the shop. There were four of us working there. I was the only educated young person from the city. The others were locals. We took turns at doing the cooking. We had a cart for bringing down the things we purchased in the mountain areas. I learnt to do everything except kill the pig.

Depressed? No, I wasn't depressed. We educated young

people were meant to be "re-educated by the poor and lower middle peasants" and I accepted this completely. Indeed, I was rather to be envied. I wasn't in the remote countryside. I didn't have to work in the fields and I got wages of 26 yuan a month. That's what I earned for all those years. When I was moved to the commune shop, I went on working as a sales assistant. Then they wanted to train me as a buyer. I really didn't want to do it. I didn't want to have to travel around. I was thirty and I wanted to settle down.

I began to try step by step to get back home. As I wasn't so very far away and I had a job with a wage of 26 yuan a month, it was going to be hard for me to get back to the city. I didn't have the same priority as young people who had been sent down to work as peasants. My first move was to swap jobs with someone working for the Capital Iron and Steel Company. He was a driver whose family lived in Huairou County. So I moved to Capital Steel as a worker and he returned to Huairou but went on working as a driver. Next, I started to hunt for someone else to change jobs with me so that I could do the sort of work I had done before. Of course it was difficult. Especially finding someone who wanted to move to Huairou County. And I had to arrange everything myself, although of course my friends and relations helped me to look. My family didn't do anything much. All the time I was in Capital Steel I kept on asking. In the end I found someone who worked in a department store in the factory town who wanted to swap with me. I worked there for a year and then I was transferred to Beijing. I've been working here four years.

No, this isn't my son. He's my classmate's kid. I'm not married yet. (Her friends interrupt at this point to tease, "She hasn't got a steady boyfriend yet. Why don't you find her someone? Zhou Ruchang's daughter is still single too."

— authors' note)

You see the old lady on the platform? She was our Dean of Studies. She organized this celebration. That's why everyone stood up and clapped when she appeared. They are hoping to use the anniversary to get more money for the school. The school was founded with money from an American woman, Mrs Bridgman. It was called the Bridgman Academy. Later that was changed to Bridgman Girls' Middle School. It was a private missionary foundation. During the Japanese occupation it was taken under government control as the Beijing Number Four Middle School. After the war it became private again under its old name. After Liberation, it was first known as the Number 51 Middle School and then as the Number Twelve Girls' Middle School. After the "cultural revolution", it went co-educational and under the unified system it was known as the number 166 Middle School. In 1951 it received a grant of 180,000 yuan. Of course it was one of the best schools in the whole country. This year it got 160,000 yuan. At its lowest, in the 1970s the grant was 60,000 yuan. How do I know all this? There is an exhibition on the history of the school by the entrance. Also, my elder sister told me a bit. She was at school here and then she did Chinese at Beijing University. She sang *Kunqu* opera very well and was a keen opera fan. When she graduated she wrote to Jiang Nanxiang — he was the Minister of Higher Education then — to ask for a job connected with opera. Fancy having the cheek to do that. In those days people were really.... Anyway, she was given an editing job in a publishing house which dealt with opera. The school has asked her to help produce a commemorative booklet and to persuade all the old girls of the school who became famous to write for it. She has done it all in her spare time. Did you hear the old lady on the platform? She said that they have petitioned the municipal government for extra funds so they can expand the school. Doesn't she talk in an old-fashioned way?

I heard that Peng Xiaomeng was invited. She was in the year above me. No, she wasn't the one who gave Chairman Mao a Red Guard armband on that famous 18th August. That was Song Bingbing. Peng Xiaomeng went on to the middle school attached to Beijing University. She was the one who wrote the article "Long Live the Rebellious Spirit of the Red Guards" and a couple of other similar ones. No, it wasn't the Qinghua University Middle School. That's where Luo Xiaohai and that group were. Chairman Mao wrote them a letter. I don't expect Peng Xiaomeng will come; she brought her followers back here during the "cultural revolution" and they beat up the teachers and the principal. No, I didn't join any of the groups. My family belonged to the "five black categories". I wouldn't have been eligible. We were driven out of our old house to live in a little place nearby. We still haven't got back in. The policy of restoring houses to their owners hasn't been carried out. We've handed over the deeds, but still no sign of the house. Do you see that woman? She is the daughter of Gu Zhutong, a high Kuomintang officer. We weren't in the same year. She's wearing a badge with her name on it. Does it say her name is Gu Hong? Gu Zhutong's three daughters all graduated from this school. The daughters of other famous people were here too. Yes, I have a good memory for names and things like that. It has never been much use to me, but anyway I remember them.

I get 54 yuan a month. I don't know what grade I count as. It's all rather mixed up. Do you know what grade we are? (She addressed this last question to her colleague who replied, "We're paid as graduates of technical schools anyway. How come you get 54 when I only get 52 yuan a month?" — authors' note) I know why. It is because of my year working in Capital Steel. I got the extra two yuan there because it was heavy industry. I went on getting it after I transferred. I see now I made the right choice when I chose technical school. If I had gone to senior middle school it would all have been wasted because the universities stopped recruiting in the "cultural revolution". Two years ago, everyone who had attended technical school had their wages raised a grade. I get quite a good bonus, about thirty yuan a month. We accountants get the average bonus. Sales assistants working in the electrical department could get as much as 50 yuan. It's only been like that for the last few months. Since June there has been no limit on bonuses. Before that, we only got ten or twenty a month. Next year, when the city carries out the economic reforms, we'll have to pay tax on bonuses. We won't be able to get so much then. Especially accountants and people like me; we can't increase our bonuses. We are going to have winter uniforms as well as these suits. They haven't been made yet. We get shoes as well. Not these ones. They are prettier than this pair. (At this point her colleague excused herself in order to go up to the front for a look around. — authors' note)

...It's not that I haven't been introduced to any men. People have found me so many I can't even remember the number....

I've got a boyfriend at the moment. He's 44. He's got a fifteen-year-old child. His wife died from some illness. He is all right. At first I wanted to go on picking and choosing, but I picked and chose men and they did the same with us. Then I saw that even my two sisters, for all their ability, felt frustrated with their home life, so I stopped. He'll do. We'll probably settle soon. A forty-year old like me ... well yes,

I'm only thirty-five, but I feel as if I'm forty....

Where did you buy that commemorative book? I want to buy a copy too. No, I won't take yours. The principal gave you yours. You should keep it to read. It's meant to help raise funds. They are asking three yuan a copy but it only cost about one yuan fifty to produce. I know about it. I asked my sister to get me a copy but she told me to ask my class representative in the school association. She didn't bother about me. She was too busy with all she had to do for this reunion. (Her colleague came back and they stood together looking at the book.—authors' note) Look, here's someone who was at the school in the thirties — she's a member of the Party Central Committee now. And the head of Fudan University, she was here then too. Teachers, directors, writers, and well-known doctors.... What a lot of famous people. Who is this? Oh, the first principal of the school. If he were still alive today he would be 180 years old! Come on. Let's go and buy a copy. Here's yours back. Sorry, but we'd better go and buy it now. If we wait till the end of the meeting, there will be even more people.

Translated by Delia Davin and Cheng Lingfang

A Young Worker

We stopped a young man at the Xidan Market in Beijing.
We'd guessed right: he was a worker.

Zhao Pingguang is a 22-year-old stoker in a steel mill.
It's heavy work; only men do the job.

SURE, I'll talk to you, but let's get one thing straight right from the start: I never read the papers or any magazines. I'm so buggered at the end of the day that all I feel like doing is falling asleep in front of the telly.

Best if you ask me questions. Anyhow, we can just talk casually.

My dad's a worker, so's me mum. My two brothers are workers, too. I've got a sister, though. She married a fella from the outer suburbs and she flogs books.

Suppose I've got the most education of anyone in my family. At least I finished senior middle school. My elder brothers only made it to the end of junior middle school. The oldies are both illiterate. They still use a seal to sign for their wages every month. Not being able to read didn't make much difference for their generation; they lived off their skills. Things are different now, like my senior middle school diploma makes it easier for me than my brothers. They still have to sit for the senior middle school exams if they want to be Grade 3 Workers; I don't have to. But I'm only a Grade 2. I haven't been in the job long enough yet.

That's right, it all depends on how long you've been working. Once you've been there the right number of years it's pretty much a sure thing that you'll get upgraded — if you aren't a complete slackarse, that is. Anyway, it means a raise of a few bucks.

I went to Jinshifang Primary. We were all street kids there. You wouldn't find anyone from a "good family" in the dump. I started in '69. You couldn't really call that school; we mucked around all day. My dad was in the Workers' Propaganda Team that occupied Qinghua University. The old man can't read a word, but there he was giving all those university people shit. The "cultural revolution" screwed me up from when I was a kid, but that's just how it was: "All power to the proletariat."

I saw this movie a few days ago. There was this line in it that said: "People with money don't have to study; they can hire people who have studied." All you have to do is change the word "money" into "power" and you have the "cultural revolution" down pat. It was a foreign movie: all foreigners are crazy about money. But we are crazy about power. School was a complete waste of time. Back then they said, "To have power is to have everything." But once Lin Biao bought it the word "power" wasn't that popular any more. The word was the only thing that changed.

"Studying to become an official" was criticized, and everyone talked about "studying being useless". You should have seen us: all these little seven-year-old farts running around criticizing this stuff. Gees we were full of crap. I don't believe any of it now: studying is real useful. Sure, my teacher only made 50 yuan a month, half what my dad got, *and* he was much older than me dad.

I started studying seriously at junior middle school. By then everything had changed and as I've always gone along

with the crowd I started working. I went to No. 8. We were
the last year to get there because we lived near the school.
After that they changed the system and No. 8 became a key
school — everyone had to pass an exam to get in. Kids in
the lower forms looked down on us and said we were all
duds. It was really weird — we didn't get to study the stuff
they were doing in first year until we were in third year.

I finished my first three years of junior middle school in
1979. By then you could only get into college, tech or senior
middle school by passing an exam. I felt like giving the
exams a miss and going straight out to work. I figured I'd
end up as a worker either way. But they didn't give me any
choice. It turned out that they wouldn't allocate you a job if
you'd only finished junior middle school, so I'd end up
unemployed. There was no way I was going to hang around
selling bowls of tea on the street like all those other guys
who were "waiting for work". I had no choice but to go on.
Of course I wanted to go to a college or a tech. If you could
get into one of them it meant a meal-ticket for life; but I
bummed out. There's courses that accept people with low
marks like me: cooking schools and horticultural schools.
But I wouldn't go near them. Me, end up as a cook? You
must be joking. The Forestry Bureau runs the horticultural
schools — they're even worse. You slave your guts out
studying and graduate as half a peasant. Shit on that for a
lark. My senior middle school was a normal one: No. 35.

After school I became a worker in the steel mill. I was
lucky because I could take over my dad's job. If it hadn't
been for that I'd probably still be waiting for work.

He got out of the propaganda team ages ago. You know
the saying, "Cadres back to your offices, workers back to
the factories. The 'cultural revolution' is one big mistake."
No, I didn't make it up. Everyone says it, easy to

remember, You can forget about him being retired and all that, he's still at the mill going strong. All he did was give up his place to me. He's a Party member, and didn't want to end up as a "gentleman pensioner" who's hired by other factories as an "old expert". Expertise pays and he could be rolling in dough if he wanted.

On my first day in the new job they sent me out to sweep the streets. All the new workers have to do a spell in the "factory beautification brigade", and it was six weeks before they gave me proper work. Some guys ended up with good jobs, I got stuck with a real lousy one. I can tell you, if I'd known they take note of your attitude to work when you're sweeping the damned roads I'd have bloody well done better. But I'm a bit slow on the uptake, and I was sloppy about sweeping the streets so I did myself in real badly. Those six damned weeks have decided the rest of my life. No, my dad didn't have a clue about the system. When he started out as an apprentice he had to clean the nightsoil pan for his foreman. There were some blokes who were even slacker than me, but they had "roots" — you won't see a section head's son out there feeding the furnaces.

What are the best jobs in a steel mill? "Working with lathe, pliers or casting can't be beat; Riveting, forging, welding are pretty neat; But if you're sent to make moulds, better to quit." Making moulds is not quite as bad as what I do. My job is to feed the furnace. It doesn't require any training; you just keep on shovelling coal into the furnace. You're sweating from the moment the work day starts. It's 50° to 60° centigrade in there all year round. There's this character who came in the same time as me. They put him in the repair shop and he spends all day fooling around. The reason you have it so good, arsehole, is that you took that work sweeping the roads seriously — that's what I think every time I see him.

It's a long way from where I live: an hour by bus each way. I give the mill ten hours of my life every day. I lived in a factory dorm for a while — six to a room, but it was incredibly noisy; then I kept losing things: meal tickets, money, clothes, everything. I gave up and moved back home. They eventually found out who was doing the stealing and the bastard was given the sack. He's opened up a small restaurant and now he's doing better than any of us. I hear he's already made 6-7,000 bucks. Bloody rip-off joint too, if you ask me. I went there once and had a beer. It cost 50 or so cents a litre like elsewhere. "Do you water down or something?" I said, "It's so damned weak." "Yeah? And what are you going to do about it? You haven't got any proof. Go on back to your lousy 40 buck job where you belong." I was pissed off as hell with him and I split his head open with my bowl. The fuck had stolen my meal tickets and never paid me back. He didn't dare make a complaint to my factory himself; he had to lump it. But his old man had the nerve to ring up and put me in. The head of security called me in but I told him, "Don't take any notice of the complaint you got about me from the factory and business regulation office. The officer who spoke to you is Little Landlord's old man." We all called that guy "Little Landlord". His dad's been working in the office for a couple of years but before now no one ever took any notice of him. Lately he's doing well for himself 'cause he's the one who gives out permits to new businesses, so of course he's very popular. Life's like that: you never know which cloud's going to piss on you.

I'm not in the Youth League or the Party. Just look at me — reckon I'm the type they want? I'm no progressive element; not that I'm a reactionary either. I love my country but. There's lots of Party members who are not good. There was this one who lived over where we do. He applied to visit his mother in Japan, and we haven't seen any sign of him since he left. Hear he's started up a business over there. What do you reckon of that for a cheat? I wouldn't go even if I did have relatives overseas, but I don't. Don't even have any relations outside Beijing; we've always lived here. Don't take any notice of the way I'm going on. I really love my country and that's straight from the heart.

I can't really think of any good examples. But it's obvious. Just look at our mill. They haven't got a clue about making proper use of the foreign machinery they've bought. They finally got this technical expert from Hongkong in who was supposed to be the representative of some company or other. Couldn't see the admin people for all the arse-licking that was going on. The man could do no wrong. If the truth be told none of them have the fain st about technical things. They spend all their time drinking tea in their offices. People go on about China going to the dogs if we had a say in the running of things; but we're all in big trouble if they take over, believe you me. They buy their technical expertise with our money. They're the pits, who needs them? It'd be quite a different matter if they could learn something new. Bugger it. The section head — a heavy in the mill — pointed at a crane one day and asked what the '10T' painted on the side of it meant. Bloody embarrassing if you ask me. A few months back they gave that lot the boot and put in a bunch of intellectuals. But they're all bureaucrats like the rest, except they're into organizing gardening brigades, canteen committees and that factory beautification office. Let them do what they want. They're all supposed to be downwardly as well as upwardly mobile — either officials or normal workers —

none of the people I've seen can manage it.

My biggest worry is finding a wife. Even with bonuses and extras the best money I can make of a month is a little over 70 yuan. Yeah, sure, but I don't look any good. My family's no help, and the girls I go for wouldn't give me a second look. Plus the fact that my job's not the best. Come off it, I'd never go to a marriage agency. All they care about is getting all your particulars down and then matching you off with someone. I don't have anything going for me; it'd be a lost cause. If I had 3,000 yuan I'd be sitting pretty — colour TV, new lounge settee and a fridge would all be in the bag. "Fragrant flowers are never in want of bees," — if I had money the girls would be all over me like a rash. But what am I supposed to do, steal the money?

If you ask me that's a load of bull. Love my foot: it's a material world, believe me. Hasn't my boss married another worker? Let's face it, workers look down on peasants and cadres feel superior to workers. And I'm just the same — there's no way I'd ever marry a hayseed. I don't care what they say about the villages being rich nowadays, it doesn't make any difference to me. Marry a peasant and you end up a 50-50, half in the city, half out. Then if you have a son his residency permit stays with his mother in the country; he'd still be a peasant. I don't want a "half-caste" for a son.

Leisure time activities? Playing cards. I go skating in the winter and swim in the summer. Never read, but I do like the movies. I get sleepy when I read; it's the same when I watch the box. That's how things are when you're a worker. I'm doing my bit for society so I reckon I haven't wasted my life. I've put my lot in with socialism.

As I said I just go along with the mob, so I guess I feel the same as everyone else: the country has a future. We're all in it together, and my future depends on that of the rest of the country. I'm not giving you any "Party line", it's really what I think. Give me credit for that much political awareness. You shouldn't take all that slinging off I do too seriously, deep down I know what's what. Apart from the Communist Party I don't think any one could keep this place — a thousand million people — going. I really love the Communist Party.

I can't make any comparisons. There's tons of other workers about apart from me. Some are more politically progressive than me, others aren't so positive. I'm just an average fellow. I've never seen people like me being written up in the papers.

Don't take my picture, no, don't. I said don't and I mean it; you shouldn't waste the film.

Translated by Geremie Barmé

The Song-girl

*There was something about the atmosphere in the coffee
lounge when she sang the song that was positively electric.
A lot of people in the audience applauded when her act
was announced. She was in a silver lamé evening dress,
Hongkong style, the hotel had specially bought for her
with foreign exchange. She was a little restrained but
obviously irrepressibly happy. She kept saying "Thank you,
thank you all...." while clasping the microphone in both
hands.*

I didn't sing it well at all. You really think so?

... I hate speaking to reporters. To be quite honest I don't
trust them. Once these reporters came along to listen. They
applauded along with everyone else, but when they wrote
about us they said the floorshow was indecent and frivolous.
I was told that the assistant manager had brought two
reporters in while I was still making up and I was nervous as
anything. But I forgot all about it after my first song.

I don't express myself very well. Why don't you speak to
the hotel manager or the head of the band? We're a group.
You've seen all of us: there's five in the band, only four
today as one singer didn't turn up tonight. If I say anything
wrong it'll affect all the others. The manager is very
supportive. In the day this is a restaurant that serves
Chinese food, but from 9:30 on it's a cabaret. No, please, I

don't know anything about politics and the management will be upset if I say something wrong. It could make things difficult for me here, and I don't want to get the sack.

If you honestly like our music then please write nice things about us. It's not easy for us; in fact, things are very hard. No, I'm not speaking Guangdong dialect; I said it's hard, you know, to be allowed to work here.

We're very strict as a group because we want to keep working as long as possible. Anyone who turns up late has to pay a fine, and if you don't show at all, like that singer tonight, you're fined a few days' pay. We make about ten yuan a night, so she'll be losing quite a lot of money.

We're very professional about our singing, 'cause if you're slack the audience will hiss you. A lot of them really know their music and they're out there listening to see if you sing the song right or not. If you're only out one note or get something wrong, the band can tell immediately and they tick you off at the end of the performance. Then you go home and put on your earphones and listen to how the song's done by the original artiste. I don't think it's fair to say that we're pandering to the audience; we're very serious about our art. There was a while there before the law campaign when Guangzhou was in a real bad way. Someone from the band had to see us home after the performance every night. And if anyone sleeps around then they're criticized by the others. We had one singer — she was very good, could sing just like that Hongkong singer Bi Ji — but she was caught sleeping with a foreigner so we had to give her the boot. But we know that wasn't really like her and we're sure she'll change. We had to make her go for the sake of the band, so we'd be allowed to keep performing.

You're right, we don't perform in the usual stuffy way. But that's because we're singing popular songs. You have to

sing and move on the stage in a different way; the whole
style is more relaxed. The aim is to have some sort of
communication with the audience. The cabarets they have
in Shekou and Shenzhen are much freer, just like Hongkong. Their singers are allowed to speak to the audience and
people can even choose songs, though you have to be able to
sing what they've chosen. There's some things that aren't
allowed to be sung, so the singer makes her apologies and
that's the end of it. Deng Lijun is okay, though there's a few
exceptions like "Plum Blossoms" or "When Will You
Return", and there's a few others you're not allowed to sing
like "I'm Chinese". But you can sing anything apart from
the few songs on the banned list. If it wasn't for my job here
I'd go and sing there too; it'd be great. Why should I quit?
— what'd happen if they decided not to let us sing
anymore?

We don't dare look at the audience too much — people
say we're trying to manipulate them if we do. Then we'd get
into trouble. You can't let yourself dance around the stage
too much either as you'd be accused of being lewd and
they'd make things hard for us. We get it in the neck every
time something goes wrong. When they were criticizing
spiritual pollution back in the spring, they went around
busting people for the possession of porn videos and all
that; and they closed down all the coffee lounges. And that
wasn't the first time. Later on the municipal cultural bureau
made us all register and take a test to make sure we were all
up to a certain standard. Because we're more popular than
the professionals and we perform in the hotels — that
makes it pretty heavy — we've only been working together
again for the last few months.

They've fixed a ratio for the number of foreign songs you
can sing: it's one foreign song for every four Chinese.

Luckily Taiwan and Hongkong are counted as part of
China! Anything's okay as long as it isn't reactionary or
pornographic, don't you reckon? Anyway, the people in the
audience only come here because they like the songs we do
and our style of performance. Basically all the hotel guests
are from Hongkong or Macao; but the people we get here
are all local youths. Lots of them own small businesses or
run street-side stalls. Small fry. They make a little money
and are prepared to pay five yuan for a ticket. For that they
get a glass of coke and can sit and listen to the music for a
couple of hours. It's a pretty good deal, don't you reckon?

When I'm not singing I like to sit at this table and watch
the audience. No, really, look at their expressions, their
eyes....I don't look directly at the audience when I'm on
stage, and so I can't take in everything. But I'm really
moved the way they get so involved and sit there all silent.
Music's an amazingly powerful thing. I sit here looking at
them all the time and never cease to be amazed.

I'm alright? You really mean it? But you're sure I haven't
said anything that'll get us into trouble? I've been singing
with them for three years now. We're an established group.
I'm at the point where I know singing isn't all that easy.

How did I get started? You'll never believe me but I
never sang as a kid, not a bit. Nobody in our family is
musical. The guitar? No one I knew played one. We don't
even have one now. No, I can't play an instrument. Both my
mum and dad work in a laundry. None of our neighbours
are involved with music either. So there was no music
anywhere around me when I was a kid. No, not even
Guangdong music. You can work it out for yourselves: I'm
twenty-one now, so that means I was three when the
"cultural revolution" began. That's right, the Red Guards
all sang "Sailing on the Seas Depends on the Helmsman"

and "I See the Pole Star When I Look Up". I seem to remember that those songs sounded good, but I can't really tell; I was too young.

The most vivid memory I have is of the three minority songs they played over the radio after National Day the year Lin Biao died in that plane crash. There was a Tibetan folksong, "The Brilliance of Chairman Mao", a Korean one called "The Yanbian People Love Chairman Mao", and another one. I was in my first year of primary school and they played the songs over the loud-speakers between classes. I remember just standing there listening. Every day I'd go back home and sit by the radio and listen to those same songs, first on the provincial radio station and then again on Central Radio. I couldn't get enough of them — what wonderful songs!

My brother started me off singing. What, him? Can't sing a note. No, he sells cassettes and records. Naturally, at first he had to do it on the sly. Now he's got a permit, but it's not quite the same thing. In 1977 he was selling tracks of Deng Lijun. There were a few others, but mainly it was her stuff. Sometimes he got stuck with dud material: one song at the start and the rest an empty tape or really badly recorded. We call tapes like that "write offs". It meant you had to listen to them right through. People who wanted to buy tapes also wanted a demo, so I heard the songs a lot of times. That was when I was in early high school. All the girls got together to write down Deng Lijun's songs. That's because everyone had only heard bits and pieces and there were mistakes or foul-ups. I sang along with the others and they all reckoned I had a good voice. Then there was a craze for Xu Xiaofeng for a while and everyone said I sounded just like her; then Xi Xiulan, and people said I sounded just like the people I imitated.

My brother took me along to a friend's place for a test.
That was Teacher Lin's place — he's the one who plays the
trumpet in our group now. Everyone calls him Teacher Lin
'cause he's a high school P.E. teacher. He's not at all like
me. Before the "cultural revolution" he was a bugler in the
Young Pioneers, and in the "cultural revolution" he joined
a Guangdong opera troupe for a while. That's when they
were modernizing Guangdong music, so they added the
trumpet.

He got out his guitar and asked me for a note so we could
harmonize. I said there was no need and started singing
straight out. I did a couple of different singers with nothing
but a guitar as accompaniment. Altogether I went through
five people. Teacher Lin said I had a natural feel for music,
then he asked me which style of singing I felt most at home
in. I had no idea what he was talking about. I told him I
could learn anything I had to.

Teacher Lin was in the first group involved with cabarets
in Guangzhou. He's been in the business for four years now;
he's a veteran. One night he took me to a cabaret and asked
the band to give me a trial run. He asked if I was scared. I
said I didn't know what he meant. I was wearing clothes my
brother had borrowed for me. I got up on the stage and sang
when they started playing. Everyone applauded when I'd
finished; it was the first time I experienced the thrill of
singing for people. When we got back home my brother
asked me why I'd been singing up at the ceiling? I said I
hadn't realized; I just sang. All I was thinking of was the
song. No wonder Teacher Lin had asked me whether I was
scared, but I didn't have a clue what he was talking about.

That's how I got started. Later Teacher Lin gave me a
musical score when we were rehearsing some new songs. He
told me to try it. I said I couldn't sing something I'd never

heard. He told me to sing straight from the score and I said I didn't know what he meant. Everyone in the group was amazed that I couldn't read music at all. It was the first time I'd ever heard of sight-reading music. There's lots of singers who can't read music. I'd simply never learnt — none of the schools I'd been to taught it. But I've got an ear for music, according to Teacher Lin and the others in their 30s, anyway. They're very surprised. Of course, I can read music now—the guys in the band taught me. I listen to them; they know about such things and they said I'd sing even better if I learnt.

Some cabaret singers are unemployed youth. People like us have normal eight-hour jobs, we get off work and come here and go on till midnight. It's pretty exhausting, but great fun. If they didn't let us sing or there were no more audiences, life would be really boring.

After work each night we all go and have a snack at a street stall. We talk about singing and lots of stuff. I can never get to sleep when I go back home because the songs are still going through my head. So I lie there thinking of how I can improve on each song. We're as serious about our singing as any professionals. They reckon we're too casual, but we think they're just too old-fashioned. Anyway we get happy and enthusiastic audiences every night. Let them see how they'd go on our stage. They're so straight-laced nobody'd come to listen.

Our band's always improvising with the music, so it's different every night. Professional singers would never be able to cope with our style. We use electronic effects; all pop songs do. A lot of songs have to be sung in Guangdong dialect to sound right too.

"Papa Can You Hear Me Singing" doesn't seem to be Guangdong dialect. It's Fujian dialect. I don't understand all of it. Something like what the man who collects empty wine bottles sings. My version's a copy of Zhen Ying. Zheng Xulan's? I haven't heard it. Sure, it's a song about love. I've never really had a steady boyfriend; no, really. I just get the feeling that this is a very sad, also powerful, song. So that's the way I sing it.

Love? I don't believe there's as much of it as they make out in songs.

At the moment I sing in the style of Zhen Ni. My voice is suited to imitating her. Sing in my own style? The audience would never accept it. They judge you by whether you sound like some singer or not. Our male singer — he's very popular — models himself on Raymond Tam. Haven't you noticed? He even looks a little like him. When they closed the cabarets down we hired a truck and went around the villages singing. Of course they wanted to hear us! We got much bigger audiences than in the city. Peasants have more money than city people, so we made much more than we do here. The only problem with it was that it was far too tiring — a trip of 100 kilometres every night. On the return trips the only one who would be awake in the truck was the driver; everyone else was out cold. And the following morning it would be work as usual. Since everyone at work knows you make far more than they do every month — about 300 yuan — you have to work especially hard so no one's got any reason to complain about you.

My full-time job? I sell shoes.

Translated by Geremie Barmé

Compatriots

The coast is plagued by violent tropical typhoons through-
out the month of August. The typhoons are enough to scare
most people off, but we worked the fishing villages on the
coast of the South and East China Seas at the height of the
season.

We spent four days at the well-appointed Zhoushan
Taiwan Fisherman Reception Centre of Zhejiang Prov-
ince. It plays host to over one thousand Taiwanese fisher-
men a year. Acting on the latest but tardy news we retraced
our steps to Shipu Harbour in Xiangshan. But we were too
late; then we met a Taiwanese fisherman by chance at....

SURE, that's right, we're fraternal compatriots. Back on
Taiwan we call you "mainland compatriots"; over here you
call us "Taiwanese compatriots". Anyway, we're all compatriots no matter how you put it. The authorities on both
sides agree that there's only one China and we have to be
reunited.

So you thought Taiwanese only spoke Fujian dialect?
You're wrong there. They were already busy popularizing
mandarin when my father was at school. My Mandarin's
okay, isn't it? Oh, thanks very much. Now you've made me
feel embarrassed.

My home port is Chilung, but we anchor at Shimen.
That's the northernmost harbour in Taiwan. It's about ten

nautical miles from Chilung. That's right, lots of names are the same. We have a Chinshan Harbour nearby, just like Jinshan in Shanghai. And there's lots of others like Xingang, Chaozhou and Hukou. In our history class in high school the teacher told us about the Hukou rebellion and how the Father of the Nation, Sun Yat-sen, led the "Second Revolution". Someone in the class asked if it was the Hukou in Xinzhu. "No," the teacher replied. "It's over in bandit-held territory." Oh, that's right, I shouldn't call this side "bandit-held territory"; it's the mainland of the motherland, isn't it? What do you call Shanghai then? Uh-huh, a city under direct jurisdiction. In our text books it's called the Special Municipality of Shanghai. But everyone knows Peiping is now called Beijing.

That's a real tough question. I don't have a clue about politics so I really can't say. Reckon I'll just wait and see what happens. Sure, it'd be better if we were reunited: at least it'd be easier on fishermen. We wouldn't have to worry about mooring here or taking things we'd bought back home with us. If it was like Hongkong or Macao where fishermen are registered with the authorities on both sides and are given permits then we'd be much freer. There they can live with the two "isms": capitalism and socialism; but they all have the same aim, everyone wants to make money by catching fish. They're free. Even as things are now our people know where we have been, but no one tries to stop us. They can't expect us to float around waiting to capsize if a typhoon comes along or the boat breaks down, or if we have an accident. After all, one of the Three Principles of the People talks about democracy. But there would definitely be some bother if you took too much mainland merchandise back with you. There's no worries if they are only small things, but I wouldn't try my luck on buying anything big. Sometimes we might miss the tide and we only take on a small catch, so we have to do a little business on the side to make up the difference. Maybe buy fish in bulk and resell it in Hongkong, that type of thing. They accept US dollars here; sometimes they even take Taiwanese money. We're in the same position as mainland fishermen — we've got lots of our own money but not much foreign currency. Sure I know things like that. We talk to the local fishermen; we know.

We've taken shelter from the wind lots of times. Though we've got a pretty up-to-date boat that's got lots of horsepower and we can follow the shoals of fish from the northern bays right over to the Japan Sea, if we strike a typhoon and can't outrace it we have to take cover wherever we can. The Vietnamese are lousy, they never let us take cover in their harbours or even let us anchor. They really are crazy. the South Koreans are friendly to us, you know, "the Republic of Korea". You're in thick with the Communists in the north, aren't you? I know. The Koreans are quite happy to have us go there, but they make us pay through the nose: charges for fresh water, repairs, then there's mooring fees and lots of other odds and ends. But here we're all Chinese and they don't charge us anything. We're even welcome to go ashore and take a look around.

There are lots of places you can go: Shipu, Shenjiamen, Dongshan, Chongwu. Usually, if we've been fishing in the waters off south or east Fujian we go to Dongshan; if we've been in the East China Sea, though, we take cover in Shenjiamen on Zhoushan Island, off the coast of Zhejiang. The authorities on Taiwan know all about it. They see these harbours as bases the Communists use for doing "united front" work. They've got the same type of set-up, reception centres for mainland fishermen in distress. It's the same idea, a form of psychological warfare; each trying to show its best face to the other side. The bureaucrats here tell us that you're still poor and working to catch up, but that's not what they say on our side. All they ever talk about there is our good points, that we're rich and we have built up a base for the recapturing of the mainland. You know, there are poor people there too, and very few people spend their time thinking about retaking the mainland. They don't give a damn about politics.

I was really scared the first time. We'd heard the place was crawling with militiamen who were just waiting to have a go at us. But other people who'd been here said it was alright and everything went smoothly. Typhoon warnings aren't to be taken lightly, especially in the case of a boat like ours. We don't have the horses to make it back home fast enough, and we'd never survive in the open sea. We had no choice, so we followed some other boats into Communist waters and lay anchor in Shenjiamen. I'd forgotten all about being scared even before we dropped anchor. You see, there were all these other Taiwanese boats already in the harbour. I knew there wasn't anything to worry about.

We work in pairs—two boats trawling a large net. One boss. Didn't go ashore that time. There were too many boats seeking shelter and the commies, no, sorry, the mainland authorities, couldn't cope. Even so, the local leadership sent people out to see us and they supplied us with vegetables and fresh water as well as with some pictorials and propaganda material. They asked whether we needed any help. We don't need a thing, I was thinking to myself; it's when the wind dies down and we leave for home that we'll be needing help. I was worried that our people would persecute us. But it was all okay: we all agreed not to say a word when we got back, and if anyone asked we'd just say that we took cover on an uninhabited island in the Zhoushan Islands. Actually, if anyone checked they could have told we were lying. Our boat's good alright, but it's not that good. It has one major fault: she doesn't sit steady in the water when she's empty. If there's an eight point wind blowing you'll get tossed from port to starboard, she rocks that badly. No one would believe we'd survived a typhoon without taking shelter in a harbour. It was a pretty flimsy story to say that we'd been on a nameless and uninhabited island in the Zhongjieshan Islands. You could have seen we were lying by just taking a look at the course we'd plotted and our charts. But when we got back nobody said a thing, though they sure as anything knew.

I told the wife when I got home but it didn't phase her at all. "Don't tell anyone else," was all she said. But she told me to get her some powdered pearl cream the next time I came. It's far more reasonable here on the mainland. They sell it on the sly back home but it's ten times cheaper here. That's a big saving.

No way. We threw all the propaganda stuff they gave us into the sea. That really would have got us in trouble. The Communists told us, "Have a look at it and throw away what you can't take back." They understand our position.

The second time around we headed straight for the mainland buoys without even waiting for the navy to warn us we were entering your waters. We followed mainland boats into Shenjiamen. You're not allowed to force your way into a harbour or grab an anchorage either, so we dropped anchor outside the harbour and requested permission to enter. The man at the reception centre said, "But you've already got yourselves an anchorage." We had to laugh. That time they asked us ashore to live and they took us on a tour of the sites at Putuo. It really is beautiful.

About the same, you know, the standard of living and that. I don't know anything about politics. Our authorities are always going on about the high standard of living on home base, and how it proves that we're politically enlightened and that the government's policies are right. You people on the mainland are supposed to be living in extreme despair and suffering; you have to have ration cards to buy anything; and the army has limitless power. All this proves that the system is rotten. But I've seen things for myself and both sides are about the same. It says a lot about the situation. The people on the streets here seem to be happy, and there's enough things in the shops. I haven't seen any proof that the political system over here is no good. So you can't trust what our authorities say. The things they base their claims on don't even exist. As for the rest of it, it's all too complicated and I just don't know.

After those first two times? Well, I've anchored at the harbours of Hui'an and Shipu, sometimes because of a typhoon, or just for repairs. Some people say what I've seen in the Communist zone is an elaborate fake, psychological warfare. But I've seen badly dressed people here, and even some beggars, or what looked like beggars, I'm not too sure—so I don't accept that. You're not offended? You sure? Thanks. It can't all be make-believe, otherwise they'd have got rid of the beggars too, don't you think? I wouldn't say this to anybody when I go back though. People would get the wrong idea and say I'm politically unreliable and that I've been brainwashed.

No, we're a private company, nothing to do with the government. We're all mates on the boat, we stick together. No one would turn his mates in. Anyway, we've been working together for so long that you'd know if anyone was on the payroll. The authorities have approved the radio operator and he was appointed by the fishermen's committee. But he's all right, he wouldn't tell them what we've been doing on the mainland. He's just the same as us — talks with the Communist authorities and goes out shopping, just like us.

We buy medicines mostly. Yunnan *baiyao*, Tiger Bone Wine, tonics as well as famous mainland wines. But good wines aren't all that easy to come by. You can get them in Hongkong, but they're more expensive. I've bought a few other things too, like the fruit and vegetables we have on board. But we eat all of it before we get home. No, none of us buy handicrafts or jewellery; you have to have money to buy things like that. We do buy things to give as presents, but you have to do it on the sly.

Things are improving here, I've seen it for myself. Now you can start your own shop and peasants and fishermen aren't all "collectivized" as they were before. It's good. I'm sure you'll catch up with our standard of living soon. No, we're still better off than fishermen on the mainland. Really, I've got my own phone and motorbike. In Chilung and Taipei there are lots of tall buildings; they're very modern. We've got our own "Ten Major Construction Projects" too. You sure you don't mind me going on like this? Yeah, I've spoken to lots of people here. But then there are many ways in which you are better off than we are in Taiwan. Though you shouldn't forget that since our economy really took off we've achieved a lot. Take free medical care, for example, you've got that here, well, so do we; unless you want to go to a private doctor. There you're right. Internationally Taiwan is worse off all the time. Lots of countries, particularly America have betrayed us. That's just the way things have gone. China's a huge place and powerful, so the sooner we're united the better for us internationally. Isn't that so?

Mainland compatriots are very friendly to us and treat us specially. Though sometimes we do have disagreements: fights over fishing zones. Your authorities have regulations about fishing zones that can't be trawled for certain periods. Our boss always tells us to go ahead because the Communist laws don't apply to us. So we go charging in and we end up in arguments. Then sometimes they say the mesh of our nets is too fine and the mainlanders haul them up and we get into a fight. If the mesh is too fine the fish you take in are small and that's bad for the fish replenishing their shoals. But we're not the ones who decide on the size of the nets. Okay, so we fight and if someone gets killed it's no matter for international law, is it? We're all Chinese. Exactly, problems arise on both sides, but there's times your mainland fishermen are in the wrong; they're a minority. The locals on Liuheng Island sold us a cargo of frozen fish that they told us were fresh. We didn't find out until we tried to sell them in Hongkong. We lost a lot on that deal. But everyone on board said it was the fishermen, not the fault of the Communists. We understand that, in the same way that what we do doesn't represent our people. Anyway, that kind of thing is really common in Taiwan.

I was born in 1959. Our family's from Chilung. My father took up fishing during the Japanese occupation. I went to the Sea Produce College after finishing high school in 1967, and I've been on the sea since that.

I'm in a small company and have a share in this boat. No, that's not quite right. The education level is very high, and there's not enough "white collar" jobs for people with my education. It's not that easy to find work. You even find university graduates climbing around construction sites. I don't think I should talk about my private life. Remember,

I've still got to go back to Taiwan. Sorry.

Thanks. Just let me say I hope we meet again after the country's reunited. I guess it'd be best if you didn't repeat anything I've said tonight to the captain or the radio operator if you happen to bump into them ... alright. Thanks for everything.

Translated by Geremie Barmé

Ready, Set, Go

He has contracted to run a large-format literary magazine.

IT isn't a decision I made on the spur of the moment; though it all came about rather suddenly. I was the editorial department director of the magazine and after returning from a business trip I was told that our editorial department had been disbanded. This had come about because although there's an ever increasing number of literary publications, including major literary journals, those that specialize in printing serious literature have gone into a decline. Despite strenuous efforts to compete by making our layout more attractive and adding new features, as well as putting out special issues of novels and biographies, we just couldn't improve our sales. Naturally, that meant we were losing money. We're under the control of a publishing house, and it was their decision to cease publication.

We're still all working in the publishing house in the usual jobs, publishing books. We are editors, after all.

I thought about it for a month.

No, I didn't hand a request in to the leadership just like that. Nor did I go to one of the bosses to get his support. I've been in this game too long to think I could get things done that way. If I was only able to convince one of them the whole project might be rejected out of hand, or it might be put on a back burner if any one of the executives said they had their doubts about the whole business. All it'd take was one word, a hint of doubt, and things would be very tricky in the future. At present we've got a collective leadership. I've been working with these people for years now, so I went around to see them all at home individually and told them what I was planning. I asked for their understanding and support. They ended up by passing my proposal straight out.

I'm keeping my old position but I've stopped drawing a salary. The new journal officially starts publication on January 1, 1985. The publishing house has elected this project as an experiment in the remodelling of the organization and revitalizing our work, so they're given me a loan to work with. The editors I've hired on contract have to pay the publishing house 10,000 yuan annually. I pay their wages and so on.

No, there's nothing to feel nervous about. Yes, I'm fifty-three this year, a state cadre and Party member. I joined the revolution in 1947 and took part in the Tashan blocking action in the Northeast. I've been working as an editor for many years. I've never suffered politically, though I led attacks on other people before the "cultural revolution". That happened when I was working in the provincial arts office.... I'm an editor of the 7th grade now and I make over 100 yuan a month. I've got two children, one's out at work and the other is at university. Basically, I've got no interest in being a bureaucrat; anyway, I'm too old now to get very far. Nor am I interested in a high position, fame or money. There's only one thing I really want, and that's to make a go of the magazine that I've spent the last few years of my life working on.

Of course you can't expect a literary journal to pay for itself. It's impossible to say whether we'll lose money, especially the way things are these days.

So I've started things off with a magazine correspondence course. I wanted to target in on young people who are interested in getting a higher degree by doing a correspondence course, so we've been using the magazine. I didn't have any authority to issue diplomas myself, so I got in touch with the people in charge of tertiary education in the provincial government as well as the universities that give degrees. They're supporting me, and now we're printing all the teaching materials for private students in the province. By doing it this way I can get university professors to give lectures to our students, eight hours a week. Although it's a correspondence course, the teacher still has to put in a certain amount of time in a contact teaching situation. One of the problems they've found with the television university programme is that the only contact teachers and students have is through the TV set. There's no direct stimulus for the students. They sit there glued to the set and invariably get bored. On this level our course can compete effectively with the TV universities.

My magazine also provides its readers with information on how to pass exams as well as publishing self-improvement teaching materials. There's a knack to passing exams, especially the way the examination system is set up today.

The students pay us nine yuan a year; that includes the fee for contact hours. We don't make much on the magazine, hardly anything. After all, there's no way of telling just how many students will end up with a degree at the end of three years. Plus the fact that the more studious young people are always poor. So we can't expect to make very much. Yet as there's such huge numbers of young people wanting to qualify for degrees at present we do have a sizeable circulation. Even though we don't make much on each magazine sold, we do manage to make a small profit.

I got the idea from a few editor friends of mine who are working down in Shenzhen. They're all experts at business. They told me that if I wanted to publish serious literature I'd need a solid commercial back-up. A correspondence magazine is just the thing. I'm only the manager, and I've got seven young people working for me. Previously they were all school-leavers. All top quality people — if they weren't they couldn't handle the job. We had an accountant who couldn't stand the pace and he quit after a few days. We're serious about the work we're doing. In our office you don't find people sitting around all day drinking tea and reading the paper. I'm choosy about who I want working for me, but once I've hired someone I leave them in complete charge of their side of the business.

The teaching programme is only one aspect of our operation. There are a number of other things, some that are already underway, others that I'm still working on, honing the finer points. Once I've got things sorted out for a new project I start it right up.

I'm not using the usual postal system for the distribution of my literature journal. The good thing about the postal network is that you can get your publication into the villages — they have post offices everywhere. The problem with that is that they won't let you commission school-leavers to do your distributing, let alone allow you to distribute a magazine yourself. They make you use their systems, and they take a 20-30% cut per copy for their trouble. If you distribute yourself you don't end up paying more than 10 *fen* a copy for the service; you save your money.

No, there haven't been any businessmen in my family.

My father was a country vet. Generally speaking I'm not just in it for the money. I'll have to rely on other economically viable projects for the foreseeable future to keep the literature journal going. But my abiding interest is in the journal.

Understandably I keep an eye on the latest publishing trends. At the moment we're seeing a falling off in the popularity of journals that specialize in serious literature, while there's been a dramatic increase in the sales of political and current affairs magazines like *Red Flag* and *Outlook*. Presumably this reflects the needs of people involved in the Party rectification for relevant study material; though there is a greater likelihood that with the economic reform programme taking hold in the countryside and the cities, people in all professions are becoming vitally interested in the stability and relevance of Party policies. This is for the simple reason that these policies have a direct influence on their own financial well-being and provide a standard by which they can gauge their own activities. Everyone is doing deals, but people want to know whether the things they are doing are legal, how far you can go and for how long. And, most importantly, if you can be assured of legal protection. And so on. Nowadays every article and line of Party policy is of vital importance to people.

I've been witness to the massive increase in the popularity of "popular literature" myself. For example, magazines specializing in crime and suspense like *The Woodpecker* have huge sales. They calculate their distribution in terms of millions of copies sold, and there's others like *Tales From Central China,* or *Forest of Martial Arts* that sell over 900,000 copies a month. Journals that concentrate on serious literature like mine can only sell about 60,000 copies. Some magazines that were selling a hundred thousand or a few hundred thousand a month have fallen off to 30,000. Of course they're losing money. Relatively speaking we're not doing too badly. That's why we're confident about being able to keep our heads above water. Another thing is that publications like *Popular Cinema*, *Reader's Digest*, *After Eight Hours* and *Four Corners* — magazines that specialize in the entertainment field and information — are seeing a steady increase in sales.

What's my editorial policy going to be?

In our view serious literature is the only legitimate form of literature. Though it's something that might not sell well, these are the works that are going to find a place in literary history. The view they present of life is more earnest, and it's for this reason that anyone involved in the publication of a journal of serious literature feels a sense of duty in the work they do. There are the "Big Four" in the field already, I know: *Harvest, October, Dangdai,* and some say the journal in fourth place, *Flower City*, has been replaced by *World of Novels*, or, according to some, *Zhongshan*. Anyway, there's been a change there. They're all very big and sell a few hundred thousand copies each issue. There's no way we could ever compete.

The tenor of critical opinion over the last few decades has been to condemn adventure stories, martial arts and supernatural fiction as being unworthy of publication, but the fact remains: this type of writing has massive popular appeal. It's the same overseas: serious literature has a small readership while popular romance and such has a huge audience. It's a normal state of affairs. The problem for us is; how should we view it in critical terms and what should our reaction to it be? If I decided to take on *The Woodpecker* on its own terms I think we'd have a good chance of competing. Readers can never get enough of the stuff. The fact that we spend all of our time editing new books and our own bookcases at home are full doesn't mean that much. There's hardly any books in the countryside. The 800 million people who are on the land are increasingly better off, but a lot remains to be done, and there's a complete vacuum when it comes to cultural life and entertainment in the countryside.

Somebody wrote a book about the legendary Yang Family Generals called *Twelve Widows March on the West*. One publisher was hesitant about taking it on. He thought it lacked literary merit. But another publisher took it, and it ended up selling over one million copies! Neither of you has ever heard of it, have you? There's lots of books like that around. In America anything that sells 500,000 copies is regarded as a best-seller. If it goes through ten reprints and sells over 500,000 copies it is a run-away best-seller. But here in China we have a population with a massive appetite for literature. And it's an appetite that is all the more voracious because of the way in which we've approached popular literature in the last decade or so. The average reader is interested in a good story; that's the tradition of popular literature in China. Maybe our problem is that we're still struggling to justify popular literature in theoretical terms, while at the same time trying to improve the readability and literary value of the material that is published. Then there's the thorny matter of taste. I'm definitely not defending the view that a work that isn't elevating is automatically trash.

I'm not going to be too adventurous with my magazine. I want to produce something that appeals to all types of reading tastes. We plan to print serious literature including translations of the better foreign works of the '70s and '80s, and there'll be sections of popular literature as well, and it's our hope that we'll be able to do something about improving the quality of this type of literature.

It's hard to say for sure just what the future holds. There are lots of capable people with ideas around at the moment. Not long after the author of *A Biography of Chiang Ching-kuo*, Liu Yiliang, was murdered, many publishers and magazines were looking for copies of the book so they could publish it. But the first issue of *March Wind*, the journal of the Chinese Handicapped Association that's coming out in January, stole a march on them by announcing that they were going to serialize the whole book.

Then you have the literary journals run by the various provincial writers' associations. The associations will keep them afloat no matter how badly distribution slumps. In the end they'll be forced to make internal administrative reforms and introduce a contract system like ours. As the economy opens up even further and the flow of information becomes increasingly liberalized and faster, the needs of the population will inevitably become fragmented. This will probably mean increasingly heated competition between journals for readers.

I'm very confident about my new journal. As I've said, I've got a solid financial basis from which to work and I'm not worried about losing money by publishing serious literature.

Translated by Geremie Barmé

The Builder

December 1984.
   Fang Yichun, 34, manager of the Harbin Xinyang Construction Company. In four years he turned a street-committee-run repair and building team into a big construction company with fixed assets of three million yuan, liquid assets of seven million yuan, and a work force of two thousand.

I came back to the city from Heihe State Farm in 1971, and stayed at home waiting for a job like a lot of other educated youngsters who'd come back to town.* We were waiting for the authorities to allocate us in batches to state-owned factories and mines, or to large collective service enterprises. It depended on what you happened to get into.

As I thought about it, the best possibility would be to get into a state-run factory as an apprentice. But after going round in circles and having to start from scratch as an apprentice again I was pretty fed up. What I'd learnt was carpentry, and after over a year of waiting for a job I joined a maintenance and building team run by the Xinyang Street Committee office. There were twenty or so unemployed youngsters and six women in the team. We mended centrally heated walls, built little chimneys, and went from house to house asking, "New Year's coming: do you want

---
* After years spent in the countryside.

your walls painted?" When we hadn't got enough work it was a chance for the "social monkeys" — the ones who hung around the streets all day — to make a pile. Whoever got us a job was in charge. They padded the worksheets for the job, took the extra wages, and kept everything that was left after paying off the actual workers. They didn't give a damn about building up our capital. After a few years I became the head of the team because I could get jobs too. Nearly all my lads were youngsters who'd come back to the city. We used our spare cash to buy some fixed assets because we really wanted to make a go of it in the building industry. During that time I had several chances of being assigned to a regular job, but I didn't take any of them up. Although working for a street committee doesn't sound anywhere near as good as working for a big collective or a state enterprise, in those outfits you're stuck in whatever job you've been assigned to as if you'd been screwed to it. You can't do the jobs you'd like to do. In 1976 the street committee asked me to give them a written undertaking that I wouldn't complain if they stopped trying to find me a regular job. I gave it them. For one thing, I was interested in the building industry, and glad to be making run-down places into something presentable. And for another, you got a lot more money being paid by the job than workers in state factories did. When my father and mother retired after that I didn't take either of the vacancies that came up.* By 1979 there were over two hundred people in the maintenance and building team, and I was in charge of half of them. A building team is labour-intensive: you don't need too much capital or technology. At that time a lot of units were setting up their own building teams, so there was less

---

* It is customary in China for retiring employees to be able to pass on jobs to family members in their place.

and less work for us to do. The "social monkeys" had all made their pile and cleared off. The street committee office was hopping mad, and we were on the point of going under.

Everyone put me forward to take over. When they were starting to contract the land out in the countryside in 1979, I suggested that we should contract for the maintenance and building team. There wouldn't have been the slightest chance of making a go of it in the old way. I wanted to run it as an enterprise. I had to have control over finance and personnel. Practically nowhere would give you the right to hire and fire then, and not enough places do now, but the street Party committee agreed. Their only condition was that I had to turn the losses into a surplus within a couple of years. In the previous seven years we'd lost nearly 60,000 yuan. If I made a go of it they'd give me a black-and-white television worth 520 yuan, and if I failed they were going to fine me 360 yuan. I told them they'd better dock my pay by thirty yuan a month in advance as we went along as they'd never be able to get all that off me at the end. Well, after I'd been running the show for a year we'd made 56,000 yuan profit, just a few thousand short of what we needed to clear off the deficits that had built up for years on end. I got my television. Of course, I've replaced it with a colour set. Ages ago. The team leader under me's got one too: he's on a contract with me.

We've only got four iron rules. One, each level of the company works on a contract basis. Two, payment is for work done, calculated by the job. Three, cadres get paid according to their responsibilities. Four, managers and technicians get paid as much as or more than workers.

Flexible methods? In the old days the maintenance and building team was scared of building anything big, and the city's construction committee wouldn't let us either. Our technique and equipment weren't up to it. But if we were going to hold our own we had to find a way to put up big buildings.

We heard of a unit that wanted an apartment block of 2,400 square metres put up. They'd given the job to the city's Third Construction Company. The company wasn't at all helpful, and it made all sorts of demands: The customer had to provide the transport to take the builders to and from work, pay cash on the nail for overtime, and let the builders eat in their canteen. We got in there fast. We made no conditions at all, we guaranteed we'd use good quality materials, and our price was lower. If they wanted to see what we could do we told them to look at the building we'd put up for the street committee office a couple of years earlier. They agreed, but the city's construction committee blocked it. The construction committee took a very dim view of our maintenance and building team. So I headed over there to tell them that there was a new man in charge — me — and I'd been a team leader before and put up big blocks. We'd already built one, and we were going to carry on building them. If we messed things up we'd give up the idea of building. The construction committee was OK. They agreed to let us have a go.

We finished the project on time, and it was a quality job too. From then on we won the right to put up big blocks. We built a whole lot of them, one after another. By 1981 the building industry throughout China was learning from the Luohe East Wind Construction Team. What they'd done had been submitted to Comrades Deng Xiaoping and Hu Yaobang and approved by them. I suppose East Wind was the first model of urban reform. We went along to learn from them too, and it only took one look to tell me that everything they'd done we'd done already, like cadres being promoted and demoted, workers being hired and fired, and flexible wages. They were a building team under a street committee too, but there were only three hundred of them. We were already up to six hundred. We were made a test case for "learning from East Wind and copying East Wind" in Harbin. We got support from everywhere in copying East Wind and moved ahead even faster.

A year later we were a company. Being a company meant we'd gone up in the world and came under the district authorities, though in fact we insisted on staying under the direct control of the street committee. For one thing we liked them, and for another — and that was the main thing — we wanted to stay unofficial. We didn't want the district putting state cadres in, and we absolutely weren't going to guarantee people jobs for life. The structure of our company is very simple. At each level there's only one person in charge: no deputies. The technicians and management in each site get a standard wage of 98 yuan, which is doubled by the supplement for special responsibilities; and as we work Sundays and public holidays that brings their monthly pay up to 240 yuan. But there's a condition: if they're not up to it, they lose the job and their pay goes down straight away. Our workers get paid more than in state enterprises too, though of course they have to work harder and for longer hours. In the last few years we've had over a hundred people defecting to us from state and big collective enterprises. What happens when people retire? Hold on — I'll come back to that in a minute.

In 1981 we became one of the "big four" in the Harbin construction industry, and in '82 our job at the Longjiang Machinery Factory was made a provincial silver-medal project. In '83 we completed a job that was an all-round high-quality one. All-round high-quality jobs take more time and material and cost a lot more too, but a company's reputation matters much more. State-run outfits used to push collective ones out, but now we're giving state enterprises the elbow. When we finished our first big apartment block we started putting up the exhibition hall beside the Songhua River, and after we'd been on the job for a month we were very politely given the boot. They said that it was a top priority item, and the mayor was taking a personal interest in it. If they let a street committee building and maintenance team do it and we'd made a mess of it they'd have been in a very awkward position. But this year we very politely saw the city's First Construction Company off. It was for a big block at Harbin University. The First Construction Company moved in with all their gear before the contract had even been signed. They were sure they'd be staying there. But we showed that we could do it for five per cent less than them, and in a year instead of their year and a half. And we could guarantee a top-quality job. Could they really get such a bargain? Was it possible? The clients went to ask the city's constrution committee, and the construction committee told them it was on: they knew from experience. Give it to Xinyang, they said, and they'll give it top priority. Give it to the First Construction Company and they'll treat it as a routine job. So that's how we were able to see the state-run company and all its equipment off the site ever so politely. Now the state-run outfits get scared at just the sound of our name. No harm in that: a collective can buck the state enterprises up a bit. Now we've got six site units and a transport team. We completed over eleven million yuan's worth of work in 1983. I went to Xi'an for a meeting and had another look at East Wind: they're still the same size.

I think technically competent management is important.

Every section has an engineer in charge. One engineer volunteered to leave a state outfit to join us. He used to be on 78 yuan a month; he gets 240 here. I've run eight courses in technical management for section chiefs and technicians. I encourage people to study and improve themselves. I announced at a company general meeting that the company would pay the study costs of anyone who passed the exams for the civil engineering department of the spare-time university. There was one lad who passed the exams and his site unit didn't want to let him study because it'd interfere with his work. On top of that the spare-time university wouldn't let him in because they were worried he'd leave the construction company after he graduated as he was only a temporary worker with us. As soon as I heard I called him to my office and asked him about it. He'd come seventh out of four or five hundred people taking the exam. That was quite something. I decided there and then to put him on the permanent staff and let the company pay his fees. So it wouldn't hit his site unit's accounting I transferred him to the company's technical safety section. Once that news got out the youngsters were keener on studying than ever. But I also announced that they had to get a graduation certificate, and that they couldn't leave the company for six years after that. Study anything else? Of course the company wouldn't foot the bill. You can't study classical literature at our company's expense. The reason I want everyone to study is so we'll build better and make the company even better.

I've only got a junior middle school diploma. But not long ago I passed the national exam for managers. In non-state companies we don't choose and promote our cadres for their paper qualifications. Besides, the general view of qualifications isn't as straightforward as it was a while back. As I see it what the country's most short of now is managerial talent, not people with diplomas.

Me? I reckon I'm managerial talent. When I was a group leader I was always thinking about how to get my group to do the work properly so that we'd all make a living. I'd never been any sort of cadre before then. No, now I mention it I was a detachment leader in the Young Pioneers at primary school. That was all.

We pay insurance for all our regular staff to the insurance company, fifty to a hundred yuan a month depending on their wages. When they retire they get about 110 yuan a month. Those are our welfare benefits, and they're no worse than in state outfits, are they? But the company only pays two thirds. One third comes from the workers themselves. That stops workers running off to other units in mid-career. The company loses most, but you're out of pocket too. Everyone can work that sum out. Our sickness benefits can compare with state ones too. Everyone gets three yuan for medical expenses a month, and if there's anything left over you keep two-thirds of the surplus. All hospital bills are met by the company, but you don't get a penny in sick pay. Medical expenses are covered, however serious, but we won't have people fiddling sick leave. We issue suits of Western clothing, heating allowances, and food subsidies. We help our workers to build their own houses too. There's no retail shop selling building material in the city, so people either have to ask their units for it or else pinch it. My rule is that if you steal anything you're fined at ten times its value. But if our own people are building their houses we let them have the stuff cheap. We only charge them two *fen* for a brick that costs five *fen* plus two *fen* for transport.

Last year there was a big fire in Harbin. Hundreds of homes were burned down, and two of our workers were affected. I went to the scene of the fire with our Party secretary. They'd gone to stay with friends or relations, so we didn't find them then. The next day the company vacated some office space for them to stay in, and we all chipped in to fit them out with a new set of kitchen things. One of them was on our permanent staff, and he lost two thousand yuan's worth of stuff in the fire. We gave him 2,500. The other was a temporary, and he got 1,500 yuan. It brought tears to their eyes. State factory workers didn't get rehoused for ages.

In the last few years dozens of our people have been given jobs in state outfits but come back here. Our Party secretary went, and he was back three days later. Everyone says they'd rather spend the rest of their working lives in our company than go to a state outfit. We're very choosy about who we take now. Most of the lads in the original maintenance and building team were kept on, and they're nearly all in the key jobs on the worksites. They're all on 246 a month, and every one of them is a ten-thousand-yuanner. I've already forked out 400,000 yuan on housing for our staff. You don't get it on seniority or on how little living space you have already. It's a reward for good work, and you're allowed to keep your old place too. We've built twenty-two flats so far and we make an open assessment to decide who deserves them. I got given this flat first because I've done more for the company than anyone else. That's a fact. The workers don't have any objections. They all said: give the first one to the boss. Two workers got flats too. They found us a lot of work. Nearly all the worksite cadres have been given flats.

As company manager I have a lot of power. People are hired or fired on my signature. We don't have any personnel problems within the company, but things are very complicated outside. I still find it hard after knocking around all these years. The trickiest stuff is to do with getting the building jobs. There are a lot of construction outfits now, and the competition for work is ruthless. The clients used to ask us out to a meal and plead with us to put up a decent building. But now it's up to the builders to take the clients out. On top of that, the middlemen want hair-raising commissions: a yuan per square metre. So on a ten-thousand square metre project they get ten thousand yuan for nothing. But I absolutely refuse to do anything too outrageous. I always say to the workers, "You may think that I've got a lot of power as the manager, but if anything goes wrong I have to carry the can. If there's trouble I'm the one who gets put inside." The only way we can and do compete is through high-quality work at lower prices.

Another headache is the way everyone wants hand-outs these days. Anyone who's starting a magazine or an advertising paper always asks you for a grant. First of all comes the invitation to a meeting. If you don't go and all the people they've invited are senior comrades it looks as though you're being stuck-up. But if you go and eat their meal or drink their tea the next thing is they're putting their hands out for money. It's two or three thousand every time. A couple of days ago a film company turned up and said they wanted to make a TV play about us. They came straight out with a demand for 60,000 yuan. What the hell did they think they were doing?

Now I'm the manager, my wage is 115 yuan a month, the same as a grade fourteen state cadre. On top of that I get a responsibility supplement and other things that bring it up to 290. The joke is that I get more than the mayor. Of course some people object to me making this much. "We've been making revolution all these years, and this is all we get, you so-and-so." What I'd like to ask is how many of them does it take to do as much work as I do? Last year I got 4,000 in bonuses. I gave 2,000 to the canteen manager for entertaining: it has to come out of my pocket, not company funds. This year policies are even more flexible and the company can pay — I can't go on shelling out that sort of money for ever. People can say what they like, but nobody's really got at me yet, and they won't be able to either. The situation's changed.

Keeping a business going isn't enough for me. I have to build businesses up. I've invested a million yuan in importing Japanese colour photograph printing equipment so I can compete with state colour prints. There's only one state place in Harbin that does colour prints. They take a fortnight to process a film and charge 1.50 for a four-inch print: Private traders in Guangzhou can do that for only 38 *fen*. I want to get into the travel business, and build a hotel to compete with the service in state hotels. And I'm interested in trade too.

That's the way I operate. To get to the root of it, my idea is never give up.

As I was an only child I didn't have to go to the countryside or the mountains.* But during the "cultural revolution" my father was branded as an active counter-revolutionary because of something he'd said. In fact all he'd done was to make a remark about how Jiang Qing had acted in films in the thirties. There really was nothing to it. But it happened just when factional fighting was getting going, and as he was a minor official he got caught up in it. He was sent back to his old home in Shandong. He even took his appeal to the State Council, and it drove him round

---

* In the early 1970s many school-leavers were sent from the cities to the mountains and villages. An exception was normally made for only children.

the twist. Even when he was rehabilitated he was left with a black mark against his name for a long time for having said something wrong. The company of the army's construction corps* I went to was on the frontier. Most people had rifles. As I told my political instructor about my shady background he didn't discriminate against me. When I saw that other people were going places and getting to university or into the Party I didn't even dream of doing that myself. I was grateful enough just to be holding my gun. I really wasn't as good as they were then. But of all my fellow-students at school I've probably gone the furthest.

Translated by W. J. F. Jenner

---

* During the "cultural revolution" many youngsters were sent to the army's construction corps farms in Xinjiang.

The Lone Goose

*Xiao Huiying, 23 years old. She gesticulates as she talks.
We sat on the stone flags of Tiananmen Square whilst the
sun set and we talked till midnight. She talked; I talked;
sometimes we both sat in silence.*

SOVIET literature is a bit closer to our experience than
American literature. I find that I can learn something about
other young people from young Soviet writers. There's a
novel about young people in a modern Russian city called
What Do You Really Want? After I'd read it I thought: it
isn't so much a question of wanting things; if I want
something, then I'll get hold of it somehow, but it's not
that, it's a question of counting for something. What am I
really worth? In most people's eyes, I don't count for
anything. I haven't got a proper job, I haven't got a unit to
take care of me. All I've got is my residence permit; I'm an
ordinary citizen. But I'm not just an ordinary citizen, am I?

Look, the square is full of people. They've all come out to
enjoy the cool breeze. Their houses are bare; naturally they
haven't got air conditioning.... Lots and lots of people in
Beijing haven't even got an electric fan. Our country is poor
and of course we want to change it, but how? All we can do
is struggle towards prosperity. Unfortunately, far too many
people want to get rich but far too few really want to escape
from the wilderness of poverty. We don't have a proper

spirit of enterprise; we're either held back by conservatism or else we force our way, fight to the death. I don't think that we have the fanatic strength to fight, though plenty of people have been forced into it. At the same time, lots and lots of people are weak. So, whether we're talking about emotional life or social life, I'm very much on my own. I don't really care if other people understand me or not; all I want is for them to acknowledge my existence. It's difficult because lots of people think I'm eccentric or mad. Mad people are still people, but just because they're mad they're excluded from the human race.

My father is a worker and my mother is a housewife. Whenever they shouted at me that I was mad, wicked or reckless, I used to think to myself that they were pretty mad, too. Neither of them even went to primary school though their brothers went to university. I've never been able to understand how a capitalist family and a factory owner's family could produce such oddities. They must be changelings. My grandfather had a fur shop; he's dead. My mother's father ran an ink factory; he's dead, too. He died of fright during the "cultural revolution" when his house was ransacked. Nobody beat him, he frightened himself to death. With a background like I've got it's hardly surprising that my educational achievements aren't up to much. Naturally, I didn't go to university after graduating from middle school. In 1979, I joined the "army", not the People's Liberation Army, but the army of young people "waiting for jobs". I'm fed up with it. I used to fight with my parents and say awful things to them: "I can't understand how you had the energy to conceive me when you didn't have enough to eat." I was born in 1961, during the three years of natural disasters. I think I understand it now: the more difficult life gets, the stronger the desire to survive; and the desire to survive manifests itself in ways that are very different from man's high moral image, or the image of so-called humanity. In that way, everybody is odd; what they ostensibly revere is exactly the reverse of this struggle to survive with its animal aspect. Human nature and human integrity are complicated.

Yes, I often think I could write something, too. At the very least I could write a few short stories. But I've never written a word, I'd never make any money by writing. And if I were to write down my thoughts, I'd be emotionally broke. There'd be no sense in making myself the subject, stripping myself bare; I'd rather read other people's books.

Of course you know all about it. All the novelists you just mentioned are overseas Chinese women writers or Taiwanese women writers, and their stories are pretty intimate, sort of exposing intimacy. You talk quite freely about it, but would you write as freely as they do? I don't think you'd dare. You have to allow the young ladies their "face". I really liked *Two Women of China: Mulberry and Peach*; admittedly, not in the edition published by the China Youth Publishing House. There are a lot of writers and a lot of books I don't like, especially "clever" new styles like ghost stories and Qiong Yao. The people who recommended her to me said her love stories were really good but after I'd read her, I felt cheated. She's never been in love, not like me. She's written lots of stories but she doesn't write about the pain of love and how it never ends, so what's the point? When you've lost your love, part of your heart dies and the wound never stops bleeding. It's true, when I read *Two Women of China: Mulberry and Peach*, what impressed me wasn't the plot or the love story but the power of the novelist.

In the spring of 1981, the street committee sent me to

work doing odd jobs in the bus company. I made just over 10 yuan a month. Not long after I started, I met a boy. He worked in an oilfield. We quickly fell in love. It was incredibly quick but we were very much in love. When I think about it now, it's easy to see why. We were separated, so we created mythical sweethearts, made them up according to our own ideals; it was a love story that we wrote ourselves. I used to save up my leave and sneak off to the oilfield to see him. I went to see him twice. At night, I stayed in the girls' dormitory; by day, I watched him at work. Then I quarrelled with my family over some small thing and I went off to stay with him for a fortnight. He was very loving and treated me very well but I saw a lot of him and my feelings grew less strong; we became pretty "alienated" as they say. But after I'd calmly assessed my feelings, I still wanted to marry him. Even if it meant losing my Beijing residence permit, I'd still marry him. I was quite willing to go and work in the oilfield. Naturally, he was very pleased. You probably don't know that oil workers are always on the move and their working conditions are bad, so even girls from small towns don't want to marry "oil rats". "The oil workers shout real hard and they'll marry a wife without a residence card." In fact you do get a residence permit, but it's a rural one. But the problem was that he wanted me to stay in Beijing, to give him a way out. He hoped that I'd be able to get him work in Beijing but there was no way I could. I told him there was no possibility of his getting to Beijing; even the children of some high officials had difficulty getting back to the capital.

Then he proposed that I should swap jobs with a woman at the oilfield whose husband worked in Beijing. She was prepared to pay me 2,000 yuan to swap jobs and residence permits with me. That really went against my principles.

I've always tried to keep my fate in my own hands. But at that time I didn't have as much control over my fate as I do now. I wanted to be independent. So the idea of changing my life for 2,000 yuan lost all interest. I went back to Beijing. I didn't cry, I just left without saying a word. When I arrived at Beijing station, I went to the post office and wrote him a telegram saying, "Two people's dreams of Beijing are destroyed." Which two people? Me and the woman who wanted to go to Beijing. I didn't explain but I supposed he'd understand it. When I was paying for the telegram, the station clock struck six and I burst into tears. I grabbed the money back and wouldn't give the money to the clerk. He didn't understand me; he just said, "Next time, pay first!" I was neglected. When I'd stopped crying, I paid. The clerk looked at the telegram and took the money without a word. But as I turned to leave, I heard the post office workers saying, "Mad!" Normally I'd have sworn at them, but I didn't have the strength. Then I knew I was finished.

I still love him. I don't know if what I love is a story I made up; if it was a brief pact for happiness that I'd signed with heaven, an illusory story. When I got home, my parents wept with relief. They'd been terribly worried. They thought I was dead. When I came back, they were so happy, it was as if they'd found a daughter. How could they know I wasn't myself? When I went back to the bus company, I had to write a self-criticism. I wrote it, explaining why I'd gone off for twenty days without asking permission. But they didn't let me explain, all they wanted to know was what I did and who I was with. I realized that they thought I'd gone off for "immoral purposes"! I was furious, "Take my trousers off and examine me; then you'll know I'm not a tart!" The end result was that they said I wouldn't acknowledge my mistake, my attitude was very bad, I refused to mend my ways and disregarded discipline. They threw me out. I was very apathetic. When I left I even said to them, "Thank you for your concern. It reminds me of those who wanted to erect memorial arches to heroines who preserved their chastity. The emperors of the past could learn from you." Honestly, at that time I could have been persuaded and the fact that they didn't try was a failure of their policy. I do think that some of the people who carry out government policy at the lower levels are really useless. With anyone else, faced with that sort of contradiction, if they hadn't solved it, the victim would have fallen into the muddy pit of thieves and whores and created even worse problems for the country.

Perhaps it's a common failing. A few days ago, there was an article in the paper about an old Party member who'd killed his son for thieving. He thought he was saving the people from harm, so he broke the law against murder and was arrested. Then there was another article about the manager of a shop who caught an employee stealing money; he'd stolen more than 3,000 yuan of public money. He didn't call the police, he just made the employee hand over the money, told his father about it and that was that. He wanted to save his comrade and probably wanted to keep the "Advanced Red Flag" reputation of his shop. But he'd covered up a crime and broken the law, so he was arrested. It served him right, it really did. But when the government asks officials like that to retire, they always say, "We'll serve the people for a few more years." Poof!

When I became a loner, I felt more energetic, more determined to grasp my own fate, and I gained more self-confidence. For over a year now I've been "upright, lofty and at the head of my fellows" as they say on television advertisements. It pretty well applies to me. For a few months I didn't read anything, see any plays or listen to any classical music but spent all my time learning to type so I could support myself. Then I joined a typing service made up of young people "waiting for work" which produces English language documents for some of the long-term resident foreign companies which stay in the big hotels. Now I earn between 300 and 400 yuan a month, which is an astronomical figure, especially compared with "real" salaries. I've finally become a "heroine" to my school-mates. When I go back to school on Founder's Day, all my schoolmates and teachers cautiously congratulate me, avoiding the issue of my dismissal by the bus company. I think to myself: I know I'm capable, but do you only congratulate people when they make money? I bet you do!

When America was opening up the West, the desert sand was soaked with blood. Ex-outlaws turned gentlemen. Is that what I am? Some people despise me and say behind my back, "She may be doing nicely now but next year she'll be eating green pills. Look what happened to all those people in the sixties." By eating green pills, they mean I'll have diarrhoea, dysentery, cholera and gastro-enteritis, that I'll lose everything. Some people try to think up reforms that will help China's economy; some draw conclusions from the runaway economies of Taiwan and Hongkong; some study the Soviet Union, Yugoslavia and Romania, but some people summarize our own experience and draw conclusions from what happened in the 60s.

Every month I give my brother 50 yuan. He's just started at university and relies on me for his pocket money. The rest, I spend. I buy clothes, I eat well; lots of dishes at every meal, beer, soft drinks; I go to concerts and I buy books. I don't give a penny to my parents, nor to my elder sister. Let everyone make what they can and spend their own money; it's normal. I know that it's hard-earned, but it's easily spent. I've always loved reading and going to concerts but when I was unemployed, I couldn't afford to. Now the money is no problem.

There was a recital by Xi Xiulan. Normally I don't like folk music or popular music but I really wanted to go. The tickets were sold out but I bought one for 10 yuan from a tout and got a seat in the front row. Other people could only afford to pay 5 yuan for the back row. As it was all amplified, it didn't actually matter where you sat. As I sat there, I thought about it and concluded that I'd spent the money on buying myself a personality. I'd achieved a feeling that I was pretty good, a feeling of self-satisfaction in the face of complicated humanity.

The recital was boring so I left half-way through. Outside, people were still milling about hopefully waiting for last-minute returned tickets. They were amazed to see someone walking out half-way! I wanted to say, "I'm not like you; I've got no staying power. If it isn't something that I really like, then I'll leave half-way through." But they can't possibly understand how a 23-year-old girl can endlessly analyze herself, how she could perhaps "leave" half-way through life. Out of a thousand million people, how many really feel that they exist on this earth to carry out the great task? They are more integrated than me, or at least, if you patch them up a bit, they'll be more integrated than me. I've been too badly broken up. I'm too realistic, and too practical.

But there are some things. There was a Japanese who wanted to marry me. I didn't marry him. Here, I can earn 400 a month but what does a typist earn there? He said he'd look after me but that finished it. I'd just struggled to achieve my independence and I couldn't go back. I don't want to marry a foreigner. I'm determined not to, though I type documents for them.

I do have beliefs but I can't really explain them, sorry. No, no, I don't mind talking about them. It's nothing to do with sex because I've never gone very far; I'm still a virgin, honestly. When I was in love I lost out and if I was to go through that again, I'd be worse off. I think it could really finish me. That time I was lucky, just as I was lucky not to lose my Beijing residence permit. But it was also a terrible loss, wasn't it?

When we broke up, he said it was because I was too progressive and he couldn't rely on me. But why should he? I don't want anyone to rely on me, but I do want to rely on a man. I don't know how to explain it. Life is a puzzle. The average man in China wants a suitable wife and the sort he wants is a doll who will hang around his neck. But she must be a working doll, so she'll bring in her own grain coupons and her own wages. That's how I see it and I think that it is the tragedy my generation has to face.

You want to see me home? It's in a narrow lane and there are no streetlights. What's more, I'll have to climb over the wall because it's late and the door will have been locked.

Translated by Frances Wood

Pretty Third Daughter

She is so strikingly beautiful that men stare at her whenever she goes out.

WE are friends so you must be sure not to show me up. I've already suffered a lot for being pretty. Of course it's been an advantage sometimes too. All in all, I couldn't really say whether it's been a good thing or not.

That's a proper puzzler. Why do you want to write about me anyway? "How does it feel to be pretty?" What do you mean? Am I so different from other people?

I was born in Beijing in 1955. I already had two elder sisters and after me a brother was born. Then my father decided that was enough....He had a boy to carry on the family line. None of the others was particularly good-looking. I don't know why I turned out like this. I just don't have the ordinary Wu family looks.

Dad had a watch and clock business before liberation. Afterwards it was made into a joint state-private company with him as the manager. Later, he was dismissed for corruption, so he went into something new — he did odd jobs round a fried food shop. So soon after I was born, the family got really poor. I didn't go to kindergarten. I just played with other children in the lane. I spent the whole day in the streets. They weren't too bothered about me at home. With three daughters what does it matter if one dies? That's how it is in poor families.

As to my primary school, there's nothing worth telling. I was poor to middling. I hardly ever got a good mark. When I was in class four, the "cultural revolution" broke out. That meant another few years running free on the street. Then, in 1969, I drifted into middle school.

It was in my second year at junior middle school that I realized I was pretty. Of course people had always said I was a pretty little girl, but I thought they were just being nice. Obviously by the time we were at middle school, we weren't completely innocent about sex, but we didn't know all that much either. I was aware that several of the boys fancied me. I couldn't help knowing. They were always trying to please me and showing off.

How did they do this? Well, for example, whenever I had a period, I was sure to find a big bar of chocolate in my desk. You see, when I had a period I didn't do morning exercises....That meant the boys could work it out. I still don't know who used to leave it for me. But every time I have a quarrel with my husband, I think, "If only I had married that one." Of course it's just a dream. Anyway, kindness isn't enough. I want a real man.

You think I was lucky? Only thirteen and boys were falling in love with me. Of course they were only interested in me for my looks. I wasn't very good at getting on with people. When we finished school, we were all to be split up. There were just three of us girls going to the same production team. Before I went, I dumped all the boys' notes and letters on the table and said, "You can each take the ones you wrote." This caused quite an upset in the class. When I was older I could see how horrible I had been. Of course, if any of them had kept on after me, I probably would have ended up marrying him. What a pity none of them did. They were just like me. None of us really knew what love was. We were just fooling around.

That year I was fifteen. All of us went to work in the countryside. Well, a few stayed in town. The ones who could pull strings. Joining an agricultural production team was counted as being given a job, so you had to pass a medical. At my gynaecological examination the doctor couldn't take his eyes off me. "I ought to have a husband," I thought suddenly. The doctor was a man of course, he must have been in his forties or fifties. Getting on, but still young at heart.

My commune was in rather mountainous country. Some of the class which had been sent down the year before began to chase after me. I fell for one of them — I suppose it was because I was rather lonely. I call it love but actually I only saw him a few times. Those older school-leavers were good to me. When I went home to see my family, they helped me buy the ticket, got a seat for me, carried my luggage.... They did everything. Why? Just so that they could see a bit more of me. They liked to get a seat beside me so that when the bus went over a bump they'd be able to lean against me. Even the roughest of them was fine with me. This made me think that if I married someone who wasn't very nice he'd become nice. In fact, I could save a man. Isn't that funny? I was quite a little salvationist.

During the movement to copy the work of the Dazhai agricultural brigade, we tried to remould the commune's land. One of the older boys hurt his foot on a stone. The bone was broken and he had it in plaster. He couldn't even take the bus, he just had to sit in the village waiting for it to get better. I used to go to see him for a chat. Sometimes I would take him some chicken. The older boys often brought me some chicken or some dog meat which they

stole from the peasants and cooked for themselves....I can't
say how it happened. I don't know how he had the face. But
anyway he asked, and I gave myself. I was sixteen years old.
I used to think that it would be something very important
— when it happened, I found that it was nothing at all. I
was a girl beforehand, and when I got up I was still the same
girl. I hadn't turned into a grown woman. But all the feeling
I'd had for that boy disappeared after that. There was
nothing left. I waited anxiously for my period because I was
afraid I might be pregnant. I didn't feel very pleased with
myself but I didn't feel guilty either. I hadn't really liked
the boy, it was just curiosity and confusion. I couldn't help
it. I never thought that we would get married. That simply
wasn't on the cards. Afterwards I didn't see much of him.

Once I was back in the city, I was sent to work in a factory
canteen. I couldn't stay in that job. I had to ask for a
transfer. The reason was that everyday the queue in front of
me was always the longest, and they were all men waiting
for me to serve them. Some of them were so shameless they
wrote me little notes on their food tickets. I took no notice
at all but afterwards the person who checked the food
tickets would say, "Oh, here's a letter for you, Little Wu."
She was teasing of course. I was transferred onto driving a
crane which was very easy. As usual, everyone looked after
me. Once the crane cable snapped and a big shaft fell down
just missing one of the workers. If it had hit him it would
certainly have killed him. He was only a young fellow but he
really blew up at me. I liked him. There were very few men
who dared scold me. You're right. There wasn't anything
frightening about me. It's just that the others were so much
in awe of my looks. I admired him for having more to him. I
didn't want to drive the crane any more after that, so I
applied for another transfer and was set to work on a

grinder. That was very light work too, because it was electronically controlled.

All right. I'll tell you about Xiao Ye, the one I almost killed with the crane. Afterwards I found out his father was a very distinguished person. He'd come from peasant stock but he managed to win a government scholarship to go to study in the United States. After he came home he became a top engineer in a design institute. Yet despite all this ability, when his wife died, he married his children's nurse. Furthermore, he was really horrible to the children of his first marriage. He only loved his pretty new wife.

"I hate all pretty women," Xiao Ye told me. If it hadn't been for this strange principle, I would probably have gone after him. Life is never as simple as it seems.

Lots of people introduced me to boyfriends and young workers would come of their own accord to chat me up. Some of them would claim that they had come to discuss something to do with work. Even on the street, men would come up and ask if I had a boyfriend.

"No, I haven't," I would say, "but I don't want to find one on the street." Then I went out with a trade union official for a few months. We were introduced by a colleague. We got on all right. He was a good man, reliable, a Party member and he had prospects. But later, when I told him that I had already had sex with somebody, he didn't want anything more to do with me. Everyone has their own moral standards. I can't blame him. I admired him, he was a principled man. Up to then I hadn't cared for him that much. But after we broke things off, I felt I loved him. Too many men were just knocked backwards by my looks. And women? With women it was the opposite. I felt that all the women hated me.... They regarded me as a potential thief because they were afraid I would steal their men. Even the ones who hadn't got boyfriends somehow felt the same.

Then I was introduced to the son of someone who had been a banker before liberation. He was very rich. His family had hundreds of thousands of yuan at home. If I'd married him I would have had no more worries. But I was afraid ... very much afraid. I wasn't afraid of him; he was rather effeminate. I couldn't have been afraid of him. But I was afraid of that money. He loved me. When I got married to someone else he gave me a lot of presents, terribly expensive things.

"In future, even if things are very hard for you, I won't be able to give you anything," he explained. So I accepted them. I said, "Later I'll be someone else's wife. If you want anything from me now, there's still time. Afterwards, it'll be too late." He patted me on the shoulder. "I've never yet kissed a girl," he said: "But I don't want to spoil things." He went away.

I could never have married him with so much money. Last year he married someone with a better political origin and better social standing than mine. They set up a modern, well-equipped home. He wasn't very happy after he got married and he went off to work in the Shenzhen Special Economic Zone as an acountant. Since then, our relationship has been strictly on a business footing. I give him Chinese currency and he buys me things from Hongkong. He always shows me the currency exchange notes for the day. He plays straight. He knew that I wasn't very happy with the person I married.

"Call on me if you can't bear it any longer," he used to say. "I'd still marry you willingly and set up a new home with you." He meant that he would break up his first marriage. So I wouldn't do it. I couldn't and I wouldn't have wanted to.

I got married to a technician when I was 27. It was all based on fantasy. I had wanted to marry someone who knew how to struggle. It was too romantic. I don't want to talk about my husband. I think we've both got an idea of what may happen, even though I'm about to become a mother. Even if we wanted to make it last, it wouldn't work. It can't go on. Don't push me. Don't ask about it.

All right, let me tell you this, for example. When he knew what had happened to me in the countryside, he wasn't upset and he wasn't surprised. In fact he was happy. Why was he happy? Because I was spoiled goods. Originally he felt that I was too pretty, that somehow my value was higher than his, and so we weren't equal. When he found out what I had done with somebody else, it lowered my value in his eyes. I knew that was what he was thinking. This wasn't tolerance. This was selfishness, real selfishness.

All the same, he wasn't really so bad. The really bad person was that boy in the countryside. I remember he said that once you turned off the light, it didn't matter whether someone was pretty or ugly. It was all the same. It was all fucking anyway....That was an awful thing to say by any standards. Oh, people, people.

After I was married, men kept chasing me just the same. Some were really after me, some just liked playing about. They thought it was the thing to do with a married woman. I did fall for someone...one of those who wasn't after me. I invited him to come to see an exhibition with me and afterwards we ate out together. "Well," he said suddenly. "We are both grown-ups. We are both adults. Right?" And that was the end of it. So where do I go? Wherever I go it always seems to lead back to the same place. There are lots of things I would like to know, and yet, if I do get to know them, what use are they?

I've had some problems in my life, but on the other hand some things have been made easy for me. If I want to buy anything I always find the male shop assistants are most attentive. If I queue for returned tickets at a theatre, someone is bound to give me some. And yet I seem to get further and further from people. Can this all be my fault?

Yes. Prettiness, this is my advantage, my "capital". But I always seem to like the people who don't take any notice of it. The pity is I don't have anything else to give. No, nothing.

Translated by Delia Davin and Cheng Lingfang

Making a Trip

Beijing's golden October has always been the busy season for tourists and conferences, and with the celebration this year of the 35th anniversary of the founding of the People's Republic, restrictions were placed on the number of people coming into the city. So by late October....

It was ten o'clock at night and the ticket windows at Beijing railway station — Beijing to Harbin, Beijing to Guangzhou, Beijing to Shanghai, to Baotou — over thirty of them, all had signs posted saying "Sold out".

You even had to queue for an hour at a temporary outdoor wicket to return tickets. The young traveller behind us was wearing a striped brown Western suit with a light blue sweater and pulling a leatherette travel case with wheels on it; he seemed very upset....

MY wife's gone missing. She got swallowed up just now when we were trying to get to the train.

First I waited at the platform gate and then when the train left I started wandering around in the main station wondering what on earth to do. One of the attendants came over and asked what I was up to, and when I told him I'd lost my wife he said I'd better go and refund my ticket, otherwise it'd be too late and I'd be 20 yuan out of pocket. Look, I've still got her ticket! (He opened his fist and showed me two clammy bits of cardboard which said

'Beijing to Handan, Train No. 307. — authors' note)

Who says I'm not upset? I just burst into tears a little while back.

We work for the Fengfeng collieries and came to Beijing to spend our honeymoon. We took a bus first to Handan and then got a train to Beijing; it's been six days in all including one day's travelling.

We knew Beijing security regulations were pretty tough so we got together all the necessary documents like our work cards, letters of introduction, marriage certificate and also some national grain coupons; we knew you're not allowed to stay in Beijing nor buy any food without them. My wife's a bit timid, she's never really been anywhere before — she got sick as soon as she got on the bus and threw up all over the place. She was okay on the train though, didn't get dizzy or sick at all. Ha, who'd believe she'd manage to get herself lost just as we were about to go home?

When we first got here we asked where the hotel booking place was and got told "Just look for the longest line!" So we queued for five hours and just as we got near the front they put out a sign saying: "No vacancies today in all city and suburban hotels." It's all right for me to kip outside for a night, but what could I do about her? I remembered that one of my workmate's relatives was something like an office manager here but I didn't know where, so I decided to call home and find out. I had to wait an hour for the call and when I got through I was told that this guy worked at the Coal Ministry. We made for a place called Hepingli and found him. He was pretty nice and even asked us to stay for supper, but we decided we'd rather find a place to sleep instead. He put us in touch with the Coal Ministry's guest house but when we got there it was packed to the gills; there were even people sleeping on the landings and staircases. I thanked him and went back to that hotel booking desk and started queuing up to register for the following day. We couldn't sleep on a staircase landing, we're on our honeymoon, how could you stay somewhere like that? Besides, they didn't even have any bedding, you had to find your own if you slept out on the landing.

So we spent the night outside — my wife was just frozen. I was okay; half way through I went and got some alcohol from the station canteen. My wife wouldn't touch it though, so she just froze and got up and got some hot noodles every couple of hours. We registered again at daybreak and when our turn came we ended up being put in a public bathhouse at Hujialou. It didn't matter that we didn't know where it was because they have this computer at the station which for four *fen* tells you how to get there and which buses to take. It really was a bathhouse too. Just our luck. She stayed in the women's part and I was in the men's, so all those documents I got together were for nothing. They ran it as a bathhouse in the daytime so we had to leave as soon as we'd signed in and couldn't go back before eight in the evening. We just got ourselves changed and went out shopping. We had to take all our things with us because there was no place to leave them.

We used our map to get to Tiananmen Square, the Palace Museum, the Workers' Cultural Palace and Zhongshan Park. We wanted to see Chairman Mao's Memorial Hall too, but it was the wrong day and they were closed. My wife was still feeling out of sorts and kept getting dizzy on the buses, so we had to get off every two or three stops, rest for a bit and then get back on again. Once I said to her, "We'll just hold on for another couple of stops; if we get off we'll never get back on again." But in the end, she threw up again as soon as we got to Wangfujing Street. Then the sanitation police came over and fined us one yuan. After that, we just had to get something worked out. So we didn't eat lunches, just breakfast and then some bread and tea back at the bathhouse in the evening. That finally did the trick. We managed to visit quite a few places every day and in four days we saw the lot. The Ming Tombs and the Great Wall we didn't get to though, with long journeys like that she would have thrown up her insides. The Summer Palace? No, we didn't get there either. We just took one look at the map, first this bus, then that one and you have to change so many times, then the No. 332; more than 300 streets — it was just too far. We brought over 1,000 yuan with us, after all it was our honeymoon, so we thought we'd do some shopping here. We pushed our way along Wangfujing, Xidan, Qianmen for a whole day and spent over 300. I think the shopping's better here than in Handan, but it's not as good as Shijiazhuang. Tell me, how can there be so many people in Beijing? Shopping's impossible and they keep the lights on all night in the bathhouse to stop theft. Last night there was a power failure and they gave us each a bit of candle to use. I kept my money in my breast pocket, put some of our things in the locker and the rest under my pillow, didn't sleep a wink all night. There were people leaving during the night to catch trains. And for that they still wanted one twenty a day, and even said it was a bargain because they threw in a free bath. How come this queue's not moving? It's been two hours already — it'll be too late for me to refund my ticket. I work as a provisions buyer in our supplies department. I'm in charge of buying rice and meat and vegetables; my wife's a cook in our canteen.

She'll be in tears all right, I was myself and she'll be worse, won't she? I just don't know if she got pushed on to that train or not. A couple of days back she said, "I always heard people talk about all the wonderful places in Beijing, but who'd have thought they'd be so far apart or that it'd be so big?" She said this trip was ill-fated too. "Here we are on our honeymoon and we have to sleep apart in a bathhouse; that's a really bad sign," she said. She started crying and I had to cheer her up a bit and tell her, "Look, this is the only time in your life you'll visit Beijing and it's here we had our honeymoon, so isn't that something to remember?" Me? You won't find me coming to Beijing for a honeymoon again!

I can hardly bear to tell you what getting a ticket home was like. We queued for ages, then they didn't have an express train stopping at Handan, so we got tickets for the No. 307 which ends up at Handan. We couldn't buy reserved seats and on top of that the train arrives at 4 in the morning, so we'd freeze to death at the other end. Anyway, we're going home; so not having seats doesn't really matter. There's probably a lot of people who didn't get anything at all. As soon as they opened the platform entrance people just burst in, the ticket collectors couldn't hold them back, they had to close up again and shout: "People who board the train without a ticket will be fined! People without validated tickets will be fined." But whether people had tickets or not they just pushed themselves through, and before I knew it my wife had disappeared. Since I didn't know if she'd gone through or not, I didn't dare move and just waited by the entrance. I stood there until everybody had gone through and they were just about to close the gate when this ticket inspector said to me, "Are you getting this train or not?" I told her my wife had disappeared and she said, "You've still got three minutes till the train goes, why haven't you got the station announcer to page her? If she's on the train she can still get off." So I got them to page her and while they did that I went back to the platform to wait for her. The train had gone, so what was I supposed to do? I went to get them to make another announcement and the lady there said, "Look, if a woman gets lost she's not going to get on a train by herself and if she got off she's not going to just sit around in the waiting room; she's more likely to be wandering around in the square outside." So I asked this woman if she'd be good enough to page my wife in the square and she said, "You've got a good sense of timing! There's a drive against noise pollution and there's just been a directive that we've got to disconnect the loudspeakers and stop broadcasting in the square. I'll make another announcement to the waiting room, the main hall and the front of the station but I can't broadcast to the whole square." So I waited till she did that and then went looking round the square but couldn't see her anywhere in all those people. So I came back to the station again and that's when the attendant saw me crying and told me to refund my ticket.

She hasn't got a ticket or any money and I've got all our documents. All she's got on her is two yuan which she was going to use to buy a snack when we got on the train. I've got our new clothes and shoes, she's just got the bag with all our toothbrushes and towels in it. Oh yes, she's got our seal, so she can use that! What can you do with that? Collect salaries, claim provisions; you always need a seal for that...and she could maybe flog something for a bit of cash, maybe flog her watch. I mean she could sell it; our speech is a bit less obvious than Beijing language. Couldn't she sell her watch for a train ticket?

There are only three people in front of me now; as soon as I've refunded the tickets I'll go to the station announcer and

see if she's there. If she's on the train she'll be okay, she
won't get sick. And there's no problem when she gets to
Handan, we've got an office there. She should be able to get
herself home, she's 23, and nobody's going to kidnap her.
Hurry up and refund your ticket. Don't let that guy in front
of you jump the queue.

Hey, how come they didn't give me the right money
back. Oh, no wonder; they've taken off a service charge. I
guess that's fair enough. We'd better go to the police now.
(We went with him to the station police who told him:
"We'll get everything sorted out; we guarantee that nobody
will get lost." Then we went to the station office where the
duty attendant declared, "We intend to take steps to
contact the 307's next scheduled stop. If his wife's on the
train then everything will be all right." — authors' note)
There's no point in my getting all upset, I'll leave it to the
police and the station staff. I guess I'll put up at the station
tonight just in case she didn't get on that train. I'll go back
to the police after a while to see if they've found her or not.

Whereabouts do you live? Next time I come to Beijing,
would it be okay for me to stay at your place?

Translated by Carole Murray

The First Guests

The first day that the Yanjing Restaurant opened its doors to Chinese guests. The Western dining room. A grey-haired man and his wife.

THIS sort of place *ought* to be open to everyone. In the 50s when they built the Friendship Hotel, they said it was an "experts guest house", specially for Russian experts, and even if the restaurant was empty, they wouldn't let Chinese eat in it. I went in once and sat down and all the waiters rushed up and said, "Comrade, this place is for foreign experts." I laughed and said, "I'm an expert, too; can I have the menu?" The food wasn't very good.

It's the same in Hongkong. At lunch-time in the expensive restaurants, they're always "fully booked" but they'll always leave a space for a foreigner; when a foreigner comes in they suddenly aren't "full". I went into one and said to the waiter, "Bring me some lunch. If a foreigner comes in, I'll give up my seat."

I've travelled a lot but I've only seen that in China and America. There are some places in America where they won't let blacks in. And what does it signify? Some of the white people in America believe in "racial supremacy", but what about us? Some people don't have enough self-respect. So when a reporter from the *Beijing Evening News* asked me what I thought just now, I said, "I haven't tasted the food yet, so I can't comment on that, but a restaurant certainly ought to open its doors to local residents!" What else could I say?

I mentioned Hongkong just now, but that was the old Hongkong. I spent 5 months there in 1949. In those days you could employ a housekeeper from Guangdong for 60 HK dollars a month but you couldn't get one now for 600 HK dollars! Prices seemed high in those days, but the cost of living was incredibly low compared with today. A packet of good cigarettes cost a dollar and breakfast was only a few cents. Nowadays, a few cents wouldn't buy anything.

A few years ago I went to Germany on assignment. I saw a big Coca Cola bottle in the shape of a thermos. It was quite well-designed so I thought I'd bring it back to show my wife but then I thought it was rather heavy and rather a silly thing to carry all that way. So I didn't.

I hadn't been out of the country for years and suddenly I got the chance. Everything was frighteningly expensive and I felt like walking in Wangfujing with only a few cents in my pocket. All I brought back were some coffee beans. Instant coffee tastes awful, even Nescafe. It's nothing like coffee you've ground yourself. ("He is always on about coffee. He couldn't survive without it. When he was criticized in the 'cultural revolution', his worst crime was 'drinking coffee like water'!" His wife interrupted. — authors' note) Well, coffee *is* water. The rebels didn't understand. ("What can I get you?" The waiter arrived. They ordered 7 yuan worth of food and the waiter turned to us. "What do you want?" After we had ordered, he turned back to the old couple."Do you want anything else?" When they said no, he said, "If you do want anything, just ask," and went off. "Want anything, want anything!, It doesn't sound very nice. He ought to say 'Do you want anything to eat?' or 'Do you want

to order?' And we still don't know if the food is any good,"
said the wife. — authors' note)

You're right, and they ought to ask you first, as a woman,
isn't that so? Still, we've come here to eat, let's not worry
about anything else. In the paper it said they've got a very
good Western food chef. There's everything on the menu,
hors d'oeuvres, entrees, sweets. And for seven yuan we
ought to get something, it's not just there for decoration.
(We thought that though they'd certainly spent less than
anyone else in the restaurant, they'd made the most informed choice. — authors' note) All we like now is to eat. After
the "cultural revolution", all our furniture, carpets, sofas,
everything was burnt and smashed to bits but we didn't buy
any new ones. What matters is eating well. We haven't got
any savings, we can't keep money. At the Red House Restaurant in Shanghai, they have a full French menu and their
grills are very good. The cakes at the Moscow Restaurant
aren't bad, as long as you stick to their speciality, cream
cakes. Kiesling's in Tianjin is also ordinary. ("Better than
Beijing," said his wife. — authors' note) That was in the
50s. Eating out in Beijing isn't bad. Last week we went to
the Zhiweiguan in Xinjiekou; they've got the best soup-
filled *ravioli* and *hundun* dumplings in Beijing. It's Hangzhou cuisine, and I was born in Hangzhou. They say the
chef comes from Hangzhou, too, and he really isn't bad. It
isn't far; we took a 19 bus to Xidan and then a 22 which
stops right outside.

I've eaten local food all over the world and the worst was
in Germany. I spent quite a few years there and the more I
ate, the more I began to think that the one thing the serious
Germans weren't serious about was food. Mind you, I was
there when they were at their poorest. I went back in 1981
and, my goodness, they certainly paid attention to eating

then! But it was really the service that was marvellous; the food wasn't that good. In 1945, I was in Austria. All we Chinese wanted to eat Chinese food but we hadn't any money and we couldn't get the condiments, so in the end we used to eat plain noodles. Have you ever eaten plain noodles? For several hundred Chinese, it was an emotional experience; we ate them and wept.

That Christmas in Bern, there were Nestle's chocolates and candied fruit everywhere. I was at the consulate and I stuffed myself with Nestle's chocolate, "the best in the world". The people at the consulate were furious but they didn't dare say anything as they were afraid of me.

I've been to all the Western food restaurants in Beijing except Maxim's and Minim's. It's not worth going to them. Do you know what those two words mean? One means "the biggest", the other, "the smallest". The biggest is for foreigners, the smallest is for the Chinese, so I don't want to go! (Pierre Cardin has opened two restaurants in Beijing, Maxim's and Minim's. — authors' note) There's one very funny thing about Beijing; the fast food restaurants are more expensive than ordinary restaurants. We've been to all of them and they're very expensive. They give something a foreign name and put the price up. Fast food isn't very competitive here because Chinese people have a lot of time. They can go to Tanglaoya and eat dog or invite guests to a Western food restaurant; they don't go out to eat in a fast food restaurant.

Every few days, we get on a bus, then we stroll about and finally look for a place to eat. We came here because we'd noticed an article in yesterday's paper saying that it would be open today. Foreigners have become "locals" and we locals have become "foreigners".

The steak isn't bad, perhaps a tiny bit tough. (When the

food came, they carefully arranged the table, fork to the left, knife to the right, and ate very correctly. The wife talked as she ate, "It's all back to front — they haven't brought the soup yet. Still, we can't wait for it, it might take forever." — authors' note) In Jakarta, they always overdo steaks and they are very tough. If you complain and ask for another, it will be exactly the same. Indians can't really cook, either. The best food in the world is Chinese and the best Western food in China is found in Hongkong.

My name? It's Hang Xiaozu. ("You've been talking to us for so long, I thought you must have recognized him!" His wife interrupted. — authors' note) That's right, I was part of the "Two Aircraft Companies' Uprising". Do you know it? It was a long time ago and most people have forgotten me by now. Over the last two years, though, I've been to quite a few social activities and quite a lot of people seem to re-member me. Some people can't believe I'm still alive. When I go abroad, some old friends ring up and say, "Are you the same Little Hang?" I am, but I'm Old Hang now.

I come from a very poor family. My father and elder brother were out of work for a long time and we had to sell all our possessions to survive. From when I was very young, I had one aim in life: to be an engineer, a radio engineer. What was radio like in the 1920s? There were big radios and receivers, a lot more antiquated than today's "old-fashioned" wirelesses. Radio only has a short history and it has changed very fast in the last 100 years. When I was in middle school, I used to help my richer school-mates to make radios. I didn't do it for money; it wouldn't be right to develop one's skills and charge money at the same time. I was happy to have the chance to try.

When I went to university, I was in the electrical en-gineering faculty — nowadays it's a very diversified subject, but in those days, there was just one faculty and it taught electrical engineering. We were divided into two groups, one for electrical engineering, the other for all the other electronic specialities we have today. I studied for two years but my family was so poor they could no longer afford the fees and I had to struggle to find the money myself. I built two radio stations in Hangzhou. There used to be only one official one which didn't broadcast during the day. Some of my fellow students got me to set one up, just for their own enjoyment. With that, I was able to finish my studies. What's more, I became quite well-known, and after I graduated, I was employed by the Hangzhou telephone company to set up a broadcasting station. In those days, the telephone company ran the broadcasting station. Though I worked in broadcasting, we didn't have electricity at home. So I used a charcoal stove for the solder to weld parts. I made my own accumulator and fixed up an electric light at home. A rich neighbour saw it and got me to make more accumulators which he was to sell, but he couldn't get anybody to buy them because they were really truck accumulators and he didn't know any truck drivers. Later another man managed to sell them because he knew the right sort of people. Watching them sitting there waiting for customers, I made up my mind never to become a businessman. After the victory in the Anti-Japanese War, anybody could get rich by shipping goods about on planes. I didn't do it. I couldn't do it. I could live well enough by my skills.

When I was at school, I was chairman of the student society. At that time, there were so many massacres, May 30th, March 18th and so on. We organised the students to go out to burn Japanese goods on the streets and demonstrate. At that time we felt that China was weak and oppressed, demonstrations or burning foreign goods were not

enough; we had to learn modern technology, to study technology for the sake of our country.

After I'd been working at the radio station for a while, I
passed an exam to enter the Europe-Asia Aviation Company, which was jointly run by Chinese and Germans. I
don't think there was much Chinese investment at the
beginning but it was later built up to 51% when it became a
"company managed by Chinese with joint Sino-foreign investment". Yes, there were joint ventures in those days.
When I joined the company, it was very small and the
technology was kept from the Chinese. When they were
repairing the planes, no Chinese was allowed to look — it
was really frustrating! We could only act as assistants.

I worked in the electric section. The German in charge
wasn't trained in electronics; he was an aircraft radio
operator, very uncultured. He'd been shot in the leg when
he was chasing sheep by plane over Inner Mongolia, so they
kept him at the company headquarters on ground service.
The Chinese manager didn't get on with him very well.
He'd studied radio engineering abroad but his knowledge
was theoretical rather than practical, so they both despised
each other and constantly quarrelled. I was promoted very
quickly; it was really a form of natural selection.

In those days, there was no radar navigation equipment
on board the planes; they used to rely on the navigator and
his maps and his knowledge of the terrain. I was almost
killed as a result. There was a newly arrived foreign pilot
who wasn't a very serious character. We flew along the
Yangtze and he got lost. He couldn't work out where we
were, he didn't know the cities and he couldn't locate Nanjing. I knew, and I knew we were headed for Suzhou but
there was a sound-proof window between us, so he couldn't
hear what I was saying. He couldn't understand my gestures

either but I knew what he was doing, he was bringing the plane down. We came down at Mocheng Township; I'll never forget the place. He was stupid, he just stood there whilst I ran off to telephone the company. The first thing the manager said was, "Who is that? Goodness! We thought he'd killed you, too!" Soon after that, they imported a larger plane with radar. The German didn't dare use it. I studied it in secret. It was broken and they had decided to send it back to Germany for repair, but I insisted on doing it myself and when I succeeded, my reputation soared. The manager had wanted it repaired because if there was no radar, the pilots wouldn't take off and the company would lose money!

I also copied the radar apparatus. I didn't dare say anything about it; I did it in secret. My salary was quite high at the time, so I bought the necessary equipment and built it at home. When the boss wasn't about, we tested it and we'd finished it when he came back from leave and we tried it out successfully. What's more, we improved it, incorporating American design features. After that, the manager sent me to Germany to do research. I was amongst the last to go to Germany. It was in 1940, during the Second World War.

The three others who went with me went into the Hansa Air Company but they didn't want me. They said, "He's the one who made the radar! We can't let him steal any more technology!" I asked to go back but the embassy was too busy packing up to leave and nobody did anything about it, so I stayed. After war was declared, I went to work for Siemens on aircraft radar and I stayed till 1945.

Life was very hard. Although wages were high, there was nothing to eat. The English bombers came over every day, so the chances of dying were pretty high. We were ordered not to run when we heard the sirens but to stay put. I used to calculate where the English bombs would drop and whether we were within the radius, but they weren't that accurate. They did bomb us once, but fortunately, it was my day off. The Germans didn't pay any attention to our political background, they let me work and do overtime.

When the war was over, I went to Vienna. When the five nations, the United States, the Soviet Union, Great Britain, China and France, won the war there was no Chinese flag at the victory celebrations. I went to ask but they said, "There is no Chinese flag!" I told them I had one. I had bought a Chinese national flag in Hongkong and put it beside my bed. I had also asked an overseas Chinese woman to make me a party flag. Naturally, it was the Nationalist flag, the Kuomintang flag, because I didn't know anything about the Chinese Communist Party at the time. All I knew was that there was a "dissenting Party" which made the Kuomintang feel uneasy. The overseas Chinese then pushed me into organizing an overseas Chinese committee. From then on, we could write "official documents", and had a seal and the position to make contact with the authorities; it was all "legal". At that time, Lu Keng, the correspondent of *Central Daily*, was with the army, officially accompanying the American army in Europe and, like us, he ate "plain noodles". ("In the 'cultural revolution', Lu Keng got us into trouble. The people who were investigating me wanted to know what was the relationship between my husband and Lu Keng and Dai Anguo," his wife interrupted. — authors' note) Those two are the only journalists I've ever been friendly with — well, Dai Anguo was my superior.

Lu Keng was very patriotic then. I still miss him. I'd like to see him again. His articles are still very good. What? He's back in America? When he returns, we'll eat plain noodles together.

The nearest Chinese consulate was in Switzerland, so I went there and the consul told me to take a refugee boat back home. Really! We weren't refugees, we wanted to go back to revive the nation. Later, I received money from home and went to France to attend an international aviation meeting. I stayed there six months and then my money ran out. And, once again, the embassy wouldn't have anything to do with us! Fortunately, there was a meeting of overseas Chinese in France and they asked me to report on the Chinese in Germany and Austria. At the meeting I criticized the embassy very strongly and so did everyone else there! The next day, the embassy sent me a plane ticket and told me to get out fast. I took a French plane to Jakarta, and then flew on to Kunming with China Airlines and in Kunming I boarded one of our own planes back to Shanghai.

By then the Europe-China Company had already become the Central Aviation Company, the larger of the two airlines in China. I became chief engineer and everyone supported me, just as before. In those days, what the chief engineer said was law; there was no discussion about it.

The Kuomintang was very keen to rope people in. I was a non-Party personage; they were polite to me. They even sent me to America for an inspection tour because they said I'd suffered in Germany. Soon after I got back, the Kuomintang ran away to Taiwan and they ordered Central Aviation to leave, too. We kept procrastinating, but we couldn't delay for ever and moved to Guangzhou. That didn't work out, so we moved to Hongkong. After that, we rebelled and came back to China. The "Two Aviation Companies' Uprising", that was us and China Airlines. The Aviation Ministry and CAAC are writing a book about it. They've been working on it for two or three years and it's almost finished.

The "Two Aviation Companies' Uprising" was the result
of the Communists' activities. The Number Two at Central
Aviation had shared a room with Premier Zhou Enlai at the
Whampoa Military Academy and he had connections in the
Party. I also participated; I was one of the members of the
committee that was set up during the uprising. There were
seven of us. Some didn't come back. Some came back to
China but left again later. I stayed. In November 1949, we
proclaimed the uprising and then came back to Guangzhou
to discuss it. The main question was remuneration. One
idea was that Hongkong dollars should be equated with
Chinese currency. That didn't work. Take me; I earned
4,000 Hongkong dollars a month, and how much was that
worth? With 4,000, you could buy a car at that time. Another idea was that we shouldn't lose out, that our standard
of living should be maintained. I favoured this method. The
manager didn't attend the meeting, so I represented the
Central Aviation Company and I finally managed to convince everyone. What had we come back for? To suffer?
How could we fix a price for the Communist Party to pay?
The Party cadres didn't attend the meeting either; they
wanted us to decide.

The general manager of Central Aviation came back but
he left afterwards. I was also a chief engineer, and so was
comrade Pan Guoding. He got divorced and returned to
China. He's a good man. But how he suffered in the "cultural revolution"! He wasn't used to life here and he hadn't
enough money; he sold everything he had, bit by bit. When
Zhou Enlai heard about it, he was very concerned and said,
"We shouldn't let Pan Guoding sell his possessions; we
must pay him enough!" Zhou Enlai also helped me. During
the movement against "three evils" and "five evils", I was
criticized but Zhou Enlai intervened and said, "Hang

Xiaozu can't do such bad things. If he were like to do that, he'd not have come back." So, one day I was being struggled against, the next, I was deputy leader of the struggle group.... Every time I saw Premier Zhou Enlai he would take my hand before I could say a word and say, "The aviation expert...." He arranged for me to go and work in Tianjin because just after liberation there were no foreign-style houses in Beijing and he was worried that I wouldn't be able to accustom myself to life in Beijing. In Tianjin, I was head of a secret factory and held four other posts concurrently such as the telecommunications engineer of the CAAC. At first, my salary was nearly 600 yuan a month but in 1952 I asked for it to be lowered and now it's about 300. Things were cheap then and China was in the middle of full-scale reconstruction and I felt uneasy having so much. Anyway I didn't come to work for money. Later, the factory came under the control of the Headquarters of the General Staff and I was designated as grade 2 engineer. In 1958 I began to do space-craft work. That was considered to be army work and I was given the rank of colonel. There were only two technicians. Both colonels and some people were unhappy about it because they'd been making revolution for most of their lives and they didn't get the same rank as a "returned aviation expert". In fact it was only an honorary rank — but my salary was higher than a major-general!

We got things done in the 50s; it wasn't so good in the 60s; people were dispersed, there was the "cultural revolution". Now I'm semi-retired. There are still things I can do and I've told the leadership, "It's not self-interest, but if there are any problems in the space programme, I can still help." I still go to the office every day. The chauffeur fetches me in the morning and I sit in the office and read the papers and I come back home at midday. I have to go because sometimes I want to borrow some equipment! I repair televisions, colour televisions. I don't bother with the old black and white sets any more. A lot of people ask me to do it, so this old man repairs televisions for other old people! There are lots of sets waiting at home. Not so many of my colleagues come now; they don't want to bother me. If your television breaks down, you can send it to me, but don't tell all your friends!

In 1981, I went back to Germany after 30 years. It was fine once I got there; my German and my technical skills are still there. All my colleagues at Siemens have retired and the young workers all thought of me as part of a previous generation. One of my instructors came back from Africa and drove a long way to see me — he really couldn't believe I was still alive. Alive, and still capable of doing a lot. If you've achieved something, you still get the rewards.

When I was abroad, I thought out ways of saving foreign currency for the country. Tinned food is cheap and I'm used to it, so I ate a lot. I didn't go to restaurants, except for banquets. The comrade who went with me was supposed to take care of me but I took care of him because he didn't know any German. Just before we left, he wanted to buy a colour television and I took him to a lot of places and we bought a broken set for just 40 yuan. He wanted to know if I could repair it; of course I could! I worked on it and it's fine. I suffered on the plane on the way back because I hadn't got any cigarettes. I wasn't saving foreign currency, I didn't buy any at the airport and they didn't have any for sale on the plane. I looked at my compatriots, each with two cartons of good cigarettes. I was dying for just one packet. They were members of the men's volleyball team, returning home after a series of matches. When we got to Beijing airport and were waiting for the customs inspection, I saw my wife waiting for me outside and shouted at her, "Throw me a packet of cigarettes!"

I'm resilient. During the "cultural revolution" I was struggled against for eleven months, but a few days ago, when the ministry asked me, "Who punished you in the 'cultural revolution'?" I said, "It was nothing, they weren't bad, I'm grateful to them!" They sent me off to cadres' school and I was the leader of the kitchen team, because I know about food! And the day before yesterday a Party cadre came to shake my hand and said, "I criticized you in the 'cultural revolution', I was wrong," and he wept. I said, "I meant it when I thanked you. When I was locked up, you went to buy tobacco for me." He's a good man. ("Just look at my old man. He was struggled against a lot during the 'cultural revolution', but he's still the same as ever. He even thanks them. They struggled against me; it was terrifying. They said I was the wife of a spy — they said I was a spy.... They took our carpet and our leather sofa away; we've got nothing left," the wife said angrily. — authors' note) They didn't get anywhere struggling against me, so they tried her!

The last time I went to West Germany, a comrade said, "Old Hang, don't go to see your German ex-wife!" How could I do that? She's in East Germany; it's more difficult for her to get to West Germany than it is for me, coming from China.

None of the children lives with us. Nor do we give them any money; we want them to be independent. We have a seven-room house with two toilets, large and small kitchens, all the rooms in use, all provided by the state. Perhaps I'd have acted differently in a different house. Only one of our five children went to university and is now a teacher in a middle school.

Oh dear, your shrimps aren't very good. When we had a banquet to celebrate the 30th anniversary of the "Two Aviation Companies' Uprising", we had crayfish, as thick as your arm and as long as this, served with a cream sauce... beautiful!

Translated by Frances Wood

The Hulan River Returns to the Sea

December 1984 in Heilongjiang.

We'd been asking about this restaurant for two days running.

Everybody knew that a few years earlier this place, owned and run by two sisters, had been in all the papers and on television, but nobody knew where it was or even if it still existed. Some people even insisted that they'd gone out of business and closed down.

MY sister said to come and talk to you, so here I am. Actually, it's been a good couple of years since anyone came to interview us.

I guess we should start with the opening of the restaurant. I was jobless and my sister had come back from working in the countryside. She used to be with an army land reclamation team and came back in '79. There was only my dad working then. My mum was a housewife. So what with an extra mouth to feed and me with no job — nobody wanted me — times were hard. They said nobody wanted me, but I wasn't up to much in school, so I guess I got my just deserts. I didn't have much option; the state didn't assign me to a job, so there wasn't much I could do. My sister got the odd bit of work with the neighbourhood committee embroidery workshop, but she got less than one yuan a day for that. They couldn't work too late in the evenings because they were worried about using up electricity.

So when we heard about the government policy relaxing a bit on private enterprise, the two of us sat up half the night working out how we could open up a restaurant. We did a rough estimate of finances and decided it ought to be a money-making proposition. We didn't calculate it down to the last penny; we just thought we'd give it a go. If state places could do well then we couldn't lose. We didn't know then that state places were subsidized up to the eyeballs. If we had, you can be sure we wouldn't have gone ahead.

We went to the neighbourhood committee. In those days it was still called a commune, an urban commune I guess you'd say, and they told us, "What do you think you're doing barging ahead like this just from hearing rumours? If you make a mistake, then what?" My sister said to them, "What do you mean by rumours? Hasn't it been reported on TV? It's straight from the Central Committee." But they said that anyway it hadn't been put into practice yet, that the official directives still hadn't come out and they couldn't be sure it was okay. A couple of days later, the both of us went back and this time they said to us, "Write out a proposal; we'll stamp it and send it on." So we wrote out an application. They added the line, "The signatories insist on making this application; please handle as you see fit." Then we took it back and went first to the bureau of commerce. They said it wasn't anything to do with them and sent us to the educated youth office. They didn't want to know either, but they were quite nice about it and told us if we were going to open up a restaurant it should be a seafood place because there was more money in it. They said we should notify them just before we opened and they would draw up a letter of congratulations. Anyway, after we'd gone through all the motions, we then had to go back to that commercial office — it wasn't called the bureau of industrial and commercial administration then, it was just an office — and they approved it all right away. Our licence was number 001, the very first privately owned restaurant. After that we went to the cereals bureau, the aquatic foodstuffs company, the health and sanitation bureau, the commercial bureau again and so on to arrange for our supplies of oil, grains and fish; then we got a health inspection certificate and finally we were in business.

The premises? Actually it was our own place, originally 13 square metres for commercial use, and that got upped to fifty-four in 1982. The day we opened, the educated youth office got the press here; then Xinhua News Agency came and the television and radio people got into the act and made a big fuss about us. When we opened they said we were the first private place in the whole city—that was true enough, we had the first licence; afterwards it turned out we were the first in the province, in the whole northeast and ultimately first in the country. I guess we were.

The money wasn't bad. In those days the deal was that you got your first three years without paying taxes, but it's not the same now. After that people just got one tax-free year. That first year we made over 2,000, an average of over 100 a month each. The second year we expanded a bit and took on a couple more staff. One was my brother-in-law — he wasn't married to my sister then — he'd come back from the countryside too. The other one was one of the neighbourhood kids who was unemployed; he's working in a factory now, he's taken over from his old man. We worked altogether ten and a half months in that second year and made over 4,000, so our average income stayed the same as the first year. Of course my sister and I took a little more, it was our place! But the other two did okay, after all one was a relative and the other was a close mate, so we had to do right by them.

Yes, sure we went into it as much as we could beforehand. What happened was that a lot more private places opened up, and for one thing there were a lot of retired chefs whose cooking skills were well above ours; on top of that prices for seafood kept going up all the time. Even ending up with a few thousand was quite something. As we say in this part of the country, it's wonderful. What else did we want to have?

At the end of the second year, the neighbourhood committee asked us if we wanted to go in with them in the Hulan restaurant. Their reasoning was that with two restaurants in the same road, neither of us was making that much. We'd be better off joining forces and edging out all the small road vendors around. My sister wanted to do it, but I wasn't all that keen. The Hulan was collectively owned and there'd be a lot less flexibility. It was too strict; if we went into it we'd be state employees and would have to do what people said. So the two of us thrashed it out and finally she talked me into it. She said we'd be better off in a collective place even though it might not be quite up to a state-owned enterprise. It would still give us a pension, labour insurance, sick pay and work disability benefits. Take mixing flour, for instance. We'd had two accidents within three months of buying our flour mixer. The first time my brother-in-law caught his fingers in it but managed to pull them out before he got too badly hurt; the second time it was me, I got my thumbnail taken off. It hurt so much I was up all night long. If I'd been disabled because of that, we'd have had to close down. But if I injured my hand at the Hulan they'd have to support me for the rest of my life, am

I right? So being in a collective, you're better off. There are other advantages too, like you don't have to worry about your basic supplies, nor whether or not you're making money, so it's not a bad deal.

When we'd made our minds up, we went down to bargain with the neighbourhood committee. Our first condition was that we wanted to put in three employees, not just two — our brother-in-law had to be included as well. They agreed, and even made it two workers and one cadre — my sister was to be deputy manager. The second condition was that they should purchase our equipment, like our flour mixer and our other kitchen stuff. They came right out with an offer of 950 for the lot. Our third thing was that we could keep our old premises, that they wouldn't knock down our new 40 square metres; that would be our accommodation. We got a bit of flak on this because the restaurant premises were classified as "temporary commercial premises" and couldn't be converted to residential space. Anyway we've managed to live in this 40 metres up to now, but when the state wants it back we'll have to dutifully return it to them. But when do you think they're going to get round to putting up high rises on *this* street? We'll face that one when it happens. At any rate, that's where we're living now.

So everything got settled, and on the 1st of January, 1983, we officially joined up and they announced on the spot that my sister was appointed deputy manager. The manager was the same person who'd originally started there in '58 during the "great leap forward".

The Hulan has over forty workers now, plus several long-term people who are on contract. Now everyone in collective and state places is on contract; we were ahead of our time and it turned out to be the right thing to do. We're open for breakfast, lunch and supper, nine hours in all; we work in two shifts and get one day off a week. You couldn't work things that way in your own place! You've got to slog your guts out from morning till night worrying about losing money. In summer you have to take a cart and sell snacks by the river and in winter wander round the streets selling stuff, it's no joke. So being at the Hulan is a lot less wear and tear.

The money's about the same, maybe a little less than being self-employed but that doesn't matter much. My sister gets just over seventy a month. I'm in charge of the rice and cereals section and get a little more than she does, just over eighty. It's not to be sneezed at, that bit extra; it does make a difference!

Well, yes, there are people who say we've taken a step backwards. But I don't see it that way. We were the pioneers in opening up a privately-owned place, and we're the first in this joint venture too. Maybe we're the first again in the whole country, the trend now is toward joint ventures. Whether you like it or not, that's the way things are going.

The benefits are good. When we had our own business we didn't go to a film for over a year. Now we get tickets given to us by the state and even time off to go.

We've got a higher social status too. We're official employees now; my sister's a cadre and she's in the Party too. D'you think you'd be in the Party if you were self-employed?

So there's a lot less to worry about.

Everything's taken care of.

Why bother with the responsibility system? Do you think it's manageable with forty to fifty people? You still have to knock yourself out like being self-employed and there's no guarantee you'll succeed. The Hulan is edging into profit now; we handed over more than 9,000 last year which was not bad going. If you work it out carefully, we don't make as much as we did with our own place; there we handed over an average of about 100 yuan a person. There are too many restaurants around these days, but it's not our problem to worry about any more.

It's like when they go to Weihu Mountain, Yang Zirong wants to but Luan Ping doesn't: "It's a matter of choice, you can't force people against their will"; oh right, it is Hu Biao, not Yang Zirong.

Him? Oh, we sure went a lot of trouble over him. When we joined the collective, we originally thought of bringing him with us but the neighbourhood committee disagreed. His residence papers weren't with our local committee, so they refused to have him. He said we just abandoned him, that we kicked him out because we were looking after ourselves. We'd only been at the Hulan a couple of days when he came and threw a brick through the glass in the main doors. The manager called the police and they got him and made him fork out 36 yuan in damages. That shows you how the system works; if it'd been a private restaurant, would the police have jumped to it like that? So it's better working in the state system. Anyway, it wasn't our fault; he wasn't registered in our neighbourhood. It's all right now, he's got a secure job as a factory worker.

To be honest, I wouldn't eat here if I were you. They're not such good cooks, the food's not wonderful. If it's somebody we know we can give them bigger portions, but if it doesn't taste like much what does it matter?

Translated by Carole Murray

The Third Wave

He has taken a leave of absence from his work to set up a company. He is 31.

NOWADAYS, Alvin Toffler's book *The Third Wave* has itself become a wave. Not only is there the book, there's also a film. I saw it at the beginning of the year (1984). Someone brought a video of it back from abroad: it looked as if it were a big secret. Whoever took it to some work unit to borrow a video recorder to show it was questioned left and right, and he had to do it through pulling strings. But when I went to Sichuan in the summer, I found it had already made its way to some of the smaller county towns. Although *The Third Wave* is quite an achievement, I think it should be classed together with science stories for youngsters and utopian novels. John Naisbitt's book *Megatrends: Ten New Directions Transforming Our Lives* has turned out to be more useful and inspiring to us.

I first read about the third wave three years ago in a magazine article. Toffler divides civilization into three stages: the first wave is the agricultural age; the second, the industrial age; and the third, which we are just now entering, is called the age of information. When I first saw this analysis, I felt terribly excited; I sensed a challenge. I asked several friends of mine also involved in creative literary work to have a look at it; unfortunately they were totally absorbed in toiling away at their respective literary tasks.

That's right; I have worked at literary creation. I've written three novels and several novellas as well as the script for a play. I can write as many as 10,000 characters per day. Naturally this makes me feel quite good about myself. People are writing a lot about the economic reforms, sticking in bits about struggles over government policy — basically imitations of the Manager Qiao stories.* I prefer to write pieces reflecting the unity between high technology and lofty emotions these times require. This point of view is the same as that in *Megatrends*. However, I haven't written anything for more than half a year; this has surprised people who know me, because I stopped just when conditions were excellent for writing. I feel that in its present state, literature is an "industry" in decline; it lacks vitality.

I suppose I have "cast down the pen to follow a trade", but ever since I entered the world of economic activity, I have felt things are extremely promising in it.

Nowadays everybody wants to do a little business, wants to make money; they all go on and on about establishing companies. The spirit with which we all organized "combat teams" during the "cultural revolution" is now being employed to organize companies. Everyone is climbing on the bandwagon and at the same time trying to knock the others off. You start up a popular technology development corporation; I establish one too. I'm scared to death you'll steal my rice bowl, so I plot ways to edge you out of business, either by absorbing you or paying you to close up shop. Actually, most of these companies have yet to get any

---

* Stories about the problems of a factory manager in instituting reforms, published by Panda Books as *All the Colours of the Rainbow*, © 1983 by Jiang Zilong.

business done and make any money! A lot of people don't run their businesses well at all.

I've heard you can make a bundle by establishing a small newspaper. Let's say there are 27,000 Chinese characters in your first issue. Each copy will cost you about two *fen* to produce, while the cover price will be four *fen* or even five. Anyway, you will sell them to the distributor at three *fen* apiece. If you produce, say, 100,000 copies each time, you'll make a clean 1,000 yuan. If it's a weekly, that makes 4,000 yuan a month. Carry a lot of thriller-type stories, adventures, or whatever — not love stories, those haven't been too popular lately, although Qiong Yao's are pretty good, and you don't even have to pay her royalties; she's in Taiwan! So why should you stop with just 100,000 copies? What's more, you can publish serialized fiction. This week a case will have been solved while another series in the same issue will just be getting off the ground. This way, the readers will have to buy every issue! You can carry advertisements as well; that means even more money. Not bad, eh — have I figured it exactly or haven't I? When I asked around about this prospect, small papers had already been set up with much fanfare in many places. They proceeded to cut each other's throats by such ruses as sweepstakes which lured readers with prizes of several hundred yuan. Then I heard the authorities were taking measures to stamp out these "indecent" papers! Isn't that a laugh? Yesterday I went to place a long-distance phone call, and while waiting for the call to go through I noticed a booth near me with three guys jammed into it so tight they couldn't shut the door. One was saying: "I can't get there tomorrow morning, damn it! Don't you know you need official permission to buy an airplane ticket in Beijing? I'm getting on the train tonight; I'll buy a ticket from the conductor after I get on. How much money can you hold on to there in Guangzhou? Tomorrow I'll withdraw a few more thousand for you; we have to get those goods no matter what! You still don't know my damned account name? It's 'Elegance, Incorporated'!'' The guy next to him in the booth, who was wearing a polyester suit, hastily grabbed the receiver and shouted: ''Wait a second, wait a second! I have a few things to say to you.'' But what more could he have to say? They're all like this — it's really a scream. They all have the zeal of revolutionaries, but both their communications and their grasp of theory are inadequate. Not many of them know what they're doing. Whatever we do seems to start with a headlong rush into action, only to be destroyed by competition.

I've worked at many different jobs, but never in the business sector. Just like everybody else, when I was 16 I was sent to the countryside. I went to Heilongjiang Province to do farm work in a production and construction corps. I was then a ''whelp'', because my father was a ''reactionary academic authority'' and my mother a ''spy'', so I had to work like a horse. Then — you can use the cliché ''first love'' if you wish — I became enamoured of a woman, a ''girl of iron''; she was our company's assistant political instructor, an educated youth from Harbin, a real go-getter, two years older than myself. She really understood me. At any rate, her world was warm and wonderful enough to me at that time. Then representatives from universities came to choose students. Quite a few old workers recommended me, while the company cadres recommended her. She came to see me, had a cry, and hoped aloud that I would let her go, as she was sick to death of the work there. I couldn't say anything to that; I felt like a real hero. How was I to know she had already ''sold'' me to the company cadres, telling them I refused to draw a clear line between myself and my family? She had put me out of the running long ago. The night before she left, the company held a banquet to send her off. While they were eating, I stood outside the window and watched. Her face was flushed with drink; she was very beautiful. Later that night, I had someone tell her to meet me at our old trysting-place, the primary school. It was a damn farce, but I just wanted to hear her say a few words. There was no heat in the room; it was terribly cold. When she finally came, she snapped, "So what is it you want?" making me feel like a fool. I hit a window with my fist; naturally the glass broke, making a messy cut on my hand. I hated myself for being such an ass; apparently she did too, for she turned on her heel and left. Suddenly, I lost my eyesight. I had to crawl back to my dormitory, and several days passed before I could see again. I wrote a long poem: "Song of the North".

The next year, when it was nearly time for the university recruiters to come round again, I had already become leader of the machinery platoon. This machinery platoon was actually a bunch of tractor drivers. Just as spring ploughing was beginning, the campaign to "criticize Lin Biao and Confucius" was reaching its peak. The company commander, who was in charge of production, wanted to concentrate on the spring ploughing, but the company political instructor, who was in charge of revolutionary affairs, called for a halt in production and a big criticism meeting. Actually the conflict between these two leaders was a personal one. What was it all about? Well, once the political instructor's younger brother had an argument with the company commander's wife. They fought and fought, and somehow the woman's trousers came down. Immediately she accused the politicalinstructor's youngerbrother of rape

— but do you think he was really capable of it? Anyway, that's how the whole vendetta got started. To tell you the truth, when I saw how distraught the company commander was over the whole thing, I really felt sorry for him; corps headquarters had sent people to keep a very sharp eye on the progress of the spring ploughing. But the political instructor was the one who had control of people's files, and this had direct bearing on the possibility of my attending university. He probably thought of me as a real intellectual. I found myself in a difficult position, right in the middle of things. Then corps headquarters sent me to work on a "Criticize Lin Biao and Confucius" exhibit, so I hoofed it on out of there. In the daytime I worked on the exhibit, while at night I returned to the company barracks to encourage my mates in the platoon to work overtime on the ploughing for the company commander's sake.

At this time I ran into another problem in the corps. We were living in temporary quarters above the corps' auditorium on the same floor as two women announcers who were also in the corps. One night late, I heard a piercing cry from one of the women. I hadn't fallen asleep yet, and I rushed into the hall....The next day, the corps security section made an investigation, asking me what I knew of the matter. I said I knew nothing. Later, I heard the investigation revealed the girl had been messed with by her boyfriend. She was the daughter of an old farm worker who insisted on pressing charges against the man since he had come to the corps alone without being sent from anywhere, hence her father had forbidden them to have contact. Actually this is not the way things were at all. I saw who came out of the girl's room: it was a shop assistant in the corps store, some relative or other of the deputy corps commander. When I went bounding into the hall, I ran smack into him. That was the truth of the matter!

Soon it was time again for the recruitment of students. Being in the corps headquarters, I had the chance to make friendly contact with the recruiters and the people in the workers' propaganda team. If you made a pleasant impression on them, they might feel you were a more reliable choice than just any old witless fool foisted upon them by others. However, it was not these people who made the final decision; the final decision was made by officials in the company on the one hand and the corps on the other. In the company, three platoons recommended me; by the time they sent some of their old workers to be delegates to the meeting at which the decision was to be made, I had already visited every house and home to do persuasive "work" on my own behalf. The political instructor was wary of me; although I had helped him write an important critical article, he didn't show what was on his mind, but just looked at the company commander. The company commander was a good guy. He was grateful to me for having helped him out at spring ploughing time, but he also understood the politics of the situation, so he pretended not to agree to choose me. When the political instructor saw this, he decided to choose me, whereupon the company commander grunted as if assenting grudgingly. The old worker delegates roared their approval, and that's how the company approved me. In the corps, I heard that about twenty candidates had been put forth from various companies, and that aside from those who were sure as shooting to get in through pulling strings, my only serious rival was a deputy commander of the armed company. The armed companies were the darlings of the corps, and moreover this guy had quite a name in the corps, was an "educated youth", a middle school graduate and a Party member! I knew my rival's qualifications like the back of my hand; the only thing to my credit was that I was the "potentially educable offspring" of politically dubious parentage. This hardly accounted for anything in the company, where the political instructor felt he had been duped and wanted to drop me in favour of another candidate. So every night I rode my bike back to the company barracks, which were a considerable distance away, while in the daytime I pressed my case at the corps headquarters.

One night late, as I was crossing the dam of the reservoir near the company compound, a man with a spade in one hand stopped me. Who was it? It was that deputy commander of the armed company. The creep had gotten nervous about having me as a competitor and wanted to "snuff" me. We both knew exactly what he was about, so we fought it out there in the dark, and after fighting we went our own ways, both without a sound. By this time, do you know how tightly I held the corps in the palm of my hand? I had possession of some materials that incriminated the relation of the deputy corps commander who had been the culprit in the incident with the woman announcer. I made the deputy commander understand that it would be best for him if he let me go without a fuss. In addition, an old friend of my father's was in charge of the railway link our corps depended upon for transportation. Finally, I had people both in the meeting where they were to choose the candidates and at the central telephone switchboard. If anything untoward were to happen, they would contact me right away, and I would call the railroad man and have him call the corps. This is how I was finally chosen to leave. In the end I sent the incriminating materials to the corps' security section anyway.

This experience of mine provided the material for one of my novels; I feel it's the best fiction I've written. Of course, it hasn't been published.

I had studied chemistry, and it happened that year they were looking for chemistry students. My graduation project was rather creative, if I may say so. But chemistry is not where my true interest lies. Later, I changed my occupation several times, working as a reporter and at other jobs.

Implementing overall economic reform to stimulate the economy has become an irreversible trend.

At the beginning of 1984, I read a few books, some related to economics, some not. Yes, it's true, in this world there's no absolute standard to distinguish what is related from what's not. For example, take the book *Hotel* by Arthur Haley. What is it? A popular novel. But doesn't it have a certain educational value? It does. Arthur Haley has used scientific methods to paint a complex, comprehensive portrait of a large modern hotel. While I read it, I started to think seriously about starting such a business.

At first, I wanted to start a hotel for domestic travellers, actually a large hotel. Investigation revealed that the present rate of available beds to travellers arriving in Beijing was one to three or four. Actually, even if the rate were one to one or even two to one, all you would need is good planning and the ability to compete. At that time, state-owned businesses could not start hotels because they were not allowed to erect new structures; they could only use pre-existing guesthouses or air-raid shelters. When I got my idea, I took a close look at various aspects of the situation and at technical details, and drew up a preliminary feasibility study. Naturally I also made some basic estimates, all of them rough; some of my friends are experts in this area. At the same time, I took another look at Arthur

Haley's *Hotel*. Haley really gives an inside view of the operation; he's provided me with quite a few tips! I find it amusing that if he knew what I was doing with his book, he would have to bow to me; after all, he just wrote *Hotel* for fun, and I'm actually going to set one up! Moreover, the place I'm planning will not simply be a business; after we show a profit, I plan to reinvest it to establish a centre for the dramatic arts and a private university — a real one, one that awards academic degrees. But where is the capital to build this hotel to come from? I thought of all kinds of strategies, among which one was to find an industrial unit from outside Beijing who needed to establish a permanent office in the capital to facilitate communication and get their products to the right customers. Taking advantage of tax reform and the responsibility system that gives the factory head independent decision-making power, they would give me the capital; I would build the structure and rent it back to them. At the same time I thought to myself: this mustn't be just any ordinary hotel. It should also be a site for business offices and should have the potential to become a communications and information centre as well as an exhibition centre for industrial products. In this case, the cost of all the interior fixtures could be reduced. Televisions, telephones, lighting and even wall paint could be supplied by the manufacturers at low cost, for their use in our hotel would be in itself a kind of advertisement, a very effective advertisement. I got in touch with a few units, and they were all very interested and supportive, but none of them dared to commit funds. They wanted to know my background, audit my finances, see if I had any financial backing. There was one group with more daring than the rest, a county government in Hebei Province; they offered me 200,000 yuan on only one condition: that they be allowed to send someone to oversee the disbursement of funds. But what is 200,000 yuan good for? Our estimate of the lump sum of capital required was more than 10 million yuan.

Another possibility was group investment; we could invite capital from rural households with incomes of 10,000 yuan or more. But after a period of contact I discovered that while peasants do want to put their liquid assets into business ventures, they don't really understand the process and they are not amenable to commercial capital management methods. They are timid and want to see immediate results; they prefer smaller ventures that they can see and touch to larger investment ventures. Even if you make them trustees or shareholders, they won't be willing; as soon as they understand they will not have direct control over people, they back off. They all want to be managers and to be first in line to manage the money.

I also thought of seeking foreign capital. It's not that I can't get hold of it, it's that it's too expensive. I discussed it with a foreign businessman who consented to sign a cooperative agreement. However, after I examined the prospect closely it proved to be unworkable. He agreed to provide all the capital necessary for construction prior to the opening of the hotel at an interest rate of about 1.35% — actually a bit higher than stipulated in the agreement. He required that the construction of the hotel be contracted by open bid. This was fine; I had originally thought to seek bids for the construction. But he wanted to know the results of the bidding, and to this I could not agree, because I had already learned that he was in the process of negotiating an investment in the equipping of a modernized construction company. He would invest money in my venture only to get the same money back from the construction company; it would be nothing more than his profiting by changing money from one pocket to the other. He wanted to make me into a middleman, but nothing doing. He shouldn't have thought that just because our women's volleyball team are third-time champions I was going to set up balls for *him* to spike, no way.

While I've been in this process of planning, the 20-storey China International Trust and Investment Corporation Building has gone up in Jianguomenwai. News has come out that across the street they're planning a 50-storey tower; they've already marked out the foundations for the Shangri-La Hotel, a joint venture with a Hongkong group, over by Purple Bamboo Park; and the municipal government has decided to allow state-owned businesses to establish "tertiary enterprises". However, in the process of planning I've come up with new ideas and schemes....I can't talk about them in detail. We've already gotten a business permit and discussed concrete problems with some concerned organizations. In future, after we are exposed to the natural selection that is born of competition, we may become an unstoppably strong group. Eventually I hope to build my hotel.

Theoretical preparations? What sort of theoretical preparations do you mean? The kind one makes by reading, or the kind one makes by investigating the current situation? I've read some books, a few things by Western economists, as well as the first volume of Marx's *Capital* and some socialist political economy. The Soviet model is no longer applicable, and neither are some of the methods discussed during the "cultural revolution" such as the "nine parts private one part public" land system or the later "tithe tax" land system....I feel the most important thing is to understand and try to predict the contemporary Chinese economic model; this involves more than just economics and political economy. I have tried to find friends and colleagues who can talk about these things, but I've found that few people understand even the basics. Some people are not even aware of reality, don't know that we're on the verge of a pluralistic, unprecedented, hopeful era.

Although our company was not the first to be established, it may happen that we "new managers", who have somewhat more determination and more theoretical training than others, may turn out to be the "third wave" that will wash up all these "old managers" with their "trade companies" and "service companies". My determination comes from my past defeats and successes....

It's possible that we will fail. I feel that economics gives me a broad scope of activity, that for a strong young man to sit home and write is a waste of his talent. The only reason I chose literary work before was to find a way to eat and be relatively free at the same time. Western theorists think that "if China's overall economic reforms do not succeed, the only remedy will be a return to the Stalinist economic thinking developed by Mao Zedong". I don't think this is a very great possibility. For not only cannot what's done be undone; if we recognize the importance of taking a macroscopic view, the reforms will not completely fail. I may experience personal defeat; this is a possibility. If by some chance I really make a mess of things, I'll go back to writing fiction. My autobiography will do nicely; my experiences and what I'm thinking and doing in the present would make a good bestseller. Even if I succeed I may write it, but not right now. I can't enter the market with a pen in my hand, can't divide myself between two careers....

Translated by Stephen Fleming

About "Chinese Profiles"

Sang Ye and Zhang Xinxin

SANG YE: A few years ago I was writing a column for the Hongkong paper *Wenhuibao* called "Personalities of the Mountains and Rivers". When the column had been going for about three or four months I got this criticism from some readers I knew well: "It's called 'Personalities of the Mountains and Rivers', so why no mountains or rivers in it, only personalities?" They were quite right. I never wrote anything about mountains and rivers as long as the column lasted. I remember that more than once I tried to explain this away by saying that my intention had always been to write about personalities who were like mountains and rivers.

Although I have been to many famous mountains and great rivers landscape has never meant much to me. Landscapes to me are static things that change little with the passage of time, apart from in such catastrophes as the Tangshan earthquake. If you go today to look at all the views Xu Xiake described in his travel writings in the seventeenth century you will find them much the same. Besides, there are still people tirelessly writing away about the eternal landscapes that have been famous since ancient times. What I want to experience and to pass on to my readers are living, moving human events. This idea is of course rather a biased one, and owes much to the fact that I started out writing news stories for the papers. Only the very best journalists can describe a still life.

Only after I had been writing for some time did I realize how superficial I was being. Even though there were some ordinary people among the personalities I wrote about, they were outstanding ordinary people, like some of the figures in the chapter on assassins in Sima Qian's *Records of the Historian*. I often felt that a column like that and interviews like that could only show an incomplete world. Had anyone asked me I could not possibly have asserted that the personalities I was writing about were carrying all the endeavours of the people.

Late in the autumn of 1983, when I had some time set aside for my own creative writing, Wang Yu, the editor of the literary supplement of the New York Chinese newspaper *Meizhou Huaqiao Ribao*, asked me to go to see Zhang Xinxin. "Tell her to keep on writing," he said, "because we've got plenty of space." A couple of months later my column in the paper came to an end, and the special feature *Chinese Profiles* by Zhang Xinxin and myself was given top billing in the paper's supplement. The people for whom *Chinese Profiles* was originally written were patriotic overseas Chinese on the other side of the Pacific. We wanted our articles to be a bridge between them and our shared endeavours here. Wang Yu, the editor of the supplement, has had a very clear understanding of the significance *Chinese Profiles* may have for both authors and readers. To this date he is still giving us a regular column with no set number of words, which goes right against the first rule of the layout of a column. As a writer who also does some editing I am very much aware of how valuable this is technically, and not only technically.

In October 1984 five literary magazines — *Shanghai Wenxue (Shanghai Literature)*, *Shouhuo (Harvest)*, *Zuojia (Author)*, *Zhongshan (Mount Zhong)* and *Wen xuejia (Writer)*—decided to publish pieces from *Chinese Profiles* simultaneously in their first issues for 1985. This brought us even more readers. Now that we were bringing *Chinese Profiles* home we made some adjustments in the contents to suit the tastes of the readership we knew best and cut out some notes that were only of significance to readers abroad. This is why we are publishing a hundred pieces in the series although we wrote even more than that. In including just one hundred ordinary Chinese people's own accounts of their lives and ideals in the book of *Chinese Profiles* we are not going back on our original intentions.

Neither the form nor the kind of material used in *Chinese Profiles* is our own invention. It has been some ten years since the value of recorded oral literature and history was reaffirmed in America. Many readers have drawn comparisons between Studs Terkel's *American Dreams: Lost and Found* or his *Working* and *Chinese Profiles*. There are indeed points of similarity, even identity, between them. It is also worth mentioning that Studs Terkel has also written a book of spoken recollections of the Great Depression. This has something in common with the collective memories of the "cultural revolution" in *Chinese Profiles* and with how we have handled them.

But *Chinese Profiles* is based on the Chinese nation. Because of differences in national environment and ecology there is hardly a single person in the book who shows the Western spirit of starting out by saying they want this and that, or of following up the failure of an old dream by dreaming a new one, even if that too is going to end in failure. The inner riches of our nation, like some grammatical usages of the spoken language, are hard to convey fully in writing, even when using the form of transcribed speech. One often needs the collision of minds brought about by cool questioning in a set environment. What comes out that way can have a dual meaning.

From a purely sociological point of view it is possible to use the explanation that these are fictional collectives to negate some forms of supposedly abnormal group consciousness. But it is precisely this group consciousness which needs no explanations that makes the oral narratives of the speakers in *Chinese Profiles* different from those in Terkel's books. In theory, every individual ought to tell a different story in a different way from every other individual. In fact you can often find either one of the following narrative methods at work, or both simultaneously: one is a way of talking that is not Chinese but like the narration in Greek tragedy: starting in the middle of the story. The other is that although they may have in common the recognition of a key point and the wish to express more about it, the narrators mention the key point only very briefly and then pass on, while going into great and repeated detail about common experiences in shared time and place.

Although there are both tears and laughter here, as well as some very flowery abuse and extremely vigorous remarks, we have not been able to use them to the same realistic effect as in *American Dreams: Lost and Found*. When noting how the use of a particular word or expression exactly caught the speaker's psychology, we often found ourselves unable to put our fingers on something that undoubtedly was there, something that taxonomists would call a marker and that a plastic artist would regard as technique.

That is why such differences as there are between *Chinese Profiles* and oral literature abroad are connected with such cultural phenomena as Chinese styles of thought and expression.

Would it be possible to use some other form, such as "onlooker's records", to show the lives of a hundred ordinary Chinese people? It should be. One of the main newspapers in Taiwan has a column called "My Other Half". It is a first-person account of a spouse, in which the "he" or "she" is shown through the eyes of a first-person narrator. Although this column is mainly about celebrities I think it's rather original. At least, it opens up one side of the situation to reveal supposedly tiny and trivial details that do not usually get out.

The background to the literature of oral record is the recording of oral literature: many works in our literary heritage are in fact reworked transcriptions.

The reason why we chose the form of oral literature to describe a hundred ordinary Chinese people is because this is a form that gets closer to reality. It can narrow the gap between the written words and the reader, and between those words and reality. We also believe that in a society in which there already exists a rather quick and direct communication network among the common people, a network that uses all available media, readers generally prefer immediacy and actuality. In addition, a work trying to portray all strata of society must choose the form that will most easily express what it has to say.

Sociologically speaking, *Chinese Profiles* may not do as well as the speaker in one of our pieces, "A Riot of Colours". Although we have tried as hard as we possibly can, we have not been able to portray everything we

experienced. On top of that there is a very great deal indeed
that we have not experienced, or failed to notice, or did not
get hold of when we had the chance to do so.

Several friends have already discussed the sociological
value of *Chinese Profiles*. As we see it, all the collection has
done has been to give a fairly full coverage of the individual
in society, especially the individual's educational standard,
private life, social interactions, and group and organiz-
ational thinking. It is natural that deviation and social
controls also come out in the collection. In addition, the
collection expresses social inequalities: stratification, gender and gender characterization. Just as my theoretical
grounding in many other areas is very inadequate, I have
only dabbled in sociology. I do not regard the collection as
research data, but as a literary work that has drawn on some
methods and findings of sociological research. Before
anyone starts judging *Chinese Profiles* by the standards of
sociology I intend to make myself scarce. But there was one
concept that gradually grew stronger and stronger during
the interviewing for this collection: cultural factors. I
wonder whether our social scientists should not pay some
attention to cultural factors as well as relations of
production. If I'm wrong you are welcome to laugh at me as
someone who doesn't know what he is talking about.

Before we chose the topic of this collection Zhang Xinxin
and I had the chance of co-operating on another topic. It
was about a "small handful of people" who are on
everyone's lips but who live in "confusion". When the
archive material had all been sorted out and we had met the
person who was to be the main character in the story, talked
to him and made some films for reference Zhang Xinxin
raised a problem: "Writing about a subject like this now has
audience appeal and may even win us some applause, but it

hasn't got much relevance today." While she made a series of decisions we wrote the first chapter of this other book, *Dusk*. After that she insisted that we drop the project. At the time I protested to her a number of times that it was precisely because the subject was so far removed from real present-day life and the central figure was so clearly in a different class fortress from us that it was a very apt and timely one for her now that she had been given such a hard time on account of her writing. Zhang Xinxin insisted repeatedly, "I'd much rather get close to life; I'd much rather write about a hundred ordinary people." So one of the background reasons why *Chinese Profiles* was completed was because she insisted on sticking to the subject. I still hope that in the future I will be able to complete *Dusk* with Zhang Xinxin. It may well be a new kind of novel in the form of news stories.

The first thing we did was to draw up a list of the sort of people we wanted to interview. In this list some of the spaces were filled in with the names and addresses of our intended narrators. Some only had their professions or ages. In some cases we only had a reminder of an area, such as, "Don't forget to include a real Taiwanese". Of the named individuals in the original list the only ones that are in the final version of *Chinese Profiles* are Aisin Gioro Pu Jie, the younger brother of China's last emperor, and Gu Jianfen. But once we had drawn up our framework even conversations with people met on trains were not just the result of chance encounters. If we didn't find the kind of person we needed the first time, we would try again; if one person wouldn't talk we would start a conversation with the next one. We ended up spending all our time rushing everywhere by train, endlessly talking and searching.

Take the Taiwan fisherman, for example. We called on a

number of people either separately or together. Some of the people we interviewed were great talkers, some had quite a high social standing and some were people in the news. We wrote them up, then tore up what we had written. The reason why we were not satisfied was simple: they had all settled on the mainland, in the United States or in Hongkong. None of them were Taiwan residents any longer. Besides, we already had people of similar standing and character in the collection. This left us with no choice. We had to find someone with roots in Taiwan, and an ordinary person too. After covering half of China visiting "Taiwan Summer Camps" and bringing back a whole lot of leads to non-residents of Taiwan, Young Zheng, a reporter on the *Meizhou Huaqiao Ribao*, suddenly came up with the suggestion, "Go to the South China Sea and wait for a typhoon." That was how we wrote that piece. Of course, because of the limits imposed by the "I'll be going back anytime now" feeling the fisherman's account of himself was not nearly as fluent and easy as those of the great majority of people we interviewed. But had he started shooting his mouth off we would probably not have been able to write it down, or to have got it published even if we had written it down. The other possibility is that he would have been punished after his return. By comparison, the people over here really are very bold when it comes to talking, expressing opinions and making judgements, even though everyone agrees unanimously that "it's only been possible these last few years...."

We only give the Taiwan fisherman as an example because everyone has shown so much interest in how we got someone from Taiwan to talk. In fact very ordinary people were much harder to get into conversation with. For example, during the craze for "Ten Thousand Yuan

Households" last year, it was not easy to find Yang Sixian, the man in "Dragon Gate" who could ride the crest of the wave without losing his clarity of mind.

We probably interviewed several hundred people for this collection. Now that the project is finished, I reckon that this year of rushing all over the place and being so sure we were right as we "wore our own boots to kick a football for the public" was both for Zhang Xinxin and myself a meaningful kind of accumulation and preparation for writing. Now that it has all been cooked and served to our customers the precipitate that remains is something rare and well worth having.

I am sure that there will be different views on how far *Chinese Profiles* is literature. In the West, where writers and their works are categorized rather more carefully, oral literature counts as non-fiction. Writers of non-fiction can be subdivided into writers of reportage, writers of actuality, writers of oral literature and so on. The *Compendium of Unofficial Histories of the Qing Dynasty* has a piece on Chu Fusheng in the section on marvels that reads:

"In the past there were people famous for their art. Mr Meng's painting, Yang Boli's poetry, Chen Wuquan's mathematics and Dong Xingfen's arts of immortality were all on everyone's lips. Chu Fusheng was famous for his pugilism."

So one or two centuries ago there were people who understood art in such a way as to include magicians and skilled practitioners of the martial arts as artists. Go back another thousand years and you will find the term we now use for economists being used to refer not to those who dealt with money and grain but to those who administered and saved their countries, what we would call statesmen. This shows how much the meaning of a specialist term can change over time; and such changes will continue in future.

An older author said to us, "In another five years you should write another book about *Chinese Profiles* five years on." We feel reluctant to agree rashly to any such expectations. All the authors of *Chinese Profiles* can do now is to thank our editors, the people we interviewed, and the ladies, gentlemen, comrades and friends who provided background material for the book or helped in other ways. Thank you.

Yes, in a few more months we won't even dare say thank you.

ZHANG XINXIN: The literary world has breathed a sigh of relief.

A few months ago a piece of news exploded like a bomb among a small circle of people. It was being said that Zhang Xinxin had stayed quiet for a whole year, kept her head down and her mouth shut, worked her guts out in secret, and written a hundred stories. It was all absolutely true! They were all going to be published in a whole lot of magazines at the same time, go off like a bomb and knock everyone off their feet.

When the story reached my ears my imagination had me badly scared for a while.

A hundred stories!

When the pieces came out it emerged that in fact they had been written by a couple of people, that they were a hundred ordinary people's accounts of themselves, that they were all just everyday, commonplace stuff, and there was a lot of padding in them. They weren't exquisitely made structures organized with supreme artistry and showing the craftsmanship that had gone into them. In no way were they stories all the more valuable for having been so hard to write.

That was all there was to them.

Honestly, that was all.

Some people asked why we had not simply called ourselves the recorders of the stories, like the authors of some similar works abroad.

They really do seem to be just records.

For a year we listened, wrote, paid attention, and gradually gained a different kind of aesthetic experience.

Every single person's living narrative was an amazing work of art.

Other people asked if we recorded it all on tape then transcribed it.

In fact we had never wanted to use a tape-recorder.

The process of transcribing tapes is not only very time-consuming: it is also a process of loss. In writing everything down a word at a time, listening again and checking, in faithfully reproducing it according to the structure of the original narration, the narrator's inner truth can be lost without one realizing it. And it is not only the narrator who loses.

Write down in a notebook the main points, figures, the actual words the narrator uses at critical moments. Remember the questions that flash into your mind during the interchange, the questions you want to ask. Or else write nothing down, just listen, ask and listen again. Sometimes it feels like sketching, trying to form a mental picture of your subject in a momentary but significant attitude.

There can be no purely objective record. Portrait-painters portray not only the sitters but themselves. Hyper-realist portraits are no different from photographs, but their main purpose is to express the painters themselves.

In an industrial age that has already created the tape-recorder and the camera, what we have done in *Chinese Profiles*, like similar books abroad and documentary films that either have us watching in rapt silence or else are so dreary that we can't take any more, is in fact to use modern techniques to find new approaches to creativity. All these methods are trying to simulate a sense of actuality and reality that comes closer to what people today can appreciate and accept. To take another approach and use a different formula, they are all trying to achieve a sense of identification. The degree of simulation should come as close as possible to the present aesthetic mentality of Chinese readers.

Sometimes I feel that there really is no point in writing fiction. What is the point in putting in all that effort to disguise a dry jujube stone as a succulent delicacy like sea cucumber? All you really have is that tiny stone, and sometimes you don't even have that. But half an hour's talk, or a few hours' talk, gives you a story, a whole human life, a sculpture that needs no reworking. A few thousand words can express it all. Pull it apart, knead it to pieces, and the flavour disappears.

If my perceptions, my story, cannot be different from those of these hundred people, of a thousand people, of ten thousand people, or if they are the same as everyone else's, writing fiction is pointless, really pointless.

April 19, 1985

Translated by W.J.F. Jenner

北 京 人

张辛欣 桑 晔

熊猫丛书

*

《中国文学》杂志社出版
（中国北京百万庄路24号）
中国国际图书贸易总公司发行
（中国国际书店）
1986年第 1 版
编号：（英）2—916—40
00650
10—E—1991 P